UF Seasons by Year/Coach

Year	Coach	Overall	Conference	Bowl/playoffs	Coaches# Rank	AP° Rank
1906	Forsythe	5–3				
1907	Forsythe	4–1–1				
1908	Forsythe	5–2–1				
1909	Pyle	6–1–1				
1910	Pyle	6–1				
1911	Pyle	5–0–1				
1912	Pyle	5–2–1				
1913	Pyle	4–3				
1914	McCoy	5–2				
1915	McCoy	4–3				
1916	McCoy	0–5				
1917	Buser	2–4				
1918	Buser	0–1				
1919	Buser	5–3				
1920	Kline	6–3	Southern (S)			
1921	Kline	6–3–2				
1922	Kline	7–2	S 2–0			
1923	Van Fleet	6–1–2	S 1–0–2			
1924	Van Fleet	6–2–2	S 2–0–1			
1925	Sebring	8–2	S 3–2			
1926	Sebring	2–6–2	1–4–1			
1927	Sebring	7–3	5–2			
1928	Bachman	8–1	S 6–1			
1929	Bachman	8–2	6–1			
1930	Bachman	6–3–1	4–2–1			
1931	Bachman	2–6–2	2–4–2			
1932	Bachman	3–6	1–6			
1933	Stanley	5–3–1	SEC 2–3			
1934	Stanley	6–3–1	2–2–1			
1935	Stanley	3–7	1–6			
1936	Cody	4–6	SEC 1–5			
1937	Cody	4–7	3–4			
1938	Cody	4–6–1	2–2–1			
1939	Cody	5–5–1	0–3–1			
1940	Lieb	5–5	SEC 2–3			
1941	Lieb	4–6	1–3			
1942	Lieb	3–7	1–3			
1944	Lieb	4–3	0–3			

Year	Coach	Record	Conference	Bowl
1945	Lieb	4–5–1	1–3–1	
1946	Wolf	0–9	SEC 0–5	
1947	Wolf	4–5–1	0–3–1	
1948	Wolf	5–5	1–5	
1949	Wolf	4–5–1	1–4–1	
1950	Woodruff	5–5	SEC 2–4	
1951	Woodruff	5–5	2–4	
1952	Woodruff	8–3	3–3	W Gator
1953	Woodruff	3–5–2	1–3–2	
1954	Woodruff	5–5	5–2	
1955	Woodruff	4–6	3–5	
1956	Woodruff	6–3–1	5–2	
1957	Woodruff	6–2–1	4–2–1	
1958	Woodruff	6–4–1	2–3–1	L Gator
1959	Woodruff	5–4–1	2–4	
1960	Graves	9–2	SEC 5–1	W Gator
1961	Graves	4–5–1	3–3	
1962	Graves	7–4	4–2	W Gator
1963	Graves	6–3–1	3–3–1	
1964	Graves	7–3	4–2	
1965	Graves	7–4	4–2	L Sugar
1966	Graves	9–2	5–1	W Orange
1967	Graves	6–4	4–2	
1968	Graves	6–3–1	3–2–1	
1969	Graves	9–1–1	3–1–1	W Gator
1970	Dickey	7–4	SEC 3–3	
1971	Dickey	4–7	1–6	
1972	Dickey	5–5–1	3–3–1	
1973	Dickey	7–5	3–4	L Tangerine
1974	Dickey	8–4	3–3	L Sugar
1975	Dickey	9–3	5–1	L Gator
1976	Dickey	8–4	4–2	L Sun
1977	Dickey	6–4–1	3–3	
1978	Dickey	4–7	3–3	
1979	Pell	0,10,1	SEC 0–6	
1980	Pell	8–4	4–2	W Tangerine
1981	Pell	7–5	3–3	L Peach
1982	Pell	8–4	3–3	L Bluebonnet
1983	Pell	9–2–1	4–2	W Gator
1984	Pell/Hall	9–1–1	5–0–1	Ineligible
1985	Hall	9–1–1	SEC 5–1	Ineligible

Forida Gators Championship Seasons

From the beginning of Football through the first championship game to the Dan Mullen era

The book is written for those of us who love the Gator Nation and Florida Gators football. You'll like the story about the University of Florida's first football season in 1906, 53 years after its founding in 1853 over 160 year ago and you will like it even more when we start talking about football. You'll love the many championships earned by the Gators.

UF's first official football game was played in 1906 but the "lads" had been fooling around on campus with weird shaped oval balls well before then as football was becoming a mature sport in America. It took until 1906 for an official UF team to emerge with its first coach Jack Forsythe and his Minnesota Shift Offense. From here, the book moves you through the Charley Pell era and to the Steve Spurrier days as both a Heisman level player and then a great coach. It finishes by looking through the seasons of Urban Meyer, Ron Zook, Will Muschamp of course on to the current season with Coach James McElwain. The championship seasons and Heisman winners in Gators football as told here are just fascinating.

This book captures the many great championship seasons and "almost" championships in Gators Football. We look at every game in every season and we take the reader through great chapters about Florida's 27 coaches to great stories about 112 seasons worth of great games (1190 games). The book often stops in time and talks about a particular great player. such as Steve Spurrier, Jack Youngblood, Emmitt Smith, Danny Wuerffel, Tim Tebow, Percy Harvin and others; or a great coach who won an SEC or national championship or two. The stories are riveting.

This book is the closest thing to an all-encompassing, full-blown encyclopedia of the greatest Gators football—a blow by blow history—with tales of the great championships. We capture all the action and all the memorable moments in the 112 great years of Florida Gators football. We even look at 1943, when the Gators had no team because of WWII. This book is your finest source for a great read on your favorite college football team as well as a great reference for when you want to see how a particular championship game in any year happened to turn out.

If you are a Gators fan, you will not want to put this book down.

Brian Kelly

LETS GO PUBLISH!

Copyright © September 2019, Brian W. Kelly Editor: Brian P. Kelly
Title: Florida Gators Championship Seasons Author Brian W. Kelly

All rights reserved: No part of this book may be reproduced or transmitted in any form, or by any means, electronic or mechanical, including photocopying, recording, scanning, faxing, or by any information storage and retrieval system, without permission from the publisher, LETS GO PUBLISH, in writing.

Disclaimer: Though judicious care was taken throughout the writing and the publication of this work that the information contained herein is accurate, there is no expressed or implied warranty that all information in this book is 100% correct. Therefore, neither LETS GO PUBLISH, nor the author accepts liability for any use of this work.

Trademarks: A number of products and names referenced in this book are trade names and trademarks of their respective companies.

Referenced Material: *Standard Disclaimer:* The information in this book has been obtained through personal and third party observations, interviews, and copious research. Where unique information has been provided, or extracted from other sources, those sources are acknowledged within the text of the book itself or in the References area in the front matter. Thus, there are no formal footnotes nor is there a bibliography section. Any picture that does not have a source was taken from various sites on the Internet with no credit attached. If resource owners would like credit in the next printing, please email publisher.

Published by: ....LETS GO PUBLISH!
Editor in Chief ....Brian P. Kelly
Email: ....info@letsgopublish.com
Web site .... www.letsgopublish.com

Library of Congress Copyright Information Pending
Book Cover Design by **Brian W. Kelly**
Editor—**Brian P. Kelly**

ISBN Information: The International Standard Book Number (ISBN) is a unique machine-readable identification number, which marks any book unmistakably. The ISBN is the clear standard in the book industry. 159 countries and territories are officially ISBN members. The Official ISBN for this book is

978-1-947402-96-6

The price for this work is:.......... $ 14.95 USD

| 10 | 9 | 8 | 7 | 6 | 5 | 4 | 3 | 2 | 1 |

Year	Coach	Record	Conf	Bowl		
1986	Hall	6–5	2–4			
1987	Hall	6–6	3–3	L Aloha		
1988	Hall	7–5	4–3	W All-American		
1989	Hall +	7-5	4-3	L Freedom		
1990	Spurrier	9–2	SEC 6–1	Ineligible		13
1991	Spurrier	10–2	7–0	L Sugar	7	7
1992	Spurrier	9–4	6–2	W Gator	11	10
1993	Spurrier	11–2	7–1	W Sugar	4	5
1994	Spurrier	10,2,1	7–1	L Sugar	7	7
1995	Spurrier	12–1	8–0	L Fiesta	3	2
1996	Spurrier	12–1	8–0	W Sugar	1	1
1997	Spurrier	10–2	6–2	W Citrus	6	4
1998	Spurrier	10–2	7–1	W Orange†	6	5
1999	Spurrier	9–4	7–1	L Citrus	14	12
2000	Spurrier	10–3	7–1	L Sugar†	11	10
2001	Spurrier	10–2	6–2	W Orange†	3	3
2002	Zook	8–5	SEC 6–2	L Outback	24	
2003	Zook	8–5	6–2	L Outback	25	24
2004	Zook+	7-5	4-4	L Peach	25	
2005	Meyer	9–3	SEC 5–3	W Outback	16	12
2006	Meyer	13–1	7–1	W BCS Champs	1	1
2007	Meyer	9–4	5–3	L Capital One	16	13
2008	Meyer	13–1	7–1	W BCS Champs	1	1
2009	Meyer	13–1	8–0	W Sugar†	3	3
2010	Meyer	8–5	4–4	W Outback		
2011	Muschamp	7–6	SEC 3–5	W Gator		
2012	Muschamp	11–2	7–1	L Sugar†	10	9
2013	Muschamp	4–8	3–5			
2014	Muschamp	7–5	4–4	W Birmingham		
2015	McElwain	10–4	SEC 7–1	L Citrus	25	25
2016	McElwain	9–4	6–2	W Outback	13	14
2017	McElwain & Shannon	4-7	3-5			
2018	Mullen	10-3	5-3		6	7

Total Games 1,183
Seasons 112
Total Wins 725
Total Losses 418
Total Ties 40 * Ties are prior to Overtime Rules
Stats from 1906 * Through August 2017

LETS GO
GO
PUBLISH

Acknowledgments:

I appreciate all the help that I received in putting this book together, along with the 210 other books from the past.

My printed acknowledgments were once so large that book readers needed to navigate too many pages to get to page one of the text. To permit me more flexibility, I put my acknowledgment list online at www.letsgopublish.com. The list of acknowledgments continues to grow. Believe it or not, it once cost about a dollar more to print each book.

Thank you all on the big list in the sky and God bless you all for your help.

Please check out www.letsgopublish.com to read the latest version of my heartfelt acknowledgments updated for this book. Thank you all!

In this book, I received some extra special help from many avid football friends including Dennis Grimes, Gerry Rodski, Wily Ky Eyely, Angel Irene McKeown Kelly, Angel Edward Joseph Kelly Sr., Angel Edward Joseph Kelly Jr., Ann Flannery, Angel James Flannery Sr., Mary Daniels, Bill Daniels, Robert Garry Daniels, Angel Sarah Janice Daniels, Angel Punkie Daniels, Joe Kelly and Diane Kelly.

References

I learned how to write creatively in Grade School at St. Boniface. I even enjoyed reading some of my own stuff as a toddler.

At Meyers High School and King's College and Wilkes-University, I learned how to research, write bibliographies and footnote every non-original thought I might have had. I learned to hate ibid, and op. cit., and I hated assuring that I had all citations written down in the proper sequence. Having to pay attention to details took my desire to write creatively and diminished it with busy work.

I know it is necessary for the world to stop plagiarism so authors and publishers can get paid properly, but for an honest writer, it sure is annoying. I wrote many proposals while with IBM and whenever I needed to cite something, I cited it in place, because my readers, IT Managers, could care less about tracing the vagaries of citations and their varied formats.

I always hated to use stilted footnotes, or produce a lengthy, perfectly formatted bibliography. I bet most bibliographies are flawed because even the experts on such drivel do not like the tedium.

I wrote 210 books before this book and several hundred articles published by many magazines and newspapers and I only cite when an idea is not mine or when I am quoting, and again, I choose to cite in place, and the reader does not have to trace strange numbers through strange footnotes and back to bibliography elements that may not be readily accessible or available. Academicians knowing all the rules of citation are not my audience. In this book, if you are a lover of Gator football, you are my intended group of readers

Yet, I would be kidding you, if in a book about the great championships in University of Florida Gators Football, I tried to bluff my way into trying to make you think that I knew everything before I began to write anything in this book. I spent as much time researching as writing. I might even call myself an expert of sorts now about the Gators, a team that I have always loved to watch, especially when the visor guy, Steve Spurrier had command of the sidelines for so many wonderful UF football years.

Without any pain on your part you can read this book from cover to cover to enjoy the stories about the many great moments in the University of Florida Football Program.

It took me about two months to write this book. If I were to have made sure that a thought of mine was not a thought somebody else ever had, this book never would have been completed or the citations pages would more than likely exceed the prose. Everybody takes credit for everything in sports writing—at least that's what I have found.

I used UF Season summaries and recaps from whatever source I could to get the scores of all the games. I verified facts when possible. There are many web sites that have great information and facts. Ironically most internet stories are the same exact stories. Who's got the original? While I was writing the book, I wrote down a bunch of Internet references and at one time, I listed them here in this article. They were the least read pages. No more. Unless I am citing a reference in a section of the book, you will not see the URL.

Since I am not a Floridian but I want to become one soon as winters in PA are very harsh and grey, I have no favorite source but I continually look for articles written by students to amplify the text I present.

While I was writing this book, because I was not sure that my citations within the text would be enough, and I was not producing a bibliography, I copied URLs into some of the book text of areas from the Internet in those cases in which I had read articles or had downloaded material and had brought articles or pieces of articles into this book. Hopefully, this will satisfy any request for additional information. If there is anything which needs a specific citation, I would be pleased to change the text. Just contact me. Your stuff is your stuff.

Most of the facts in this book are also put forth in the UF Media Guide. Our thanks for the use of this material for the accurate production of this book.

Preface:

This book is all about the great championships in Florida Gators football. Along the way to today, we note the founding of the University of Florida, the preliminaries before UF football and then we delve right into the storied University of Florida Football Program--its struggles; its greatness; and its many championships that present its greatness and its impact on American life.

I like the Gators and have always liked the Gators and I never liked the humming of the Tomahawk chant when my team, no matter which team it was, was losing. I'll bet you I was forever hoping for Steve Spurrier and follow-ons to whoop Bobby Bowden (nothing personal) and follow-ons on the gridiron even when my teams were not playing.

Another reason why I picked Florida as my state for this book, is that at more than a half a century older than ten years old and perhaps even more, I would love for some book shop in Florida to have a book-signing for me. I would come because I love Florida. After a favorite ND book has been out almost a year, ND Sports information department recently informed me that they worked to get my book into the ND Bookstore. It was selling well, and now even better.

At Gainesville in Ben Hill Griffin Stadium, maybe somebody could get me fifty-yard line seats in a game in which UF is playing against one of my old-time favorites ND or PSU, or quite frankly, any team. I'd be there with bells on and I'd be signing and after the game, after a few whistle wetters, I would be happy to sign again.

I like UF a lot but you gotta admit that it was easy for me to be a Penn State Fan all of my life and ND has always been as close as a family religion. I began to pay attention to the Gators watching the great Steve Spurrier as a coach. I had no idea he was such a great football player also, before researching this book. I promise that I will know a lot more as I tell his story and the UF Football story in this book.

Supporters who love the University of Florida will read the book and get an immediate burst of emotions such as warmth and love for their favorite team. You will love this book because it actually has it all – something about every season with emphasis on the championship and almost championship seasons. Go Gator Nation!

This book walks you through the whole UF championship journey including the three big national football championships. Now with Dan Mullen at the helm, we might be seeing another one soon. Let's all hope.

As we cover the games, we also look at the great players on the early teams who struggled to win games without big-time programs and coaches This period began in 1906. Think about the struggle of playing on a college football team when getting the right equipment was the biggest issue.

The great UF coaches are listed within the football seasons in which they coached--from season 1 in 1906 to season 111 in 2017. In other words, the seasons are examined chronologically and the coaches and certain games and certain players are highlighted within the seasons in which they were played. I sure hope you enjoy this unique approach.

Few of the UF twenty-five coaches took the team for more than five years early-on but they still produced powerful teams with powerful players. It was not until the 1930's and 1940's when UF joined the SEC that the losses began to be seen more often than the wins. By the 1950's the coaches began to put in longer tenures and the wins began to increase. When Steve Spurrier became the coach, thanks to the efforts of coaches such as Charley Pell, winning had become commonplace and he kept it going. Some think Spurrier put the football program on the map. In many ways, he sure did.

Florida Gators are a long-time football power

One hundred twelve years is a long time to be playing football. The University of Florida Gators are recognized today as one of the finest teams in the nation, ready to win a national championship at the drop of the next hat.

Preface xv

In 1933 the University of Florida joined the SEC and have been playing the best football teams in the nation ever since by competing in the NCAA Division I Football Bowl Subdivision.

Your author would like you to know that when football season closes in the second week of January each year, there is now a great football item—this book—that is available all 52 weeks of the year and in fact all 365 days each year. It does not rely on the stadium gates being open for you to get a great dose of Gator Football. Just begin reading right here.

It is now available for you to add to your Gator Nation experience and your book collection. Once you get this book, it is yours forever unless, of course you give it away to one of the many who will be in awe, and who will accept it gladly.

The book opens with its first story set shortly after the beginning of college football as a sport in America. It then moves on to the first official game with the first official coach and all the way to Coach Dan Mullen's last game. It tells a story about the football seasons and the great coaches from the first coached game in 1906 to today.

You are going to love this book because it is the perfect read for anybody who loves the Gator Nation and wants to know more about the most revered athletes to have competed in one of the finest football programs of all time.

Few sports books are a must-read but Brian Kelly's Forida Gators Championship Seasons will quickly appear at the top of Americas most enjoyable must-read books about sports. Enjoy!

Who is Brian W. Kelly?

Brian W. Kelly is one of the leading authors in America with this, his 211th published book. Brian is an outspoken and eloquent expert on a variety of topics and he has also written several hundred articles on other topics of interest to Americans.

Most of his early works involved high technology. Later, Brian wrote a number of patriotic books and most recently he has been writing human interest books such as The Wine Diet and Thank you, IBM. His books are always well received.

Brian's books are highlighted at www.letsgopublish.com. You may see most of Brian's works by taking the following link www.amazon.com/author/brianwkelly.

The Best!

Sincerely,

Brian P. Kelly, Editor in Chief
I am Brian Kelly's eldest son.

Table of Contents

Chapter 1 Introduction to University of Florida (UF) Football 1
Chapter 2 UF Launches First "Un-Official" Football Team 15
Chapter 3 UF Launches First "Official" Football Team 21
Chapter 4 The Evolution of Modern Football 39
Chapter 5 Gators Football – Next Seven Years 1907-1913 47
Chapter 6 C. J. McCoy Era 1914-1916 61
Chapter 7 Alfred Buser & William G Kline Era 1917 - 1922 65
Chapter 8 James Van Fleet & Harold L. Sebring Era 1923-1927 71
Chapter 9 Charlie Bachman Era 1928-1932 77
Chapter 10 Dennis Stanley & Josh Cody Era 1933-1939 89
Chapter 11 Tom Lieb & Ray Wolf Era 1940-1949 93
Chapter 12 Bob Woodruff Era 1950-1959 99
Chapter 13 Ray Graves Era 1960-1969 109
Chapter 14 Doug Dickey Era 1970-1978 131
Chapter 15 Charley Pell Era 1979-1984 141
Chapter 16 Galen Hall Era 1985-1989 151
Chapter 17 Steve Spurrier Era 1990 to 2001 161
Chapter 18 Ron Zook Era 2002 to 2004 193
Chapter 19 Urban Meyer Era 2005 - 2010 201
Chapter 20 Will Muschamp Era 2011 to 2014 261
Chapter 21 Jim McElwain Era 2015-2017+ 275
Chapter 22 Dan Mullen Era 2018- + ... 283
Other Books by Brian W. Kelly: (amazon.com, and Kindle) 287

About the Author

Brian Kelly retired as an Assistant Professor in the Business Information Technology (BIT) Program at Marywood University, where he also served as the IBM i and Midrange Systems Technical Advisor to the IT Faculty. Kelly designed, developed, and taught many college and professional courses. He continues as a contributing technical editor to a number of technical industry magazines, including "The Four Hundred" and "Four Hundred Guru," published by IT Jungle.

Kelly is a former IBM Senior Systems Engineer. His specialty was problem solving for customers as well as implementing advanced operating systems and software on his client's machines. Brian is the author of 211 books and hundreds of magazine articles. He has been a frequent speaker at technical conferences throughout the United States.

Brian was a candidate for the US Congress from Pennsylvania in 2010 and he ran for Mayor in his home town in 2015. He loves Florida Gators Football and can't wait to get back down to Florida again in the fall. When he comes, he'll be glad to sign your books. God bless the Gators!

Chapter 1 Introduction to University of Florida (UF) Football

University of Florida's 113th Year in 2019!

The Gator Nation celebrated 100 years of Florida football in 2006. Football was played beginning in 1906 and the 100th season was completed in 2006. The team played every year but 1943 in the heat of World War II and the 1918 team played just one game during World War I. One game in one year doth make a season.

Coach Mullen leading the Gators onto the field

The football team, though great for sure, is only one part of The University of Florida , a great institution, which the people of Florida affectionately and simply call Florida. It is a public research university that awards associate, bachelor's, master's, doctoral, and professional degrees such as the MD. The university also offers continuing education programs.

UF is an American public land-grant, sea-grant, and space-grant research universityon a beautiful 2,000-acre (8.1 km2) campus in Gainesville, Florida.

UF traces its origins to 1853, when the East Florida Seminary, the oldest of the University of Florida's four predecessor institutions, was founded in Ocala, Florida. On January 6, 1853, Governor Thomas Brown signed a bill that provided public support for higher education in Florida. From 1906 on, the University has fielded great football teams.

During the 1918 season, the Gators' team ranks were depleted by both the Spanish Flu and the loss of the many World War I volunteers and draftees. Therefore, the 1918 team played just that one game. One can fathom that the Army training camps had the best players in the nation at the time. The Gators lost L (2–14) to a football team from Camp Johnston, a U.S. Army training installation in nearby Jacksonville, Florida.

Coach Alfred L. Buser's Gators had a tough time finding a college game in 1918 and were unable to play any Southern Intercollegiate Athletic Association (SIAA) teams in 1918. In 1943, the Gators skipped the season because with the war demands, there simply were not enough players for UF to put a team on the field.

The Gators therefore have fielded a team every season since the inaugural 1906 season, with the exception of 1943 (World War II). Florida has played 1,183 games in its 112 seasons, and the Gators have a fine all-time record of 725 wins, 418 losses, and 40 ties. That's a lot of football folks. The 110th anniversary was in 2016.

Officially the University of Florida recognizes a long football history that dates back to 1906. If you are from Florida State, or some other rival school, you might not be so kind. Too often rivals ask if the Gators ever had a football team before 1990, the beginning of Steve Spurrier's 12-year tenure as head coach. That is an unfair shot that probably can be made against every struggling startup college football program. Everybody knows Spurrier and the greatness he brought to the University of Florida. But, Florida had a lot of moxie and a lot of fine results pre-Spurrier. Maybe not quite as much—but enough to take notice.

So, that is an unfair shot to suggest the Gators were noplace as the program has produced close to 800 wins with a late start in 1906 when many of the legendary teams had already been legends for thirty years or more. UF had its share of medsa medsa mediocre seasons from the 1930's on but they more or less ended in the mid 1950's when Bob Woodward finished off the decade with four nice winning seasons. And, yes, there were championships and almost championships before Florida joined the SEC.

In the 1960's coach Ray Graves, the coach who taught Steve Spurrier how to play college football had some fine teams. We can't forget that Steve Spurrier started at QB in 1964, 1965, and 1966. He could not play as a 1963 freshman. Spurrier won the Heisman Trophy in his senior season of 1966 leading the Gators to a 9-2 season. He was a consensus All-American in both 1965 and 1966. Ray Graves also had a 9-1-1 season in 1969 before he turned the UF reins over to Doug Dickey.

Mike Bianchi a Florida Sentinel Pundit wishes that the 1970's could be ink-blotted out of the Gator record. From his perspective, he saw the promotion of Ray Graves as a strategic football mistake for the UF Administration. Here is an unabashed Bianchi:

"He'd just coached the Gators to one of the most exciting, pyrotechnic offensive seasons in UF history (9-1-1 in 1969) and then inexplicably was kicked upstairs to focus solely on his athletic-director's duties so the Gators could hire Tennessee's Dickey as the football coach. The dynamic pass-happy Graves era gave way to a decade of boring, snoring football under Florida alum Dickey."

Charley Pell replaced Dickey and came in with some good ideas that had no time to develop. Pell was an absolutely super coach--one of the best in Florida's history. His plan did produce many on-the-field victories over the next five years. However, while he was using matches and almost extinguished candles to light his way in his first season as the Gators coach, he produced an unmitigated disaster. Nothing ever compared to the poor record of Charley Pell's first year. But, believe it or not, he recovered. That's what happens to championship-level coaches. They recover and improve.

Yes, it was a disaster. I had to look up his record a number of times to make sure I was right. Pell has the record, set in 1979, for the most losses in any single season in Gators football history. He wrapped up his season with a winless 0–10–1 overall record and a 0–6 record in the SEC. He did recover and he did very well and then, because the accusers were accusing, and the Administration did not stick with him, he was replaced by Galen Hall. Hall was a fine coach but Charley Pell—he was one of a kind—and the Gators fired him. Humph!

So, we can say surely that in the 1980's under Charley Pell and Galen Hall, the Gators had some nice and some very great seasons. For example in 1984, Pell and Hall combined for a 9-1-1 season and then Hall got his own Gators team in 1985, while Charley Pell was figuring out what had happened.

And my point is that Gator fans cannot and should not write off the pre-Spurrier era as no-account years. They counted big time in the formation of what now is a football dynasty, with an occasional drop but always a big rebound. Yes, there were championships before Spurrier and there were also "almost" championship. Nobody may have been counting then, but Florida's Gators had a lot of great, championship-level teams long before Steve Spurrier set the tone.

In all fairness to the huge spark generated by Coach Spurrier, when greatness is measured, consistency is big factor, and Steve Spurrier was consistent as a player and even more consistent as a coach, no matter what team he coached or endeavor of which he was a part.

And, so there is no question that Florida reached a new level of success, consistency, and national prominence when the fiery Head Football Coach returned to his alma mater in 2015. When he left after believing he had served long enough, Spurrier tried his hand in the NFL but he really did not like the change. Steve Spurrier came back to College Football but by then the Gators had their own coach

After a three-year period of mediocrity with new coaches with last names of Zook and Strong, following Spurrier's departure for the NFL, Florida brought a different kind of offensive genius to Gainesville, and some of the best seasons in school history occurred during his short tenure.

Urban Myer is a living coaching master. He, like Steve Spurrier built his own football legacy through hard work. Myer came to Florida in 2005 and soon the Gators would have their third Heisman and for good measure, Meyer would sneak in another National Championship, and another, and almost another.

The 2006 100th year celebration was a wonderful Florida Gator experience that was sponsored by Gatorade. Do you get it – Gator-Ade, named from the Florida Gators. One of the hallmarks of the celebration events was that the University honored the Spurrier coached national championship team during the season's opening weekend v. Southern Miss on September 2nd. Members of the national championship team formed a tunnel as the 2006 Gator team took the field at Ben Hill Griffin Stadium.

Each ensuing home game that year had its own 100-year celebration theme, including a throwback uniform game v Alabama on September 30. Moreover, there was a Gator Fans' Team of the Century presented by Gatorade announced during the game vs. Western Carolina on November 18. Florida was celebrating 100 years and darn well they should.

Showing that UF's hard working folks clean up very well after playing mud-ball in the Swamp, a top line black-tie gala celebration, titled "Gator Gala," was held the night before the Alabama game with an evening of dinner, dancing and live entertainment at the Stephen C. O'Connell Center. The proceeds for this event benefited the Athletic Scholarship Endowment Fund. In Academia, every opportunity for fun is s fund-raiser for a great cause.

Among other special parts of the celebration, there were commemorative tickets and game programs complete with a Gator great player card set, a commemorative photo history book and a DVD of Florida football. How about that for a celebration!

Gator fans were able to purchase officially licensed 100-year anniversary merchandise and commemorative bricks in the Gator Walk, that was constructed on the north walkway leading up to Ben Hill Griffin Stadium. Banners placed on light poles around the

Florida campus were installed to honor all who were part of the first 100 years.

Before the event, the AD commented: "Florida All-American football players. The tradition and history of Florida football is special and we are looking forward to reliving memories with our passionate fans and supporters who have helped make this program one of the best in the country," said UF Athletics Director Jeremy Foley. Foley continued:

"The University of Florida is the birthplace of Gatorade, and since 1965, we have been on the Gators' sidelines helping athletes perform at their best," said Tom Fox, Senior Vice President of Gatorade Sports Marketing. "We're proud to partner with the University of Florida to celebrate the 100th anniversary of Gators' football and support the Fans All-Century Team Voting. We look forward to seeing who the fans select."

Other highlights of the celebration included the following:

Celebration Details

- Throwback Game with special uniforms
- 204-page Commemorative Book
- DVD—Gridiron Gators
- Complimentary Poster
- Team of the Century by Gatorade
- Gator Black-Tie Gala
- Game Programs

This book that you are reading celebrates University of Florida Football; its founding; its struggles; its greatness; and its championships. People like me, who love the Gators, will love this book. Gator haters will want their own copy just for additional ammo. Yet, it won't help them! Hah!

We begin the rest of the Florida Gators football story in the next chapter, and we continue in subsequent chapters, right into the founding of the full Gator unofficial football program and then the official Gator program in 1906 after the students had been begging the argument by playing American football on the campus in intramural games.

In defining the format of the book, we chose to use a timetable that is based on a historical chronology. Within this framework, we discuss all the seasons in Univesity of Florida football history, and we highlight the championships and almost championships. No book can claim to be able to capture them all, as it would be a never-ending story, but we sure do try and I hope you think we did well after your first read.

Three Heismans for Florida

For three larger than life Florida Alligators--one time great football players, three larger-than-life statues of these UF Heisman Trophy winners will surely do. What a great tribute to such great legendary players. They are now all fully installed outside Ben Hill Griffin Stadium. Nobody in Florida or elsewhere in the country is complaining. It had to be a hefty task getting them in place as the statues commemorating those whose images they hold range in weight from 1,700 to 2,000 pounds. Try to guess whose statue is the heaviest! I am not telling!

Florida loves its greats and always reveres them. These three Florida Gator Greats in bronze form were installed in April 2011 outside the Ben Hill Griffin Stadium. The University Athletic Association board had previously, quite unanimously, approved the project. Everybody from the University of Florida Gator Nation loves the three who are still alive -- very much alive, while their images are living outside the stadium all covered in a beautiful bronze. From left to right we have Tim Tebow; Steve Spurrier; and Danny Wuerffel. Wouldn't all colleges in America like to have these three alums and Heisman Winners gracing the entrance to any of their sports pavillions. You bet they would!!!

So, who might these bronzed, frozen in time, once great actors on the Gators football field be? Don't let on that I already told you? You probably already know because I showed you their pictures on the prior page ahem! It's The bronze statues of Tim Tebow, Steve Spurrier, and Danny Wuerffel from left to right—Florida's three Heisman Winners were placed on the west side of the stadium in full regalia. The statues cost about $550,000, which was funded by private donations. Lots of people like all three of these Gator Nation immortals.

Why does UF have statues for living people?

The university anticipated this question and their reasoning is that the statues are a unique way of marking the success of several unique Gator players who have won one of college football's most significant awards—the Heisman Trophy. No laggard ever won such an award ever. These three are remarkably the best of Flordia football at a player level.

As noted, lots of other universities would love to have Heisman winners that they too could honor with similar gestures.

In addition to UF, seven other universities have won at least three Heisman's. Three universities—Notre Dame, Ohio State and Southern California - lead the list with seven apiece.

Here is the list:

- Notre Dame: 7
- Ohio State: 7
- USC: 7
- Oklahoma: 5
- Army: 3
- Florida: 3
- Michigan: 3
- Nebraska: 3
- Auburn: 3
- Florida State: 3

Even prior to the Steve Spurrier coaching dynasty, the University of Florida has had one of the most prestigious football programs in the nation.

Spurrier and Wuerffel, both outstanding quarterbacks in their day, are shown in the stadium statues decked out in bronze while passing the pigskin. Whereas Tebow, a multi-talented star quarterback with a penchant and great abilities as a runner, is shown running the football. It is a marvelous tribute to the players and a great gesture from a fine university.

The three statues were first revealed at the 2011 Spring Game. During the 2011 season, Florida honored its three Heisman Trophy winners with the life-sized statues outside the stadium. The bronze versions of Steve Spurrier (1966), Danny Wuerffel (1996) and Tim Tebow (2007) were presented during halftime of the spring game.

Onlookers especially enjoyed the Tebow' depiction. Always a sport, Tebow said: "That's fine...You have to change it up... We can't all be throwing." All three recipients were very thankful for the great honor.

"When do you ever think growing up that you'll have a statue somewhere where people will look at it and have great memories?" Wuerffel said. "It's even more special being next to two guys that I love and admire in my coach, Steve Spurrier, and my friend, Tim Tebow. That even makes it more special for me."

Spurrier threw for more than 4,800 yards and 37 touchdowns as a three-year starter in Gainesville. His most notable play might not have even been at his position. He kicked a 40-yard field goal to beat Auburn 30-27 during his senior season. Spurrier is the only person to win the Heisman Trophy (1966) and then coach a Heisman winner (Danny Wuerffel in 1996) and then win a national title. Only Gators dosuch great things. Amen!

After starting his coaching career at Duke, Spurrier returned to coach his alma mater in 1990. He led the Gators to six Southeastern Conference championships and the 1996 national title with Wuerffel at the helm. Under Spurrier's guidance, Florida won 122 games in 12 seasons and went 68-5 in Gainesville. He helped create one of the best home-field advantages in college football and even nicknamed the stadium "The Swamp."

"This is one of the best honors I've ever had in my life," Spurrier said. Wuerffel, who threw for more than 3,600 yards and 39 touchdowns in 1996, echoed Spurrier's sentiments. "There have been so many wonderful memories, from hugging a teammate after a touchdown to being picked up after a sack from one of my buddies," Wuerffel said. "This is one of those that is kind of hard to grasp at the moment..."

Tebow, not surprisingly as the most current recipient, had the largest contingent on hand for the ceremony. He had friends, family members, and a bunch of former teammates at Florida Field. One of college football's greatest players ever, Tebow had 32 touchdown passes in 2007 and ran for 23 more. He would have had 2000 more but he ran out of seasons.

Tim Tebow became the first player to score at least 20 touchdowns rushing and passing, then he became the first sophomore to win the Heisman. All three honored former players were ones of a kind.

"I feel like I'm not just a player, but I'm part of it," Tebow said. "I grew up a Gator and that just makes it that much more special."

Now that Steve Spurrier has retired from the being Head Coach at South Carolina, he can again enjoy his roots at Florida even more. The fans and administration think the world of Coach Spurrier.

On September 3, 2016, the playing surface of the "SWAMP" was renamed in honor of former Florida quarterback and head coach Steve Spurrier. For the Gators, that meant putting his name on the field in "The Swamp," Spurrier's famed nickname for the field. And, so as of 2016, the complete name is: "Steve Spurrier-Florida Field at Ben Hill Griffin Stadium." That sure has a nice ring.

Though your author lives in Wilkes-Barre, Pennsylvania, he loves the Gators and their visor capped coach and the two others. What a legacy. What a treat to be fan of the Gators. Let's keep it up!

Come up with your own chant!

For the Florida Gators, pumping it up all started in 1949 at Florida Field when George Edmondson looked at the crowd around him as the Gators were playing The Citadel. Fans were booing the team and George would not stand for it. He answered the call. He jumped up and got the fans cheering, and so began the legend of Mr. Two Bits.

Mr. Two Bits; One of a Kind!

For 60 years, Gator fans from all-across the world became eternally grateful for the man who started every Gator home football game with the phrase "Two-bits, Four-bits, Six-bits, a dollar. All for the Gators, Stand up and holler!" Wow, there was always lots of hollering.

He has his own fan championship prize and UF fans awared "Two-bits" the prize every year, He was known to the University of Florida community as "Mr. Two Bits", a long-time football fan of—and cheerleader for—the Florida Gators football team. Trying not to be repetitive, he led a traditional "Two Bits' cheer at Florida football games from 1949 until his "retirement" in 2008. Now what? It ain't gonna end!

No great tradition ends at the UF, especially for football. Since 2008, a series of University of Florida students and famous alumni have taken over the Mr. Two Bits role during pregame festivities at the Steve Spurrier Field at Ben Hill Griffin Stadium. Aren't traditions great!

Two Bits!

Nobody at UF could do anything about the number of bits-cheer as well as the legacy creator, Mr. Edmundson. But, the cheer author simply wanted the Gators to cheer and cheer loud in 1949 and then, many years afterwards.

He would be proud of how well the cheer stands today, and how well it still sounds from the stands. Edmondson used a similar routine no matter how he was able to get his cheer going across multiple scenarios.

For example, he led his cheer from either the stands or from the field. During the game, he would walk through the stands, to get the Gator fans going, and he would wait for a break in the action. Then, not bashful at all, he would then draw attention to himself and silence the crowd by holding up a small orange and blue sign reading "2 Bits" and blowing a whistle.

He actually used a real bugle during his first few years, but later, he found that a whistle was lots easier to carry. Once the surrounding fans quieted down, Mr. "Two Bits" prompted them to yell each line of the cheer with arm waves and fist pumps, encouraging them to roar after the last line.

When performing on the field, Mr. Two Bits would be introduced before kickoff and then jog out to midfield wearing his signature outfit. Then, using the same whistle and sign and even more vigorous arm waving, he would lead the entire Florida Field crowd in the cheer.

As performed at the University of Florida, the Two Bits cheer is as follows:

- Two Bits!
- Four Bits!
- Six Bits!
- A Dollar!
- All for the Gators Stand up and holler!

How about that?

Ya gotta love the Florida Gators and they sure love their team!

The university of Florida is a long-time football power

Bordering on 113 years is a long time to be playing football. The Florida Gators football team was established in 1906. This great and storied football powerhouse represents the University of Florida in college football. The moniker *Gators* comes from the notion of the Alligator so prevalently popping up in the Evergaldes and all through Florida. Florida University has become a Gator Nation because it has decided that it is Gator tough. Even Gator-Ade came to US to get its branding right.

For many years, the University of Florida football team competed in the SEC Conference, in the NCAA Division I Football Bowl Subdivision. Years and year ago when there was no SEC, right after it was formed, Florida joined in and has become a powerhouse as a member of the SEC. through the current 2019 season. All SEC teams say that the SEC is the toughest conference in which to compete in the the United States of America. I think they are right! You?

Chapter 2 UF Launches First "Un-Official" Football Team

The 1899 Florida Agricultural College (FAC) Football Players

1899: Nearly 50 years from the founding

Though the school was not called the University of Florida in 1899, the first reported football play by any of the predecessor schools that ultimately became UF was in 1899. One of four University of Florida precursor schools—known then as the Florida Agricultural School was playing unofficial football games at an intramural level in 1899. They would have loved to find another school willing to give them a game.

Football was really catching on as an American sport by 1899 and it was a tough chore for college administrators across the country to limit its play on American campuses. You may know that the 1899 "UF" intramural season came thirty years after what many regard as the very first football game ever played at the intercollegiate level. This of course was a contest held between teams from Rutgers College (now Rutgers University) and the College of New Jersey (now Princeton University). This 1869 game between Rutgers and Princeton is important in College Football History in that it is the first documented "football" game between two American colleges. For folks who like to know the results of the game—Rutgers won the game by a score of 6–4. Yes, the scoring was different in the early days

The early football games from the first were a combination of American football (like soccer) and rugby. From 1876, Yale's Walter Camp helped form the rules of the game with innovations such as the scrimmage line. Those interested in how American football came to be, might be interested in my 2017 book titled American College Football: The Beginning, available on Amazon and Kindle.

UF was a bit late getting into the game but then again, UF was not really UF until 1906 when it played its official first football game. By then, the four precursor teams had merged and the scenario for Florida was settled. By then, the Ivy League teams had been playing for about thirty years; Teams like Notre Dame, Alabama, and Penn State had been at it for about twenty years. So, it is no wonder that it took a bit of time for UF to catch up.

The 1901 Florida Agricultural College (FAC) football team actually found some games with an opponent willing to play. At the time, FAC was the representative team in the sport of American football. As you know, this team was not the modern era Florida Gators of the University of Florida in Gainesville, which began its program 1906, but it was one of its four forming institutions.

The FAC played its first intercollegiate football game in the state of Florida against the Stetson Hatters in Jacksonville as part of the 1901 State Fair. It was great to get a game. Stetson won 6–0, after a sure FAC score was obstructed by a tree stump. Think about the quality of football back then. Getting a field of suitable quality on which to play was an issue for a few more years. As previously noted, the school's first team was organized in 1899, but it played intramural for the most part as there was no other school found to play.

The FAC competed again in the 1902 college football season and found four games. They had a 1-2-1 record having played Stetson twice early in the fall. The first outing was a T (0-0) tie and the second was a big loss L (5-22). Then, in December, they played Florida State at Tallahassee on the 8th and lost L (0-6). They followed this up on Dcember 20 and won W (6-0) at Florida State, Lake City

1902 Florida Agricultural College (FAC) Team

In 1903, the Florida Legislature changed the name of Florida Agricultural College to the "University of Florida", in recognition of the legislature's desire to expand the curriculum beyond the college's original agricultural and engineering educational missions.

Ready to roll again in 1903, the University of Florida, known as the Blue and White football team (not the FAC) represented the University of Florida at Lake City in American football. Again, this was not the modern Florida Gators of the University of Florida in Gainesville but they were one of the four predecessors.

The Blue and White played three games this year. They lost to East Florida Seminary (another of the predecessors but at the time independent) early in the Fall, and then in a rematch which they won. No score was recorded in either game. They followed this up with a game against Florida State in Tallahassee on November 13, and lost the match L (0-12)

By 1904, even more teams were ready to engage. This time again, The 1904 University of Florida White and Blue football team was not the modern Florida Gators of the University of Florida in Gainesville, but were now operating with a name change. The team played several major colleges, including Mike Donahue's Auburn. They played Georgia Tech in John Heisman's first year coaching the Georgia Tech team.a bit outclassed by the new competition failed to post a win.

Every team leaves its comfort zone to move on to excellence. There was little excellence in this year but the "to-be" Gators team had surely moved out of their comfort zone. This was the results of moving from comfort to tough football:

October 1	at Alabama	The Quad • Tuscaloosa,	L 0–29
October 4	at Auburn	Auburn, AL	L 0–44
October 15	at Georgia	Macon, GA	L 0–52
October 17	at Georgia T	Atlanta, GA	L 0–77
October 21	at Florida State College, Lake City, Fl		L 0–23

In 1905, the precursor institutions were all in flux getting ready to join the big mothership that would be known forever more as The University of Florida at Gainesville. When it got itself together in 1906, the football team that it fielded took on the name of the mother university, the University of Florida or UF.

The days of unofficial UF football were over. The Gators were about to appear but the name would wait a few more years.

And, so as we now refer to it compared to the four formative schools, the modern University of Florida (UF) was created in 1905 when the Florida Legislature enacted the Buckman Act. This was the end of the four separate schools. The Act abolished all of the state's publicly-supported institutions of higher learning and consolidated the academic programs of the four precursor schools into the new University of the State of Florida (a land-grant university for white men).

"White men" was in the original wording. It was common at that time in US history. Descending from a major agricultural school, this clearly excluded women, and as it appears, those of other races than caucasian. The US was growing in understanding at the time but had not yet reached where it needed to go.

The private Stetson College, which is now known as Stetson University in DeLand was the first college to field a football team in the state of Florida. They played intramural games as early as 1894, and were one of the first team that the FAC played. Stetson, West Florida Seminary (later Florida State College, now Florida State University), and Florida Agricultural College (renamed the University of Florida at Lake City in 1903) had intramural football teams by the late 1890s or early 1900s.

Now, let's look at that first official season.

Chapter 3 UF Launches First "Official" Football Team

None of the prior games counted until the University ponied up with its official proaclamation of officialdom, Finally, after the four-school consolidation had taken place in 1905. UF football, featuring the team that would grow into being the Florida Gators was permitted to begin playing football officially for the University of Florida. 1906 Team Picture below:

And, so the 1906 Florida football team was the first official varsity team fielded by the new University of the State of Florida (now known simply as the University of Florida); during the 1906 college football season. The team finished its inaugural season with a winning record of 5–3. In recent years, this record has been contested. In our second edition, depending on what we learn to be the truth, we may go through the recommended corrections after they undergo more scrutiny, and we will correct or affirm the next time we print a new edition of this book. For now, we use 5-3.

Nobody denies that the 1906 Florida gridders were known as "Pee Wee's Boys." This was in honor of their coach, Jack "Pee Wee" Forsythe, who was a former Clemson Tigers lineman who played for coach THE John Heisman from 1901 to 1903.

<< Coach Forsythe was a real coach but he also played on the team as an end, just like Knute Rockne was an end. Forsythe used a technique known as the Minnesota shift to get the advantage over opponents. Since 1906, Florida has had a football season every year until 1943 when the war demands were such that even if a university could field a team, they would have a tough time finding another team to play.

Florida quickly joined the Intercollegiate Athletic Association of the United States (IAAUS), but remained independent of an athletic conference. Though we think that the term Gators has always been the moniker of Florida, the university did not adopt the great nickname-- "Florida Gators" for all of its sports teams until 1911. Early Florida football teams were known simply as "Florida" or the "Orange and Blue." Orange and Blue still are the identifiable marks of the team when on the field.

The Florida football teams played their home games in a variety of locations, including the university's Gainesville, Florida campus.

Buckman Act Changed Life for UF Big Time

After the Buckman Act in 1905, the modern University of Florida (still in Lake City) metamorphosized into today's Gators—well almost. The university hired coach C. A. Holton and was ready to play its first season in 1905. The 1905 Season is virtually non-existant from the records as, even with a coach, the team played just half a game against the Julia Landon Institute of Jacksonville.

The 1905 non-season was thus described by Tom McEwen as "lame duck, confusing, and troubled." Players were banned by Andrew Sledd from playing as they were behind in their studies. The captain of the 1905 team was William M. Rowlett. Of all the players from the earlier predecessor teams of the Florida Gators, only tackle William Gibbs of the 1905 Lake City team is known to have played for the new university's team in Gainesville in the fall of 1906. Most big changes eventually turn out well but the road to wellness often leaves many old traditons behind.

Why are University of Florida's Team Colors Orange & Blue?

Surely, one day somebody will come up with a better story but here is the truth. This is one of those explanations that could be true, but nobody is 100% sure one way or the other. One day maybe everybody will go back to saying, "We don't know!" In the book of colors of course, blue and orange stand for "We don't know." You'll find that explanation as good as the apparent truth. Since it is very much like "we don't know." Blue and orange it became, nonetheless.

In 1910, the Buckman Act, which we have already discussed, consolidated many of the state universities in Florida, including University of Florida at Lake City and East Florida Seminary. The big rumor on the team colors comes about from UFLC's (blue) and EFS's (orange and black). They say the colors were appropriated and mixed with the Gators mascot to create the modern Florida Gators look. Of course, nobody yet knows who "they" are.

Rule changes

At the end of 1905, there had been so little hype and so little real football action that UF had not taken a side on the looming national football controversy over "unnecessary roughness" in the game. Football was on the verge of being abolished at the US level due to all of the reoccurring violence during games. The rules made it easy for people to be hurt but Walter Camp was working on that along with Knute Rockne, President Roosevelt, and others.

Football was a sport that unfortunately had degenerated into clever but dangerous tactics such as: the flying wedge, punching, kicking, piling-on, and elbows to the face. Almost any violent behavior was allowed. Like the Roman Coliseum, all that mattered to the fans was that the other team did not win. Fatalities and injuries mounted during the nation's 1905 football season.

As a result, the 1906 season was played under a new set of rules. Walter Camp gets credit for many. The rules governing intercollegiate football were changed to promote a more open and less dangerous style of play.

An intercollegiate conference, which would become the forerunner of the NCAA, approved radical changes including the legalization of the forward pass, allowing the punting team to recover an on-side kick as a live ball, abolishing the dangerous flying wedge, creating a neutral zone between offense and defense, and doubling the first-down distance to 10 yards, to be gained in three downs.

The 1906 rules were the first installment and installments of rules to help the game and to make the game safer are continually made at the college and professional level even today.

Even in 1906, sometimes new collegiate level teams could not find other colleges to play them. So, they played whomever they could.

The 1906 Games

On Oct 13, UF played the Gainesville Athletic Club at the Baseball Park (Swamp) in Gainesville, Florida and Florida got the win, W (16–6). Then, on Oct 20 at Mercer in Central City Park. Macon, Georgia, UF could not find the magic and lost L (0-12).

On Oct 26 v Rollins at the Baseball Park in Gainesville, Florida, UF prevailed W (6–0) with 150 fans watching every play. On Nov 2, v the Riverside Athletic Club at the Baseball Park in Gainesville, Florida, UF again triumphed W (19–0), UF was feeling pretty good when they had to travel on Nov 4 to the Savannah Athletic Club in Georgia but they fell to the Club team L (2-27).

On Nov 11 at Rollins in Winter Park, Florida it was a loss L (0-5). The next week Nov 18, at the Athens Athletic Club in Athens, Georgia, UF was victorious W 10–0. The next venture of the 1906 UF football squad was Nov 30, at the Riverside Athletic Club in Jacksonville, Florida. UF collected a big win W (39-0).

Florida Fields

Though UF has thousands of acres, the acreage was not well developed for sports in the early years. Both football and baseball games as well as track meets were held at University Athletic Field. This was a grassy playing surface flanked by low bleachers. It was located on West University Avenue just north of the present stadium site. Permanent bleachers were installed in 1911, and the facility was given a real name, Fleming Field in honor of former Florida governor Francis P. Fleming. Somehow politicians get their names on a lot of things.

Football game at Fleming Field, 1924. Note Thomas Hall, background right.

From 1911 to 1930, Florida's football squads posted a 49–7–1 record at Fleming Field. This is a pre-SPurrier football record and it is not too shabby at all. Because the facility had a very limited capacity of just about 5,000 and the relative inaccessibility of Gainesville to the rest of the world in the early 20th century, many home games against top opponents were rescheduled to be played at larger venues in larger cities such as Jacksonville or Tampa. There were even other games that were played in St. Petersburg and Miami and Orlando. In 1930, about 25 years after football had begun for real at UF, things on the field were about to change for the good.

Ben Hill Griffin Stadium at Florida Field

It is an easy conclusion to deduce that The Ben Hill Griffin, Jr. Stadium at Florida Field was named after Ben Hill Griffin, Jr.

< Ben Hill Griffin, Jr.

Mr, Griffin came to the University of Florida in 1930 to study economics, agriculture and marketing. He was an eager learner and a programatist, who wished to put his newly acquired knowledge to work. Three years after arriving, he departed in 1933 without his degree. That same year, Ben Hill Griffin, Jr. received a 10-acre citrus grove as a wedding present from his father and that was his beginning of his odyssey to become a giant in the citrus, packaging and cattle industries. There was nothing Ben could not do when he put his mind to it.

As the years passed, he amassed thousands of acres of land and expanded into other businesses that made sense. For example, he got big in fruit-packing plants, cattle ranches, grove caretaking operations, banks, an automobile dealership, and he even became successful in the timber business as well as real estate enterprises.

In 1948, he founded the family-run citrus grove and cattle business, Ben Hill Griffin, Inc. From 1973 to 1990, Ben Hill Griffin served as chairman of the board and majority shareholder of Alico, Inc., an agribusiness with divisions in citrus, cattle, mining, timber and land development. Like many prominent businessmen, Ben Hill Griffin also tried his hand in state politics and served in the Florida Legislature for more than 16 years.

He was named one of the Top 50 Most Important Floridians of the 20th Century, but Ben Hill Griffin never forgot where he came from.

He credited UF with his knowledge of marketing and he was pleased to reinvest millions of dollars back into the academic and athletic areas of his alma mater. He helped students who needed a financial boost by establishing scholarships in Gator athletics and an Eminent Scholar Chair in Agricultural Economics Marketing. In addition, his contributions funded renovations of Griffin-Floyd Hall.

Because of his kindness and goodness to the University, the administration renamed the football stadium and an area of its Citrus Research and Education Center in Lake Alfred, FL in his honor. Additionally, they awarded him a Distinguished Alumnus award in 1974. In 1979, Ben Hill Griffin was inducted into the Citrus Hall of Fame, the Florida Agricultural Hall of Fame in 1987 and he is featured on a plaque outside Shands Hospital.

Facility History

Ben Hill Griffin Stadium at Florida Field for Gators' fans is the place to be on Saturdays during the fall. Also known as "the Swamp" where "only Gators come out alive," the stadium is home to the SEC powerhouse University of Florida Gators Football Team.

The stadium was rededicated in September 1989 as Ben Hill Griffin Stadium at Florida Field, in honor of the major UF benefactor, Ben Hill Griffin, Jr. In August of 2003, the fifth renovation in the history of the stadium was completed, which increased capacity to 88,548. The entire project cost $50 million and was built solely through private donations. The project made The Ben Hill Griffin Stadium at Florida Field the largest stadium in the state of Florida and one of the loudest anywhere in the country.

The Gatorzone has provided the information so that we can discuss the five major expansions from when Florida Field was first constructed in 1930. Gator fans know it as the Swamp. Why?

Well, the Atlanta Journal-Constitution would suggest that it being the Swamp, has something to do with it being "the loudest, most obnoxious and notorious piece of real estate in all of college football."

Florida Field at Ben Hill Griffin Stadium is in fact more commonly known as The Swamp. It has the reputation of being the toughest place in the country to play in all of college football. With five expansions since 1930, The Swamp can now host more than 90,000 fans and so it has become even louder than before.

The Swamp; Florida Field at Ben Hill Griffin Stadium

The Swamp did not simply appear one day out of nowhere in 1930. The Timeline of The Swamp as we know it today is courtesy of GatorZone.com. It all began in April 16, 1930 when construction begins on what would be the original Florida Field. It did not take long but it was after the 1930 season began when on October 27, 1930, construction was completed.

Construction Begins on Florida Field in 1930

The original 1930 Florida Field came with a capacity of 21,769. For those familiar with the venue, this original stadium consisted of what is now seen as the lower half of the current stadium. All that was needed after all the construction equipment was removed was for somebody to blow the whistle so that the Gators could begin to play some football.

Construction Continues Florida Field in 1930

That happened on November 8, 1930 with the dedication of Florida Field. A total sellout crowd of of 21,769 watched Florida play Alabama. It was the legendary Red Barber, a UF student, who called the play-by-play that day.

Florida Field let the Bands Play

Florida Field in the 1930's

On October 13, 1934: Florida Field was re-dedicated to commemorate the memory of servicemen who died in World War I. Overflow crowds were common in such a low-capacity stadium and so it was time for UF's main stadium to grow-up a bit.

Construction of the west stands, August 1950.

After the season on December 16, 1949 the plans were drawn to add 11,200 seats to the west stands. This first real expansion was finished on time for the 1950 season, bringing total capacity, including temporary bleachers which were also added, to 40,116. Lights were also added.

On September 23, 1950, the first night game was played at Florida Field against The Citadel. Small amounts of temporary and permanent seating were added throughout the years in non-major projects.

Sept 23, 1950 First Night Game at Florida Field

There still were not enough seats and so after the season in December,1965: construction immediately began for an east side 10,000-seat addition. This brought permanent seating to 56,164... The temporary bleachers were becoming more permanent and needed. They were moved to the south end zone for total capacity of 62,800 during the 1966 season.

In the 1970s, there was a rush to make stadium fields "modern looking," by replacing the grass with artificial turf. In April 1971, an artificial surface was installed in Florida Field.

More seats were still needed. So, in August 1982, in the third major expansion. UF completed the south end zone, bringing capacity to

72,000. An athletic training center and a skybox tower and modern press box were also built during this project.

On September 9, 1989 as discussed above, the Football Stadium was named Ben Hill Griffin Stadium at Florida Field during dedication ceremonies. As discussed above, the stadium was named in honor of Ben Hill Griffin Jr., a life-long Gator supporter and fan who had been extremely benevolent and generous to a number of sectors at the University of Florida.

On December 31, Florida took action that would change the complexion of Gator Football forever. The University of Florida hired Heisman winner Steve Spurrier, to coach the 1990 Florida Gators. Spurrier is shown below at the announcement event on New Years Eve, 1989. With the renamed stadium, and a new coach, the 1990 Gators had a newly renamed house to play in and they had a great new coach to make sure they played well.

There is nothing like natural grass for football. Rather than replace the artificial turf, on June 30, 1990: natural grass was brought back to replace the artificial turf at Florida Field. The turf had lasted about twenty years. The Spurrier era began on natural grass.

In the fourth major expansion, in September, 1991, construction was completed on new north end zone, bringing the capacity to 83,000, making Florida Field one of the eight largest on-campus collegiate football stadiums in the nation and the largest in the state of Florida. The cost of the north end zone expansion was $17 million, but there was no state funding required.

On October 12, 1991: The official dedication of the new north end zone was held, as Florida met the Tennessee Volunteers. Red Barber, who called the original dedication game in 1930, was UF's special guest of honor.

All of this space and more was about to be used. On November 30, 1991, Ben Hill Griffin Stadium was the site of the largest football crowd (collegiate or professional) in the state of Florida history (85,461 vs. FSU). During the 1991 and 1992 seasons the stadium would be the site of the 12 largest crowds in state history.

At the end of the 1991 Season: Head Coach Steve Spurrier labeled Ben Hill Griffin Stadium at Florida Field "The Swamp." Coach Spurrier said: "The swamp is where Gators live. We feel comfortable there, but we hope our opponents feel tentative. A swamp is hot and sticky and can be dangerous."

A minimal expansion of less significance to capacity was done in August of 1998. This $2.1 million video project allowed fans to catch game action on the new Daktronics LED Video Board located in the SEZ or on one of the 23 monitors located underneath the North and South endzone mezzanines.

A $4.8 million renovation of the South Endzone complex expanded the locker room, strength and conditioning area and medical training area to 51,000 square feet. The complex, which features displays on Gator Greats, also includes a 130-seat amphitheater squad meeting room. It ain't over 'til it's over.

On May 14, 2001, the fifth major expansion and renovation occurred. It cost a whopping $55 million. The mission was to expand the press level, add chairback seats on a new club level, renovate existing suites and add additional luxury suites. The press level was expanded to more than 200 working press seats and six TV/radio booths.

More than 2,900 chairback seats, dubbed the "Champions Club" were also added on the west side of the stadium. Twenty-eight existing suites were renovated and an additional 28 suites were built. The entire project, built with no state money, was completed just prior to the 2003 football season.

The current official seating capacity is 88,548, although the actual attendance regularly exceeds 90,000.

Before the 2008 season, the Heavener Football Complex opened on the southwest corner of Florida Field at Ben Hill Griffin Stadium. Like other expansions, this $28 million addition, which was funded entirely with private donations, is meant to be the "front door" of the football program and houses a museum highlighting Gator football history along with offices, meeting space, a new weight room, and other facilities for the football program.

Following the Gators' 2008 BCS Championship season with coach Urban Myer, large Daktronics HD-16 video boards were installed atop the upper deck of both endzones. The screen in the south endzone is 30 feet x 137 ft while the one in the north endzone is 25 feet by 75 feet. These screens display statistics, replays, advertisements, and other things that add to the football experience.

Construction seems to always be going on at the stadium though the 90,000 plus capacity was not increased. After the 2011 season, an extensive renovation of the 1950s-era concourse under the west stands improved restrooms, lighting, concessions, and crowd circulation patterns and added flat-screen displays for fan viewing.

On September 3, 2016, The "Head Ball Coach," Steve Spurrier was back at The Swamp on a Saturday night to be recognized for his great Gators playing and coaching career as Florida's field was dedicated to him.

The Gators changed their official field name to Steve Spurrier-Florida Field at Ben Hill Stadium in honor of the 1966 Heisman winner and Hall of Famer. Spurrier addressed the Florida crowd prior to its season opener against Massachusetts.

Steve Spurrier-Florida Field at Ben Hill Griffin Stadium

Also, in September 2016, the school's University Athletic Association Board proposed a $100 million facilities upgrade. This is to include a $60 million stand-alone football facility for players. The stand-alone facility would include an updated locker room, 3-D hologram training environment, strength and conditioning center, hydrotherapy space, team meeting rooms, coaching offices and nutrition bar.

The facility is to be built by the engineering firm HOK. When the new facility is completed, some of the redundant space in Ben Hill Griffin Stadium will be converted to other uses.

As one would think, the Gators have played the vast majority of their home contests at Florida Field since it opened in 1930. The most notable exception is the annual Florida-Georgia game. This game has been held at various stadiums in Jacksonville since 1933 with the two teams alternating being the official home team.

The only seasons in which UF and UGA did not meet in Jacksonville were 1994 and 1995, when the old Gator Bowl was being rebuilt into a venue now known as EverBank Field. This was needed for the NFL's expansion Jacksonville Jaguars. In these two years, their "friendly" neutral field contest was held both at Florida's Swamp, and Georgia's Sanford Stadium, respectively in those two years.

Steve Spurrier Field at Ben Hill Griffin Stadium Today

Over the years, Florida would often schedule another home game in Jacksonville, Tampa, or (less frequently) Miami and even Orlando. Even with their annual Jacksonville meeting with Georgia, the Gators still every now and then play a regular season home contest at another venue in Florida besides Florida Field. For example, in September 1980, they defeated the California Golden Bears in old Tampa Stadium.

Look for the construction crane at UF's Steve Spurrier Field ad Ben Hill Griffin Stadium again in the future. With the popularity of college football and stadiums over 100,000 in capacity becoming more and more commonplace, you can bet the Florida Alums and fans will soon be pressing for more capacity. Maybe one day, there will even be a seat for yours truly. It's OK with me if it is a different seat every year.

A rendering of the Florida Gators' $65 million football-only complex. [COURTESY: University Athletic Association]

In March 2018, Florida crossed the t's, and dotted the i's on the plans to solve the need for better football, baseball, and softball facilities. The fields should be ready sometime from 2020 to 2022.

After months of detailed conversations and proposals about a stand-alone football complex, Florida knew it had another problem to solve.

Its baseball stadium was squeezing space for football.
On Friday, the Gators announced their $50 million solution: Build a new baseball stadium for the defending national champions to make way for a football facility that will help that program add to its collection, too.

Both projects and an upgrade to the softball stadium are part of a $130 million facilities package approved Friday by the board of trustees to keep UF competitive in college sports' arms race.

Chapter 4 The Evolution of Modern Football

Yale vs. Columbia

There was lots of playing before playing football became official

The official agreed upon date for the first American-style college football game is November 6, 1869. If you can find a replay of this game someplace in the heavens, however, you would find it would not look much like football as we know it. But, it was not completely soccer or rugby either.

Before this game, teams were playing a rugby style similar to that played in Britain in the mid-19th century. At the time in the US, a derivative known as association football was also played. In both games, a football is kicked at a goal or run over a line. These styles were based on the varieties of English public school football games. Over time, as noted, the style of "football" play in America continued to evolve.

On November 6, 1869, the first football game in America featured Rutgers and Princeton. Before the teams were even on the field it was being plugged as the first college football game of all time. Penn State did not get a Rugby team until the early 1960's. Nobody at Penn State in 1869, from what I could find, was even thinking about the game of football.

The first game of intercollegiate football was a sporting battle between two neighboring schools on a plot of ground where the present-day Rutgers gymnasium now stands in New Brunswick, N.J. Rutgers won that first game, 6-4.

There were two teams of 25 men each and the rules were rugby-like, but different enough to make it very interesting and enjoyable.

Like today's football, there were many surprises; strategies needed to be employed; determination exhibited, and of course the players required physical prowess.

1st Game Rutgers 6 Princeton 4 College Field, New Brunswick, NJ

At 3 p.m. the 50 combatants as well as 100 spectators gathered on the field. Most sat on a low wooden fence and watched the athletes discard their hats, coats and vests. The players used their suspenders as belts. To give a unique look, Rutgers wore scarlet-colored scarfs, which they converted into turbans. This contrasted them with the bareheaded boys from Princeton.

Two members of each team remained more or less stationary near the opponent's goal in the hopes of being able to slip over and score from unguarded positions. Thus, the present day "sleeper" was conceived. The remaining 23 players were divided into groups of 11 and 12. While the 11 "fielders" lined up in their own territory as defenders, the 12 "bulldogs" carried the battle.

Each score counted as a "game" and 10 games completed the contest. Following each score, the teams changed direction. The ball could be advanced only by kicking or batting it with the feet, hands, heads or sides.

Rutgers put a challenge forward that three games were to be played that year. The first was played at New Brunswick and won by Rutgers. Princeton won the second game, but cries of "over-emphasis" prevented the third game in football's first year when faculties of both institutions protested on the grounds that the games were interfering with student studies.

This is an excerpt of the Rutgers account of the game on its web site. A person named Herbert gave this detailed account of the play in the first game:

"Though smaller on the average, the Rutgers players, as it developed, had ample speed and fine football sense. Receiving the ball, our men formed a perfect interference around it and with short, skillful kicks and dribbles drove it down the field. Taken by surprise, the Princeton men fought valiantly, but in five minutes we had gotten the ball through to our captains on the enemy's goal and S.G. Gano, '71 and G.R. Dixon, '73, neatly kicked it over. None thought of it, so far as I know, but we had without previous plan or thought evolved the play that became famous a few years later as 'the flying wedge'."

"Next period Rutgers bucked, or received the ball, hoping to repeat the flying wedge," Herbert's account continues. "But the first time we formed it Big Mike came charging full upon us. It was our turn for surprise. The Princeton battering ram made no attempt to reach the ball but, forerunner of the interference-breaking ends of today, threw himself into our mass play, bursting us apart, and bowing us over. Time and again Rutgers formed the wedge and charged; as often Big Mike broke it up. And finally, on one of these incredible break-ups a

Princeton bulldog with a long accurate, perhaps lucky kick, sent the ball between the posts for the second score.

It was at this point that a Rutgers professor could stand it no longer. Waving his umbrella at the participants, he shrieked, "You will come to no Christian end!"

Herbert's account of the game continues: "The fifth and sixth goals went to Rutgers. The stars of the latter period of play, in the memory of the players after the lapse of many years, were "Big

Mike" and Large (former State Senator George H. Large of Flemington, another Princeton player) ...

The University of Notre Dame did not get into the football act until the late 1880's. At this time, the rules of rugby kept changing to accommodate the infatuation for the Americanized style of "football" play that would ultimately become the American game of football.

Walter Camp: the father of American football?

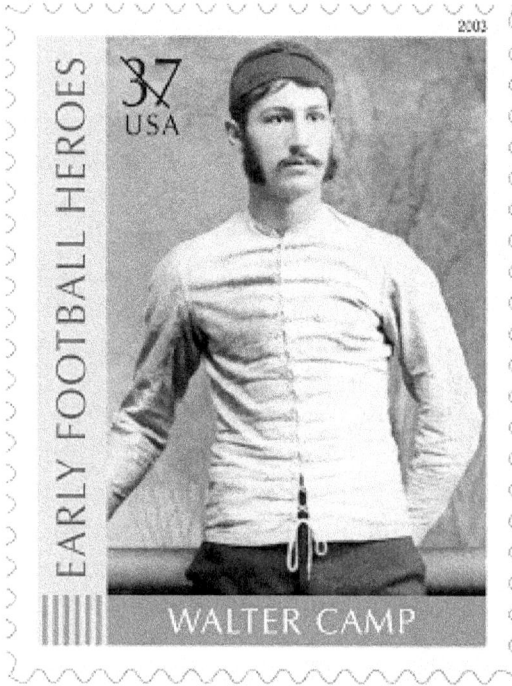

Walter Camp was a very well-known rugby player from Yale. In today's world, he would have been characterized as a rugby hero. It was his love of the game, his knowledge of the game as it was played, and his innovative mind that caused him to take the evolution of football even further. He pioneered the changes to the rules of rugby that slowly transformed the sport into the new game of American Football.

The rule changes that were introduced to the rugby and

association style (like soccer) of play were mostly those authored by Camp, who was also a Hopkins School graduate. For his original efforts, Walter Camp today is considered to be the "Father of American Football". Among the important changes brought to the game were the introduction of a line of scrimmage; down-and-distance rules; and the legalization of interference (blocking).

There was no such thing in those days as a forward pass and so the legalization of interference in 1880 football permitted blocking for runners. The forward pass would add another dimension to the game that made it much different than rugby or association football.

Soon after the early football changes, in the late nineteenth and into the early twentieth centuries, more game-play type developments were introduced by college coaches. The list is like a who's who of early American College Football. Coaches, such as Eddie Cochems, Amos Alonzo Stagg, Parke H. Davis, Knute Rockne, John Heisman, and Glenn "Pop" Warner helped introduce and then take advantage of the newly introduced forward pass. College football as well as professional football, were introduced prior to the 20th century. Fans were lured into watching again and again once they saw the game played.

College football especially grew in popularity despite the existence of pro-football. It became the dominant version of the sport of football in the United States. It was this way for the entire first half of the 20th century. Bowl games made the idea of football even more exciting in the college ranks. Rivalries grew and continued and the fans loved it! This great football tradition brought a national audience to college football games that still dominates the sports world today.

This book has little to do with pro-football or any other sport. However, there is no denying that the greatest college football players more often than not eventually found their fortunes in professional football. Pro football can be traced back to the season that Notre Dame brought forth a real football team after a two-year lapse from its last half-Rugby season in 1889. It was 1892 when William "Pudge" Heffelfinger signed a $500 contract to play for the Allegheny Athletic Association against the Pittsburgh Athletic Club.

Twenty-eight years later, the American Professional Football Association was formed. This league changed its name to the National Football League (NFL) just two years later. Eventually, the NFL became the major league of American football. Originally, just a sport played in Midwestern industrial towns in the United States, professional football eventually became a national phenomenon. We all know this because from August to February, in America, many of us are glued to our TV sets or chained to our seats in some of the most intriguing pro-football stadiums in America.

Legends existed all during the formation of football. There was Stagg, Halas, Warner, Thorpe, Heisman, Grange, Rockne and The Four Horsemen.

The Heisman

In 1935, New York City's Downtown Athletic Club awarded its first Heisman Trophy to University of Chicago halfback Jay Berwanger. He was also the first ever NFL Draft pick in 1936. The trophy continues to this day to recognize the nation's "most outstanding" college football player. It has become one of the most coveted awards in all of American sports.

New formations and play sets continued to be developed by innovative coaches and their staffs. Emory Bellard from the University of Texas, developed a three-back option style offense known as the wishbone. Bear Bryant of Alabama became a preacher of the wishbone.

The strategic opposite of the wishbone is called the spread offense. Some teams have managed to adapt with the times to keep winning consistently. In the rankings of the most victorious programs, Michigan, Texas, and Notre Dame are ranked first, second, and third in total wins.

And so that is as far as we will take it in this chapter about the early evolution of football. With so many conferences and sports associations as well as pro, college, high school, and mini sports, something tells me we have not yet seen our last rule change

Jay Berwanger, 1st Heisman Winner

Chapter 5 Gators Football – Next Seven Years 1907-1913

Forsythe   Coach #1
Pyle   Coach #2

Year	Coach	Record	Conf	Record
1906	Jack "Pee Wee" Forsythe	5-3-1		
1907	Jack "Pee Wee" Forsythe	4-1-1		
1908	Jack "Pee Wee" Forsythe	5-2-1		
1909	George Pyle	6-1-1		
1910	George Pyle	6-1-0		
1911	George Pyle	5-0-1		
1912	George Pyle	5-2-1	SIAA	0-2-1
1913	George Pyle	4-3-0	SIAA	2-2-0

1907 UF Football Team Coach Pee Wee Forsythe

Look above the picture and you can see that each year the Florida football team was above 500 with some fine years in the mix. You can see the championships from way back without anybody making them wll known to you. "Almost" championships and championships were part of the Gators tradition from 1906 on.

It was not until the 1930's that the losing seasons began to make it seem that losing wa the Gators tradition. Not so. That was 24 years after the first game. As you can see, long before Steve Spurrier brought the Gators their winning ways, it was a natural for the early teams to win and win and win.

With the creation of the University of Florida via the Buckman act and the establishment of the campus in Gainesville, the university fielded its first football team in 1906 led by former Clemson star Jack "Pee Wee" Forsythe. Forsythe coached for three seasons compiling a 14–6–2 record with a 0.682 winning percentage. Here is another photo of the team celebrating a victory over Savannah:

In addition to his coaching duties, Forsythe also played on the team as a fullback and was paid $500 for coaching and another $500 for playing. In their first game, the University of Florida football team defeated Gainesville Athletic Club 6-0 on Oct. 5, 1906 in front of a "crowd" of 150 people (the university had 100 students enrolled at the time).

The game was played on a fenced in field in Porter's community center in Gainesville so the university could charge admission. The profit from the game was $5.20. The team finished the 1906 season with a 5-3 record.

Read more: http://gatornation.proboards.com/thread/8909/florida-gators-1906-1919#ixzz4dJJdXQg6

1907 Florida Gators Football Coach Jack Forsythe
Championship caliber season

The UF official football program began in 1906. In 1907, the Florida football team posted a 4–1–1 record, due in large part to the play of star Tailback and Quarterback Willie Shands from Gainesville, who later was elected as a state senator and helped found the UF medical school Shands Hospital in 1953.

Only four men from the 1906 team returned. Captain Roy Corbett was also the athletics editor of the Florida Pennant.

The 1907 Florida football team was coached by Jack Forsythe in its 2nd season and his second season as head coach of the UF Football team.

The Orange and Blue lost on Oct 12 to the Mercer Bears for the second season in a row in Macon GA L (0-6); beat the Columbia Agricultural College W (6-0 on Oct 26 in Savannah; beat a tough Rollins College Tars W (9-4) on Nov 9 in the Baseball Park on the Gainesville, Florida campus;

The Gators beat the Riverside Athletic Club Nov 28 (picture above) at the Baseball Park W (17-0); and tied the Tars T (0-0) on their home field in Winter Park, Florida. As noted, Coach Forsythe's 1907 Florida football team posted an overall record of 4–1–1 in their second varsity season. If the teams that they played had a league, the Gators would have been the champs.

1908 Florida Gators Football Coach Jack Forsythe

The 1907 Florida football team was coached by Jack Forsythe in its 3rd season and Forsythe's third season and last as head coach of the UF Football team. Forsythe's 1908 Florida football team posted a record of 5–2–1 in their third varsity season. The fine 1908 team (5-1-1) had a lot to do with the play of Willie Shands.

<During this season and others following, Earle "Dummy" Taylor (Left) became the only UF player ever to earn five football letters. He played five seasons as a halfback and drop-kicker, beginning with his freshman season in 1908. He was quite a player. He ran for touchdowns of 43, 75 and 60 yards in a 28-3 win over Rollins in 1909. His field-goal records for a game (three), season (eight in 1911) and career (16) stood until the mid-1970s.

The team captain, William Gibbs, came in as a veteran transfer. As noted, it was the first season for the talented Gainesville young man. Dummy Taylor. The backfield had some fine players including

Charlie Bartleson, Jim Vidal, and the already mentioned William A. Shands, future state senator and namesake of Shands Hospital.

<< Forsythe There are always stories in football that are often passed by word of mouth. One such story talks of the University of Florida becoming the "Florida Gators" and suggests it originated in 1908. There was a Gainesville shop owner who ordered orange and blue pennants with a gator emblem from the Michie Company, drawing inspiration from the University of Virginia, and the notion of being the "Gators" came naturally.

Working through the Gators starting lineup without a pic, from left to right we find Malhorton at left end; Rader at left tackle, Van Fleet at (left guard, Parker at center), Videll at right guard), J. Taylor at right tackle, and Shands at right end). In the backfield, Thompson played QB, Bartleson played left half, E. Taylor played right halfback, and Gibbs was the starting fullback).

On Oct 10, The Florida football team opened the season with a loss to the Mercer Baptists at Macon, GA for the third consecutive season. L (0-24). The Mercer team must have been good eaters as they outweighed Florida by twenty pounds.

In the games at Riverside, Florida beat the Riverside Athletic Club of Jacksonville twice. The first win on Oct 10 at the Baseball Park was 4–0. Former Gator Roy Corbett coached and played right halfback for Riverside. In the second game, the AC 37-0

Early game at the Swamp (to be Fleming Field)

On Oct 21, Florida then beat the Gainesville Athletic Club W 37–5 and then Columbia College on Oct 24, W (6-0) at Lake City, FL. Then Rollins got the best of the Gators L (0-5) at Winter Park, FL. The tough state champion Rollins Tars beat the Gators in a close match. The game breaker was Rollins' Harman breaking away for a 30-yard touchdown in the second half.

In the next game on Nov. 7, Florida played the Stetson College Hatters for the first time, beating them in a close game 6–5 on the Orange and Blue's home field (Baseball Field) in Gainesville. A great kick by Dummy Taylor's for the extra point decided the win over Stetson, after a Charlie Bartleson touchdown run.

Then, on Nov. 2,1 came the second win over Riverside W (37–0.) played at the Baseball Park.

On Nov. 26, Florida finished the season with a rematch that ended in a tie (0-0) against Stetson at the Hatters' home field in DeLand, Florida.

1909 Florida Gators Football Coach George Pyle
Championship caliber season

In its fourth season, the 1909 University of Florida football team was coached by George Pyle in his first season as head coach of the Gators. This year, 1908 the University of the State of Florida officially shortened its name to the University of Florida Pyle's 1909 Florida football team finished its fourth varsity football season with a nicely played 6–1–1 set of games.

Coach George Pyle 1909-1913

On October 8, the Gators opened the season with a nice in W (5–0) of the Gainesville Athletic Club. In the next game on Oct 23 v Olympics in Jacksonville, FL, UF prevailed W (9-0). This was the second week of play, Dummy Taylor was on the mark and he kicked three field goals, all that was needed to beat the Olympics 9–0.

In this game, Moody was at left end); Wagner at left tackle, McMillian at left guard, Storter at center), Cox at right guard, Rader at right tackle), Johnston at right end and George Pile played quarterback. Shands was the left halfback; Taylor played right halfback, and Vidal (started at fullback). They all played well.

On Oct 30, Florida defeated the Rollins College Tars for the first of two times. The second was at the end of the season. In this first game in Gainesville, Florida beat Rollins 14–0 in a contest described as "fast and furious". Taylor hit McCormick on a 20-yard pass, and scored every point.

On Nov. 6, UF was beaten by Stetson in DeLand FL L (0-26). On Nov. 24, UF played Stetson again but could not get much scoring done again. This time the D held and the Gators tied Stetson T (5-5) against this tougher than nails team. UF lost L (26-0). This was the second game of another two-for against the Stetson College Hatters. It was twice in the same season for the second year in a row. The first loss was at the Hatters' home field in DeLand, Florida. The tie was at home. 1909 was the last season in which Stetson claimed a state championship

In their second game with Rollins on Nov 15 in Orlando, Florida beat Rollins W (28–3). Florida fumbled the kickoff and Rollins made a field goal. Taylor ran 45 and 75 yards for touchdowns in the first half. In the second half, Taylor had another 60-yard run. Edgerton had a 30-yard run and McCormick had one of 80 years. Game was called on darkness.

On Nov. 20, in the second game of another two-for, at the Baseball Park, the Gators beat Olympics W (11-0). On Nov 28, the Tallahassee Athletic Club came to the Baseball Park in Gainesville and were whooped 24-0.

1910 Florida Gators Football Coach George Pyle

In its fifth season, the 1910 University of Florida football team was coached by George Pyle in his second season as head coach of the Gators. This year the Gators were undefeated on their home field, with an overall record of 6–1 and a Southern Intercollegiate Athletic Association (SIAA) record of 1–1.

The season began on Oct 8 with a nice win W (23-0) vs. the Gainesville Guards at the Baseball Park. On Oct 15, UF traveled to Jacksonville to play Georgia A & M and had a great day defeating them W (52-0). Always having a tough time with Mercer, the Gators had not figured out the magic yet of beating the Baptists. In a game played at Central City Park in Macon Georgia on Oct 22, UF lost again to Mercer L (0-13).

On Nov 5, UF traveled to Jacksonville and beat the Citadel W (6-2). Then, on Nov 12 the Gators took on a once-tough Rollins team at Winter Park and beat them big time, W (38-0). On Nov. 19, Charleston played at the Baseball Park in Gainesville and were soundly beaten by the Florida W 34–0. In a season finale, UF traveled to Lake City and played the Columbia Athletic Club and won a nice match W (33-0)

A point of confusion for readers of the results of early football games is typically the fact that it is not all colleges and universities who line up as opponents. Florida began its formal program in 1906 and so, in 1910, it had been playing collegiate v Intramural football for just five years. Thus, those scheduling games had a tough time finding teams willing to play—especially if your team was really good.

Therefore, there are many schools who at this time would not only play athletic clubs who would be made up of former players who had graduated or those who never went to college and some who were still in high school. In fact, many schools across the country played High School Teams who were brave enough to face them.

It was so tough to get a good game, that mostly anybody would play anybody and there was no NCAA back then to tell the colleges and university they could not do whatever they wanted. By scheduling athletic clubs and high schools, the "lads" on the tea got a lot more game action than they would otherwise.

1911 Florida Gators Football Coach George Pyle
Championship caliber season

In its sixth season, the 1911 University of Florida football team was coached by George Pyle in his third season as head coach of the Gators. This year the Gators were undefeated on their home field, with an overall record of 6–1 and a Southern Intercollegiate Athletic Association (SIAA) record of 1–1.

This year, there were no high schools nor athletic clubs on Florida's football schedule but there were also just six games. The season began on Oct 7 against the Citadel in the Baseball Field. Florida won W (15-3). Taking the bus to South Carolina's Davis Field, in Columbia, the Gators on Oct 21 played South Carolina to a tie T (6-6).

Moving down what was a tough schedule, on Oct 25, UF took on Clemson at Bowman Field in Calhoun SC and literally squeaked out a victory W (6-5). Back Home at the Baseball Field, UF beat Columbia College on Nov 4 W (9-0).

Then, UF took the bus to DeLand Florida and played Stetson, and made the trip worthwhile with a nice win W (27-0). In its sixth and last game of the season, Florida was on the road again at Jacksonville to play Charleston. The Gators got their fifth win of the season against no losses and one tie. George Pyle knew how to coach.

**1912 Florida Gators Football Coach George Pyle
Won the Bacardi Bowl Championship**

The 1912 Florida Gators football team, the seventh season for Florida, was the fourth for George Pyle as the Gators football team's head coach. Pyle's 1912 Florida Gators finished their seventh varsity football season with an SIAA conference record of 1–2 and an overall winning record of 5–2–1. Not too shabby for a still neophyte program.

The 1912 season was marked by several exciting first-time events for the Florida Gators. Though in this book, we called them the Gators out of the chute, this was the first full season that the Florida football team would compete as the "Florida Gators"; the first games that they played against two future rivals, the Auburn Tigers and Georgia Tech Yellow Jackets (both games were losses); their first-ever victory over the South Carolina Gamecocks; their first season played in the Southern Intercollegiate Athletic Association (SIAA); and the first time they ever participated in a post-season bowl game. Florida also claimed the state championship by beating in-state rival Stetson for the third consecutive year.

1912 Gators practicing on UF Campus

Now, can any of you folks top that for a productive year of any program, institution, or business? Congratulations Gators! You make us all proud and we've been that way for over 100 years.

To bring us all up-to-date, before the season had even begun, Florida joined the Southern Intercollegiate Athletic Association. It had been playing games against teams from the conference for a few years before. The SIAA, when Florida joined was a large confederation of southern athletic programs that was the precursor to several other regional conferences, including the Southeastern Conference. This raised the profile of the young UF program, perhaps immeasurably at the time.

We all know in this chapter that 1912 was only the seventh academic year for the modern University of Florida. It allowed more contests against older football programs in the south and elsewhere. In some ways, Florida, was experiencing a baptism of fire as it faced many teams that had been playing even tougher team than the Gators. As Florida sportswriter and UF alumnus Tom McEwen wrote, "it was in 1912 when the Gators really ventured out into big-time football."

Florida played two more games this year than the last. Both were against Athletic clubs which we explained helped to keep the adrenalin flowing with a real game against unknown opponents who really wanted to beat you. The price a new team in a new conference paid in those days to be part of better football all-around was that they played less home games.

On Oct 12, UF played Auburn at Drake Field in Auburn, Alabama. The Gators performed well but lost L (27–13). On Oct 19, at home in the Baseball Field, which was renamed University Field, Florida beat South Carolina W (10-6).

Skipping a week, on October 26, UF played Georgia Tech in Jacksonville, Florida and the Gators looked good while losing L (6-14). On Nov 4, Charleston marched into University Field to take on the gators but they had a real tough time this day in Gainesville, Florida and were beaten soundly by the Gators W 78–0.

On Nov 15. Stetson, a team that was always ready to play came to University Field and were beaten soundly by UF W (23–7). On Nov 28, a tough Mercer team came with its winning bags ready to take away a triumph. When Mercer left, nothing was in the bag but a sweet grandmother's kiss for the tie game T (0-0) that they played against the Gators.

The season was not over as southern teams can play a lot longer than northern teams. On Dec. 20 at the Tampa Athletic Club, UF prevailed decidedly W 44–0. Then, on Christmas Day, December 25 at the Vedado Athletic Club in Almendares Park • Havana, Cuba, UF won the Bacardi Bowl W 28–0. Good things were beginning to happen.

1913 Florida Gators Football Coach George Pyle

The 1913 Florida Gators football team, the eighth season for Florida, was the fifth and final year for George Pyle as the Gators football team's head coach. Pyle had one a great job as coach and had ushered UF into the big-time. Pyle's 1913 Florida Gators finished their eighth varsity football season with an SIAA conference record of 2–2 and an overall winning record of 4-3 Not too shabby for an off-year in what would be called still neophyte program.

The 1913 Florida Gators football team represented the University of Florida during the 1913 Southern Intercollegiate Athletic Association

football season. The season was George Pyle's fifth and last as the head coach of the Florida Gators football team. Pyle's 1913 Florida Gators completed their eighth varsity football season with an overall record of 4–3 and their fourth year in the Southern Intercollegiate Athletic Association (SIAA) with a conference record of 2–2.
The 144–0 defeat of Florida Southern is the largest in school history

To begin the season, the UF played a team that should not have been on the field. It was like there was no D and UF could do as it pleased. There had not been enough time from the beginning of football for any tea to really know that scoring over 75 points might be frowned upon.

Nonetheless, on Oct 6. The Gators had to be all charged up to play a team that wanted to beat them as much as they wanted to beat the other team. Florida Southern marched proudly into "The Baseball Field" and expected to make a game out of it. Perhaps because of the tough competition UF had faced that never gave an inch. The Gators felt it was OK to not move an inch and they defeated Florida Southern by a frightful score of 144 to nothing. I bet after the game, they wished they could have taken a bunch of touchdowns away. We all learn by our mistakes.

Auburn, a really tough team for a long time on Oct 11 let UF have it the following week as they pounded the Gators 55-0. This score did not seem big because of the prior week's major blowout.

On Oct 18, Maryville came to Gainesville and knew there would be no mercy. Compared to Florida Southern, they did fine at W (39-0). UF was getting tough for sure and it showed it the following week Oct 25 at Georgia Tech in Jacksonville with a squeaker win W (13-3).

On Nov 8, South Carolina did not let UF score a point but go just 13 themselves L (0-13). The Citadel, like UF had been upgrading its program and they called the Gators to task on the field but lost nonetheless W (18-13).
0s
On Nov 27, at home, UF was happy to beat a typically tough Mercer team W (24-0) to close out the season.

Chapter 6 C. J. McCoy Era 1914-1916

Coach # 3

Year	Coach	Record
1914	C. J. McCoy	5–2-0
1915	C. J. McCoy	4–3-0
1916	C. J. McCoy	0–5-0

The first losing season came in 1916.

1914 Florida Gators Football Team

1914 Florida Gators Football Coach C.J. McCoy

The 1914 Florida Gators football team, the ninth season for Florida, was the first of three years coaching for C. J. McCoy as the Football Gators head coach. All new coaches are suspect, especially after succeeding a fine coach such as George Pyle.

As noted previously, Pyle had done a great job as coach and had moved UF football into the big-leagues. That made it hard for C. J. McCoy to take over and be immediately successful. Yet, his 1914 Florida Gators finished their ninth varsity football season with an SIAA conference record of 3–2 and an overall winning record of 5-2

Not too shabby for an off-year in what would be called a still-neophyte program.

McCoy's 1914 Florida Gators completed their ninth varsity football season on a four-game winning streak, with an overall record of 5-2 and an SIAA conference record of 3-2.

<<<C. J. McCoy
The season began against a tough Auburn team on Oct 10 in Jacksonville L (0-20). On Oct 17, it was back home against King's College W (36-0) Sewanee was a really tough team and they beat Florida on Oct 24 L (0-26). Southern Florida was next on the schedule in a game played at Tampa W (59-0).

Wofford visited the Gators home campus on Nov 7 and were beaten up by Florida W (66-0). On Nov 14, the Gators traveled to the Citadel and played tough enough to win a close W (7-0) at Charles Park Stadium in Charleston South Carolina. Mercer was next on November 26 for the season Finale at Mercer W (14-0)

1915 Florida Gators Football Coach C.J. McCoy

The 1915 Florida Gators football team, the tenth season for Florida, was the second of three years coaching for C. J. McCoy as the

Football Gators head coach. This was not as productive a year for Coach McCoy. They finished with an overall record of 4–3 and in their sixth year in the Southern Intercollegiate Athletic Association (SIAA), they came in with a conference record of 3–3.

1915 Gators team photo Coach Charlie McCoy on right

In 1914, we know that first-year head coach Charles J. McCoy had released a Florida team that performed in the top half of the SIAA. In 1915, McCoy also assumed the role as the school's first basketball coach.

The football team captain was tackle A. A. "Daddy" Lotspeich. At the guards were Ham Dowling, future Georgia Tech transfer, and Everett Yon, future Gator athletic director. Leading the backfield was Rammy Ramsdell, "the Gators' first quarterback of note," and the first scholarship athlete at the University of Florida.

McCoy got an assistant for 2015--Z. J. Stanley. In 2014, he had been the coach of the Maryville Scots.

The season began on Oct 9, again the first opponent was Auburn. The game was played at Drake Field in Alabama. Auburn won the game again L (0-7). On Oct 16, the Gators played Sewanee at Barrs

Field in Jacksonville and lost by the same score L (0-7). Florida Southern was an easier match but each time they get just a little tougher. On Oct 20, the Gators won W (45-0). The Gators played Georgia next on Nov 6. Georgia dominated the game L (0-37).

On Nov 13, The Citadel came to Gainesville for a Gator home game won by Florida W (6-0). On Nov 18 in another home game, the Gators defeated Tulane W (14-7). The Gators finished their 1915 season against Mercer at Macon Georgia W (34-7)

1916 Florida Gators Football Coach C.J. McCoy

Having coached for two years and believing he finally had the makings of a great Gators squad, Coach McCoy looked out and booked the most ambitious and difficult Gators football schedule to date. There were no breather teams. The best laid plans of mice and men often go astray. This was the case as the coach's plans were thwarted by a series of injuries and academic ineligibility problems. He was lucky to field a team.

It began with Gators' starting quarterback, Rammy Ramsdell. The QB broke his leg playing baseball against Auburn Tigers. The team then saw experienced guard Ham Dowling transferring schools, and tackle Everett Yon was called by the National Guard to defend the Mexican border.

Due to a shortage of men players, captain Rex Farrior, previously a center, moved to fullback. Mercer had scheduled a game with Florida, but several Mercer linemen were behind in their studies, and so the game that might have given Florida a win was cancelled.

The 1916 Florida Gators football team, the eleventh season for Florida, was the third (last) of three years coaching for C. J. McCoy as the Football Gators head coach. This was a terrible year for the Gators and Coach McCoy. The team had been depleted of first-string football talent and it also lacked depth, McCoy's 1916 Florida Gators ended their season disastrously with an overall record of 0–5 and a Southern Intercollegiate Athletic Association (SIAA) conference record of 0–4.

Chapter 7 Alfred Buser & William G Kline Era 1917 - 1922

Coach #4 Alfred E. Buser
Coach #5 William G. Kline

Year	Coach	Record	Conference	Record
1917	Alfred E. Buser	2–4-0	SIAA	0-4-0
1918	Alfred E. Buser	0–1-0	SIAA	none
1919	Alfred E. Buser	5–3-0	SIAA	2-2-0
1920	William G. Kline	6–3-0	SIAA	1-3-0
1921	William G. Kline	6–3-2	SIAA	4-1-2
1922	William G. Kline	7–2-0	SoCon	2–0-0

Florida got through the losing seasons and then moved on to championship caliber play with coach William G. Kline for three years.

1917 Florida Gators Football Coach Alfred E. Buser

The 1917 Florida Gators football team, the twelfth season for Florida, was the first of three years coaching for Alfred E. Buser.

Buser in 1911 as Wisconsin team captain

This was another bad year but not as bad as 1916. Buser's 1917 Florida Gators ended their season with an overall record of 2–4 and a Southern Intercollegiate Athletic Association (SIAA) conference record of 0–4.

Coach Buser was a great football player who was declared an All-American lineman for the Wisconsin Badgers in 1911. Buser promised to bring a Midwestern power football style of play to revive the Gators after the winless 1916 season. Captain "Rowdy Bill" Wilkinson was the team's only returning letterman for 1917.

South Carolina Game 1917 Signed Picture

1918 Florida Gators Football Coach Alfred E. Buser

The 1918 Florida Gators football team was the thirteenth season for Florida. It was year 2 of three years coaching for Alfred E. Buser as the Football Gators head coach. The Gators' ranks were depleted by both the Spanish flu and the loss of World War I military volunteers and draftees, and the 1918 Gators played only one game a loss L (2-14) to a football team from Camp Johnston, Army Training Camp.

1919 Florida Gators Football Coach Alfred E. Buser

The 1919 Florida Gators football team was the fourteenth season for Florida. It was year 3 and the last of three years coaching for Alfred

E. Buser as the Football Gators head coach. Finally, Buser brought home a winner but he did not win games he should have and it got to be too much for Florida fans.

In fact, Florida students, fans and alumni had had enough of losing. They had learned to suffer through football losses to major Southern Intercollegiate Athletic Association (SIAA) opponents such as the Georgia Bulldogs and the Tulane Green Wave, but the 0-7 loss to the Florida Southern in 1919 was viewed by many as an unacceptable failure. Nevertheless, as noted, Buser's 1919 Florida Gators completed their football season with an improved overall record of 5-3 and an SIAA conference record of 2-2. Florida Southern had surely stepped up its game.

Jim Sparkman was the team captain this year. He had just returned from World War I service with the Rainbow Division after having playing for Florida from 1914 to 1916. Rondo Hatton was a substitute quarterback on the team.

1920 Florida Gators Football Coach William G. Kline

The 1920 Florida Gators football team was the fifteenth season for Florida. It was year 1 for new coach, law professor William G. Kline as the Football Gators head coach. Coach Kline, a law professor, was a former halfback for the Illinois Fighting Illini, and he previously had coached the Nebraska Cornhuskers.

<< Kline's 1920 Florida Gators compiled a marginally better 6-3 overall record than the 1919 Gators, but their 1-3 conference record against Southern Intercollegiate Athletic Association (SIAA) competition was poor.

The Gators improved their series records against traditional in-state opponents like the Florida Southern Moccasins and the Stetson Hatters, they also suffered a shutout defeat by the Tulane Green

Wave and lost their fourth consecutive game to the Georgia Bulldogs. In a season looking for big changes, they did not come.

1921 Florida Gators Football Coach William G. Kline

The 1921 Florida Gators football team was the sixteenth season for Florida. It was year 2 for coach & law professor William G. Kline as the Football Gators head coach. It was its 9th and final season for UF as a member of the Southern Intercollegiate Athletic Association (SIAA).

The Gators played their home games at the former Baseball Field, which was renamed as Fleming Field in Gainesville, Florida. They finished the season with a record of 6 wins, 3 losses, and 2 ties (6–3–2 overall, 4–1–2 in the SIAA), finishing 6th in conference play.

1921 Florida Gators Football Team

The Gators improved their record against major collegiate competition with a notable win against the Alabama Crimson Tide (9–2) in Tuscaloosa, Alabama. Florida's two losses against the Tennessee Volunteers (0–9) and the North Carolina Tar Heels (10–14) were both competitive and close.

The prowess of the Gators football team was noticed by other coaches. Coach Herman Stegeman of Georgia wrote in Spalding's

Football Guide "Florida, for the first time, had a strong team. Aided by Dixon, the South's best punter, they combined a kicking game and a well-diversified offense to good advantage." Captain Tootie Perry was the school's first ever All-Southern selection.

Before the season began James Van Fleet, a professor of military science joined Kline's coaching staff. In the era of Knute Rockne and Hugo Bezdek bringing in championships and undefeated seasons. The entire Florida staff faced heavy pressure from the alumni for putting together a winning football team.

To this end, and so "five players were brought from the University of Oklahoma and the western states" such as Ferdinand H. Duncan and Ark Newton. Newton allegedly first attended a practice only to watch, but the captain Tootie Perry was so impressed when he saw him that he offered Newton a uniform and coaxed him onto the field. Newton's punts sailed over the head of the return men, and brought the attention of all the Gator coaches. Football was now a national big time sport at the college level.

1922 Florida Gators Football Coach William G. Kline

The 1922 Florida Gators football team was the seventeenth season for Florida. It was year 3 and the final year for coach & law professor William G. Kline as the Football Gators head coach. It was the Gators first season with the new Southern Conference SoCon, placing fifth of twenty-one teams in the conference standings.

Kline's 1922 Florida Gators finished 7–2 overall, and 2–0 in their first year as members of the new Southern Conference.

Despite having an undefeated conference record, the team played only two conference opponents (Tulane and Clemson) and so it did not get the benefit of being co-champion along with with Vanderbilt, Georgia Tech, and North Carolina.

Even before Steve Spurrier, Florida, like Notre Dame and other great teams of the day had taken to the passing game in a big way. The 1922 Spalding's Football Guide ranked Florida as the best forward passing team in the country.

The team expected to do well and did but there was an unexpected loss early in the season to Furman in a close match. Otherwise the season was very interesting for the players as they got to visit Washington D. C. and the White House when traveling North for the first time to face the Harvard Crimson, and the upset of Tulane.

In the first season of the new Southern Conference (SoCon), freshmen were barred from play. 1921 had been the best year in Florida football history. Florida had two of the South's best punters in running backs Ark Newton and Ray Dickson.

Chapter 8 James Van Fleet & Harold L. Sebring Era 1923-1927

Coach #6 James Van Fleet
Coach #7 Harold L. Sebring

Year	Coach	Record	Conference	Record
1923	James Van Fleet	6–1–2	SoCon	1–0–2
1924	James Van Fleet	6–2–2	SoCon	2–0–1
1925	Harold L. Sebring	8–2–0	SoCon	3–2–0
1926	Harold L. Sebring	2–6–2	SoCon	1–4–1
1927	Harold L. Sebring	7–3–0	SoCon	5–2–0

1920's Gators Football Team Picture

1923 Florida Gators Football Coach James Van Fleet

The 1923 Florida Gators football team was the eighteenth season for Florida. It was year one of two for the new coach Major James Van Fleet as the Football Gators head coach. It was the Gators second season with the new Southern Conference SoCon, placing fifth of twenty-one teams in the conference standings.

Van Fleet was a serving officer in the U.S. Army and a professor of military tactics in the university's Reserve Officer Training Corps (ROTC) program, and had been a standout fullback on the undefeated West Point Cadets team of 1914. Van Fleet's 1923 Florida Gators finished 6–1–2 overall, and 1–0–2 in the Southern Conference, placing third of twenty-one teams in the conference standings.

This was the first year that Florida alumni and students celebrated a Homecoming. It was a wonderful 19–7 victory over the Mercer Baptists. The Gators tied the defending SoCon champion Georgia Tech Golden Tornado this year. The highlight of the entire 1923 season was a 16–6 upset of legendary coach Wallace Wade's previously undefeated Alabama Crimson Tide on a muddy, rain-soaked field in Birmingham, Alabama in the final game of the year. Go Gators!

For whatever reason, the Junior and Senior Classes did not play much of a role in the 1923 season. It was built from sophomores. Freshmen were playing their own games at the time and the 1922 Florida freshmen had won the southern crown for freshmen squads so this set of sophomores, though without varsity game experience were expected to lead the Gators to a fine season.

The team included Cy Williams, Goldy Goldstein, Edgar Jones, and Bill Middlekauff.

There were a lot of preseason reports about what to expect in 1923. One preseason account reads: "Big Cy Williams, star Freshman tackle of last year and probably the Varsity tackle of this year, was the immediate cause of the 'dummy's' downfall for when he dove into the lifeless foe, it collapsed and Cy was deluged with sawdust. A new 'dummy' was brought out but it is predicted that it will not last long under the fierce tackling of the Gators gridders."

1924 Florida Gators Football Coach James Van Fleet

The 1924 Florida Gators football team was the nineteenth season for Florida. It was year two and the last of two for coach Major James

Van Fleet as the Football Gators head coach. It was the Gators third season with the new Southern Conference SoCon, placing second of twenty-two teams in the conference standings.

Van Fleet's 1924 Florida Gators finished 6–2–2 overall, and 2–0–1 in the Southern Conference, and as noted, placing second of twenty-two teams in the conference standings.

The Gators traveled further during the 1924 season than any other college football team in the country, and received national recognition for a controversial tie with the Texas Longhorns and a very close loss to a nationally ranked Army team. The season also produced a tie with a southern power, who had often prevailed against the Gators—Georgia Tech.

General Van Fleet Gators Coach

Coach Van Fleet's assignment was changed from Florida to the Panama Canal Zone before the season opened. However, out of respect for the team, he coached on an unpaid basis during four months of leave.

In the trivia category but also the fun to know category, more than 100 players took part in a game between the varsity and freshmen. Also, a 4-month old Florida black bear captured by a freshman, wandered onto the field on October 1. An unidentified fan placed a Gator banner on its back, and it never caused much trouble but offered some nice photographs for the fans.

Wake Forest came in to Plant Field in Tampa, Florida on Oct 18, and the Gators won W (34–0). Knowing the notion of the home field advantage, the Gator coaches and the Florida Administration were probably beginning to think about how propitious it would be for the Gators to have a nice sized stadium so traveling for popular games was not required and so that the home team could play in a home field. This dream was about five-years from fruition

1925 Florida Gators Football Coach Harold L. Sebring

The 1925 Florida Gators football team was the twentieth season for Florida. It was year one of three for new coach Harold L. "Tom" Sebring as the Football Gators head coach. It was the Gators fourth season with the Southern Conference SoCon, placing second of twenty-two teams in the conference standings.

Sebring's 1925 Florida Gators finished 8–2, and 3-2 in the Southern Conference, and placing eighth of twenty-two teams in the conference standings.

The Gators compiled their best win-loss record to date, losing only to the Georgia Tech Yellow Jackets 7–23 in Atlanta, Georgia and legendary coach Wallace Wade's undefeated Alabama Crimson Tide 0–34 in Montgomery, Alabama. The highlights of the season included conference victories over the Wake Forest Demon Deacons, Clemson Tigers, Mississippi A&M Aggies and Washington & Lee Generals.

Captain and halfback Edgar C. Jones set a Florida single-season scoring record of 108 points, which lasted until 1969.

It is a long time from season end to season begin. Practice began on September 14 with new head coach Tom Sebring, along with A. C. Tipton, Everett Yon, and Herbert Bunker. They were in charge of the first workout.

<<< Coach Sebring
Though he had graduated, Clyde Norton was deemed eligible to return to play another year. Despite losing eight players, prospects were still bright for the team. In 1925, southern teams made substantial use of the forward pass. As coach Sebring recalled, the UF 1924 QB Edgar C. Jones had "held back from calling plays for himself the year before. I told him not to hold back."

The season began on Oct 3 with Mercer at home W (24-0).

1926 Florida Gators Football Coach Harold L. Sebring

The 1926 Florida Gators football team was the twenty-first season for Florida. It was year two of three for new coach Harold L. "Tom"

Sebring as the Football Gators head coach. It was his least successful so don't be looking for a lot of W's in the game results. It was the Gators sixth season with the Southern Conference SoCon, placing nineteenth of twenty-two teams in the conference standings.

Sebring's 1926 Florida Gators finished 2-6-2 overall, and 1-4-1 in the Southern Conference, and placing nineteenth of twenty-two teams in the conference standings.

There are always great highlights even in the most dismal of seasons. In 1926. The highlights of the season were the Gators' two home field victories over the Florida Southern Moccasins W 16-0) and the Clemson Tigers W (33-0). Unfortunately, these were interspersed among four close losses to the Chicago Maroons (6–12), the Ole Miss Rebels (7–12), the Mercer Bears (3–7) and the Kentucky Wildcats (13–18), crushing defeats by the Georgia Bulldogs (9–32) and coach Wallace Wade's undefeated Alabama Crimson Tide (0–49), and two low-scoring ties with the Hampden–Sydney Tigers (0–0) and the Washington & Lee Generals.

1927 Florida Gators Football Coach Harold L. Sebring

The 1927 Florida Gators football team was the twenty-second season for Florida. It was year three (last) of three for coach Harold L. "Tom" Sebring as the Football Gators head coach. It was not so bad. his least successful so don't be looking for a lot of W's in the game results. It was the Gators seventh season with the Southern Conference SoCon, placing sixth of twenty-two teams in the conference standings.

Sebring's 1927 Florida Gators finished 7-3 overall, and 5-2 in the Southern Conference, and placing sixth of twenty-two teams in the conference standings.

Chapter 9 Charlie Bachman Era 1928-1932

Coach # 8 Charlie Bachman

Year	Coach	Record	Conference	Record
1928	Charlie Bachman	8–1	SoCon	6–1
1929	Charlie Bachman	8–2	SoCon	6–1
1930	Charlie Bachman	6–3–1	SoCon	4–2–1
1931	Charlie Bachman	2–6–2	SoCon	2–4–2
1932	Charlie Bachman	3–6	SoCon	1–6

1928 Florida Gators Football Coach Charlie Bachman
3rd place of 22 in SoCon

The 1928 Florida Gators football team was the twenty-third season for Florida. It was the first year of five for new coach Charlie Bachman as the Football Gators head coach. He had a great year in 1928. It was the Gators eighth season with the Southern Conference SoCon, placing third of twenty-two teams in the conference standings.

Coach Charlie Bachman

Bachman's 1928 Florida Gators were outstanding, finishing 8-1 overall, and 6-1 in the Southern Conference, and placing third of twenty-two teams in the conference standings behind the national champion Georgia Tech Golden Tornado (7–0 SoCon), and the Tennessee Volunteers (6–0–1 SoCon).

The Gators were as good as they had ever been and better. Florida the entire nation in scoring with 336 points, and they were remembered by many sports commentators as the best Florida football team until at least the 1960s.

The secret was the "Phantom Four Backfield" The large scores were mostly attributed to the great play of the named backfield. Its "Phantom Four" backfield included: quarterback Clyde Crabtree, halfbacks Carl Brumbaugh and Royce Goodbread, and fullback Rainey Cawthon.

This was a great name and was surely reminiscent of the Four Horsemen of Notre Dame. You may recall this group of stalwarts were put together just a few years before the Phantom Four. Coach Knute Rockne devised the lineup in 1922 during their sophomore season. During the three-year tenure of the Four Horsemen, Notre Dame lost only two games; one each in 1922 and 1923, both to Nebraska in Lincoln before packed houses. In 1924, ND got the National Championship with no defeats.

The Gators were just one win away from what could have been their **first National Championship**. It was a great season for Florida. Other backs contributing to the fine year were captain "Goof" Bowyer, sophomore halfback Lee Roy "Red" Bethea, alternate-captain and halfback Tommy Owens, and fullback Ed Sauls. Lots of stories were told about the prowess of the backfield. One story goes like this:

"There were twelve backs on the squad. Six of them could do the hundred in 10.1 seconds. Eight of them were fine punters and ten of them were great passers. And all of them are good receivers."

At ends were future coach Dutch Stanley, and Florida's first-ever, first-team All-American, Dale Van Sickel. Van Sickel and quarterback Crabtree, who was really ambidextrous and could throw passes with either hand, or punt with either foot, while on the run or stationary, were both unanimous All-Southern selections. What a team.

There were tons of highlights for such a spectacular season. Among the many of 1928 were the Gators' 26–6 victory over the Georgia Bulldogs. This was not only a great victory but it ended a six-game losing streak against the Bulldogs. And, of course, there was the controversial loss to Tennessee that ended the Gators bid for an undefeated season and more than likely a Rose Bowl berth, the SoCon championship, and the National Championship.

Let's talk about that game for before we get into season games.

The 1928 Gators were 8-0-0, after having executed a tough schedule, playing six Southern Conference powerhouse teams. They then played their final game of the season against coach Robert Neyland's Tennessee Volunteers. It was played on the Vols' home field in Knoxville, Tennessee.

Coach Neyland was sick with the flu on the day of the game. The game was played on a soft, wet field, following a hard rain. Nothing unusual. Both teams were able to score two touchdowns on the muddy field. The Volunteers missed one of their two extra-point conversion attempts after touchdowns, but the Gators missed both conversion attempts and thus lost the game by a single point, 12–13.

In what would become a trend in the series, there was a controversy about the contest. By what today is said to be "by all accounts," the playing surface had been a muddy mess. Some Gators claimed that it could not have gotten that bad by the amount of rain that had fallen. They were convinced that the home team had watered down the field in an effort to slow down the speedy Gator backs.

The loss eliminated Florida's hopes of its first conference title, and fans and players have long since mourned this missed opportunity chance to play and win a Rose Bowl. Coach Bachman later added: "We would have beaten California in the Rose Bowl. Worse than Tech did on a dry field."

Tennessee quarterback Bobby Dodd, who came from no place to star in the game is depicted on the above football card from the 1950s.

Tennessee got off to a fast start and led the scoring for most of the game; Florida only made the game close after two late rallies.

It was early in the second quarter that Tennessee made the half's lone score. It was set up by a "bullet-like" 25-yard pass from Dodd, who was running to avoid getting sacked. The pass went to Paul Hug, who was tackled at the 2-yard line. After Florida held for three downs, Gene McEver scored between the center's legs on fourth down. The ensuing extra point on a pass from Dodd to Herc Alley would decide the game. Dodd was on his way to a hero's game.

Down 7–0 at the half, the Gators got it going and scored two minutes into the third quarter. It was a play that was similar to Tennessee's score. Royce Goodbread completed a 16-yard pass to Dale Van Sickel, who was tackled at the 1-yard line. Goodbread ran over left tackle for the touchdown on the very next play. Dodd was doing it all that day. On defense, he then deflected Carl Brumbaugh's pass for the extra point attempt, denying the Gators the opportunity to tie the game.

When the fourth quarter got going, Florida had the ball inside its own 15-yard line after Tennessee had turned the ball over on downs. Clyde Crabtree ran instead of punting, and he was tackled just as he tried to execute a lateral to Goodbread near the 30-yard line. The lateral was intercepted by Tennessee's Buddy Hackman, who outsprinted Brumbaugh to the goal. So, the Volunteers second TD was scored by its defense.

The Gators later drove to the 4-yard line and with all the mud, they just could not get the ball over the goal line and so they were held on downs. Tennessee could not move the ball and after Dodd's punt to midfield, the Gators' began their final scoring drive.

It began with a 27-yard pass from Brumbaugh to Van Sickel. The Gators soon were out of bounds at the 1-yard line. Crabtree ran it in for the touchdown. This time the Gators kicked the extra-point try but Brumbaugh's place kick for the extra point was both wide and short. There were sources on the field who claim the kick was blocked. The game ended as a heartbreaker for Florida Gators history. It was a game that could have and should have been won.

Games of the 1928 Season

New Head coach Charlie Bachman replaced Tom Sebring, who was his former player at Kansas State. Bachman had attended Notre Dame and he knew how to use Knute Rockne's system. When Sebring graduated from the University of Florida's College of Law, he moved on.

Bachman did not have a lot of time but It was enough for him to know what he had. Practice was opened on September 3. He was the beneficiary of a wealth of talented players from Florida high schools, He knew what he had after just two weeks. Bachman declared his backfield material as the finest ever. The days of playing in the old Baseball Field were coming to an end but not just yet.

The season began with three home games in a row. On Oct. 6, the Gators beat Florida Southern W (26-0). On Oct 13, one week later, UF beat Auburn W (27-0). The following week on Oct 20, Mercer went down big W (73-0). With some bleachers in place, over 8,000 saw the Mercer game.

On Oct 27, the Gators narrowly beat North Carolina State at Fairfield Stadium in Jacksonville, Florida W (14–7) before 13,000. On Nov. 3, The Gators hammered Sewanee at Fairfield Stadium W (71–6). The Gators then traveled to Georgia and beat the Bulldogs at Municipal Stadium in Savannah, W (26–6) before 16,000. Clemson came to Fairfield Stadium on Nov 17 and were beaten by the Gators W 27-6 before 15,000. UF was using Jacksonville a lot more as the demand to see Gators football was increasing.

On November 29, Washington & Lee came to Fairfield Stadium and were walloped W (60-6). The Gators were ready for Tennessee. They traveled to Shields-Watkins Field • Knoxville, Tennessee on December 8, and in a muddy contest that was a nail biter, the Gators came up short L (13–12). Overall the season was great but with just two more points, and perhaps just one more, the Gators would have had a few championships.

1929 Florida Gators Football Coach Charlie Bachman

The 1929 Florida Gators football team was the twenty-fourth season for Florida. It was the second year of five for coach Charlie Bachman as the Football Gators head coach. He had another fine year in 1929. It was the Gators ninth season with the Southern Conference SoCon, placing fourth of twenty-two teams in the conference standings.

Bachman's 1929 Florida Gators were outstanding, finishing finished 8-1 overall, and 6-1 in the Southern Conference, and placing fourth in the conference standings.

Dale Van Sickel

<<<Dale Van Sickel

Dale Van Sickel is one of the greats for sure who played for the Gators from 1927 to 1929 during the Knute Rockne years at ND. Sickel did not have to leave Gainesville, where he attended high school to play for the Gators. He became a three-sport athlete in football, basketball and baseball at Florida. His great moment regarding his Gator career is that he was the first UF Gator to be inducted into the College Football Hall of Fame in 1975.

Van Sickel played end for the Gators, and was selected as a first-team All-American in 1928, and a second-team All-American in 1929. Born in Georgia, he grew up in Gainesville , playing ball for the Hurricanes. Dale's older brother Talmadge had also been an all-state player for Gainesville High. In 2007, eighty-one years after he graduated from high school, the Florida High School Athletic Association (FHSAA) recognized Dale Van Sickel as one of the "100 Greatest Players of the First 100 Years" of Florida high school football. He is generally regarded as the best high school football player produced in the state of Florida before the 1930s. He was a welcome addition to the Gators.

Coach Bachman began the season's intensive practices on the beach at Anastasia Island, some ten miles from Saint Augustine. There was a fierce battle amongst the eleven running backs featured to get the starting positions. Another good backfield was expected.

Bachman later said the 1929 team "was as good as the 1928 team and would have been better had we not lost Carl Brumbaugh from the year before. He was our passer, and he was our thinker. He could get the ball to Van Sickel. In those days, the halfbacks passed more than the quarterback. And boy did we pass. In the flats a lot, like they do now."

This is the last team that would have the old baseball field as its home field. Soon in 1930, the new Florida Stadium would begin construction with a style that could be expanded as needed. Florida Stadium would be a place to behold

1930 Florida Gators Football Coach Charlie Bachman

The 1930 Florida Gators football team was the twenty-fifth season for Florida. It was the third year of five for coach Charlie Bachman as the Football Gators head coach. Things did not go quite as well this year as they had in 1928 and 1929. It was the Gators tenth season with the Southern Conference SoCon, placing fourth of twenty-two teams in the conference standings.

Bachman's 1930 Florida Gators were not too bad and not too good. They were short of outstanding for sure. They finished 6-3-1 overall, and 4-2-1 in the Southern Conference, and placing seventh in the conference standings. After a great start in 1928, Bachman's teams had taken a downward trajectory.

1931 Florida Gators Football Coach Charlie Bachman

The 1931 Florida Gators football team was the twenty-sixth season for Florida. It was the fourth of five for coach Charlie Bachman as the Football Gators head coach. Things did not go well at all this year as they had the first three years. It was the Gators eleventh season with the Southern Conference SoCon, placing fifteenth of twenty-three teams in the conference standings.

Bachman's 1930 Florida Gators were not very good this season. They finished 2-6-2 overall, and 2-4-2 in the Southern Conference, and placing fifteenth of twenty-three in the conference standings. After a great start in 1928, Bachman's teams had taken a downward trajectory and had reached the bottom in 1931.

1931 Florida Gators

There were few season highlights but we must count the Gators' only victories over the North Carolina State (31–0) in Raleigh, North Carolina and the Auburn Tigers (13–12) in Jacksonville, Florida, both of which were fellow Southern Conference members.

Noted sportswriter Tom McEwen was quoted: "The handwriting was on the wall during that dismal 1931 season. The Gators lost five of their last six games, tying the other. During that streak the Florida offense—three years earlier the best in the country—managed only two touchdowns and a safety."

1932 Florida Gators Football Coach Charlie Bachman

The 1932 Florida Gators football team was the twenty-seventh season for Florida. It was the fifth of five for coach Charlie Bachman as the Football Gators head coach. Things were just a skosh better this year than the last year's miserable season. It was the Gators twelfth season with the Southern Conference SoCon, placing twentieth of twenty-three teams in the conference standings.

Bachman's 1932 Florida Gators were not quite as bad as the 1932 version. But, they were not good either. The Gators finished 3-6 overall, and 1-6 in the Southern Conference, and placed twentieth of twenty-three in the conference standings. After a great start in 1928, Bachman's teams had taken a downward trajectory and had reached the bottom on 1931. This was the Gators' final year as members of the Southern Conference.

Coach Bachman with a team loaded with sophomores again, predicted that the Gators would win half of their games.

Tough season for sure!

Chapter 10 Dennis Stanley & Josh Cody Era 1933-1939

Coach # 9 Dennis K Stanley
Coach # 10 Josh Cody

Year	Coach	Record	Conference	Record
1933	Dennis K. Stanley	5–3–1	SEC	2–3-0
1934	Dennis K. Stanley	6–3–1	SEC	2–2–1
1935	Dennis K. Stanley	3–7-0	SEC	1–6-0
1936	Josh Cody	4–6	SEC	1–5-0
1937	Josh Cody	4–7-0	SEC	3–4-0
1938	Josh Cody	4–6–1	SEC	2–2–1
1939	Josh Cody	5–5–1	SEC	0–3–1

After Coach Stanley, things went downhill with Josh Cody.

Coach Stanley's 1935 Gators are shown below:

1933 Florida Gators Football Coach Dennis K. (Dutch" Stanley

The 1933 Florida Gators football team was the twenty-eighth season for Florida. It was the first of three seasons for Florida Alumnus Dennis K. (Dutch) Stanley as the Football Gators head coach.

Things were a lot better this year with the new coach as the record was again above 500.

It was the Gators first season with the South-Eastern Conference. The overall record was 5-3-1 and the SEC record was 2-3-0. They tied for ninth of thirteen teams in the conference standings.

<<< Dennis K. Stanley had been a standout end on the great 1928 Gators team. To make it work for Florida, he assembled an all-Florida-alumni coaching staff and led the Gators to a 5–3–1 revival following two consecutive losing seasons in 1931 and 1932.

Before the season got going Quarterback Sam Davis was the first quarterback and captain since Goof Bowyer in 1928. An expected star on the team was Al Hickland, a 250-pound, three-sport athlete who was also the team's kicker.

1934 Florida Gators Football Coach Dennis K. (Dutch" Stanley

The 1934 Florida Gators football team was the twenty-ninth season for Florida. It was the second of three seasons for Florida Alumnus Dennis K. (Dutch) Stanley as the Football Gators head coach. Things were a little better this year with the new coach as the team recorded one more win than in 1933. This would be Dutch's best year.

It was the Gators second season with the South-Eastern Conference. The overall record was 6-3-1 and the SEC record was 2-2-1. They placed seventh of thirteen teams in the SEC conference standings.

1935 Florida Gators Football Coach Dennis K. (Dutch" Stanley

The 1935 Florida Gators football team was the thirtieth season for Florida. It was the last of three seasons for Florida Alumnus Dennis K. (Dutch) Stanley as the Football Gators head coach. Things got really bad and the losses started to roll in at a clip better than the wins from the prior two years. This would-be Dutch's worst year. He was gone the next year and his epitaph was not long.

It was the Gators third season with the South-Eastern Conference. The overall record was 3-7 and the best I can say about the SEC record is that at least there was one win 1-6. They placed twelfth of thirteen teams in the SEC conference standings. Coach Stanley's 1935 Gators are shown in the picture below

The highlights of the season included the Gators' victories over the Sewanee Tigers (20–0) and the South Carolina Gamecocks (22–0).

1936 Florida Gators Football Coach Josh Cody

The 1936 Florida Gators football team was the thirty-first season for Florida. It was the first of four seasons for Josh Cody as the Football Gators head coach. With the coaching change came no better results.

It was the Gators fourth season with the South-Eastern Conference. The overall record was 4-6 and the best things I can say about the SEC record again is that at least there was one win and one less loss. 1-5. The Gators have yet to be in last place in any conference. They placed tenth of thirteen teams in SEC standings.

1937 Florida Gators Football Coach Josh Cody

The 1937 Florida Gators football team was the thirty-second season for Florida. It was the second of four seasons for Josh Cody as the Football Gators head coach. The overall record was worse but instead of one win in the conference, Cody's team brought in three.

It was the Gators fifth season with the South-Eastern Conference. The overall record was 4-7 and the 3-4 in the SEC. They placed eighth of thirteen teams in the SEC conference standings.

1938 Florida Gators Football Coach Josh Cody

The 1938 Florida Gators football team was the thirty-third season for Florida. It was the third of four seasons for Josh Cody as the Football Gators head coach. Not much changed in the win-loss column.

It was the Gators sixth season with the South-Eastern Conference. The overall record was 4-6-1and the 4-2-1 in the SEC. They placed seventh of thirteen teams in the SEC conference standings. This was Cody's best finish in the SEC, where the tough football is played.

1939 Florida Gators Football Coach Josh Cody

Gators vs Boston College 1939
Ralph Kelleman carries

The 1939 Florida Gators football team was the thirty-fourth season for Florida. It was the last of four seasons for Josh Cody as the Football Gators head coach. This year Cody won five games for the first time and the team was not below 500.

It was the Gators seventh season with the South-Eastern Conference. The overall record was 5-5-1 and the 0-3-1 in the SEC. They placed twelfth of thirteen teams in the SEC conference standings. They won no games v SEC teams This is Cody's best finish overall but his worst record in the SEC, where the tough football is played.

Chapter 11 Tom Lieb & Ray Wolf Era 1940-1949

Coach #11 Lieb
Coach #12 Wolf

Year	Coach	Record	Conference	Record
1940	Thomas Lieb	5–5-0	SEC	2–3-0
1941	Thomas Lieb	4–6-0	SEC	1–3-0
1942	Thomas Lieb	3–7-0	SEC	1–3-0
1943	Thomas Lieb WWII			
1944	Thomas Lieb	4–3-0	SEC	0–3-0
1945	Thomas Lieb	4–5-1	SEC	1–3–1
1946	Raymond "Bear" Wolf	0–9-0	SEC	0–5-0
1947	Raymond "Bear" Wolf	4–5-0	SEC	0–3–1
1948	Raymond "Bear" Wolf	5–5-0	SEC	1–5-0
1949	Raymond "Bear" Wolf	4–5-1	SEC	1–4–1

Ten years of floundering and sometimes worse.

1940 Florida Gators Football Coach Thomas Lieb

The 1940 Florida Gators football team was the thirty-fifth season for Florida. It was the first of six seasons for Thomas J. "Tom" Lieb as the Football Gators head coach. This year Lieb won five games and kept his team above 500 overall. Despite great credentials coming in, this would be his best record.

It was the Gators eighth season with the South-Eastern Conference. The overall record was 5-5-1 and the 0-3-1 in the

SEC. They placed eighth of thirteen teams in the SEC conference standings. They won two games v SEC teams This is Lieb's best finish overall and best finish in the SEC, where the tough football is played.

Thomas Lieb, like most Gator coaches had a great pedigree. I keep thinking about how well Knute Rockne would have done at Notre Dame without talent. Who knows the problems of 1940, yet somebody was on the other side of the line beating the Gators and they had figured something out.

I am still not apt to blame coaching. Lieb was the former coach of the Loyola Lions, where he had done well and he had previously served as Knute Rockne's primary assistant and on-the-field replacement while Rockne was in the hospital during most of the Notre Dame Fighting Irish's 1930 national championship season. He obviously knew how to take players and help make them champions. But?

I have heard few good definitive explanations of the black cloud over the Gators. If there were such a cloud, why did their opponents not feel the same pain? Interesting question but I have no answer…yet. How about you?

For those scoring at home. It will be about thirteen more years before we see consistent wins from the Gators.

1941 Florida Gators Football Coach Thomas Lieb

The 1941 Florida Gators football team was the thirty-sixth season for Florida. It was the second of six seasons for Thomas J. "Tom" Lieb as the Football Gators head coach. This year Lieb fell behind the 500 mark and in his six years, he never found it again. He won four games but just one game in the SEC. So far, the Gators have never been at the bottom of the SEC, though they have been close.

It was the Gators ninth season with the South-Eastern Conference. The overall record was 4-6-0, and 1-3-0 in the SEC. They placed tenth of thirteen teams in the SEC conference standings. They won just two games v SEC teams This is Lieb's best finish overall as a coach at UF and his best finish in the SEC, where the tough football is played.

1942 Florida Gators Football Coach Thomas Lieb

The 1942 Florida Gators football team was the thirty-seventh season for Florida. It was the third of six seasons for Thomas J. "Tom" Lieb as the Football Gators head coach. This year Lieb won three games but just one game in the SEC.

It was the Gators tenth season with the South-Eastern Conference (SEC). The overall record was 3-7-0, and 1-3-0 in the SEC. They placed ninth of twelve teams in the SEC conference standings. They won just one game v SEC teams, where the tough football is played.

By the autumn of 1942, World War II had begun to affect many college football programs. Florida lost several players and most of its coaching staff to the war effort before the season, the team lost several more players during the season, leading to diminishing success as the schedule progressed. For example, the Gators began the season 3-1 but lost their final six contests

1943 Florida Gators Football Coach Thomas Lieb

In 1943, for the first and only autumn since the modern University of Florida opened its Gainesville campus in 1906, the university did not field an official varsity football team because most able-bodied men of college age were serving in the U.S. armed forces during World War II. Florida was one of seven Southeastern Conference schools that did not field a squad during the 1943 season. Because Coach Lieb was not fired, we count this as the fourth of six seasons for Thomas J. "Tom" Lieb as the Football Gators head coach, though no football games were played.

1944 Florida Gators Football Coach Thomas Lieb

If anybody today called Mr. Lieb or his successor, Mr. Wolf in to check out the scenario as it looked in the 1940's, neither would have applied for the UF coaching job. Something was wrong at UF that the best of the best coaches hired judiciously by the administration could not repair. We have discussed this already. More than likely, it was money and scholarships. You cannot get blood from a stone. The war seemed to impact the less endowed schools the most.

The 1944 Florida Gators football team was the thirty-eighth season for Florida. It was the fifth of six seasons for Thomas J. "Tom" Lieb as the Football Gators head coach. This year Lieb won four games but not one game in the SEC.

It was the Gators twelfth season with the South-Eastern Conference (SEC). The overall record was 4-3-0, and 0-3-0 in the SEC. They placed tenth of twelve teams in the SEC conference standings. They won no games v SEC teams, where the tough football is played.

1945 Florida Gators Football Coach Thomas Lieb

The 1945 Florida Gators football team was the thirty-ninth season for Florida. It was the last of six seasons for Thomas J. "Tom" Lieb as the Football Gators head coach. This year Lieb won four games but just one game in the SEC.

It was the Gators thirteenth season with the South-Eastern Conference (SEC). The overall record was 4-5-1, and 1-3-1 in the SEC. They placed ninth of twelve teams in the SEC conference standings. They won one game v SEC teams, where the tough football is played.

The 1945 backfield was made up entirely of freshmen.

1946 Florida Gators Football Coach Raymond "Bear" Wolf

<<< "Bear" Wolf. The 1946 Florida Gators football team was the fortieth season for Florida. It was the first of four seasons for Raymond "Bear" Wolf as the Football Gators head coach. This year Wolf was winless 0-9-0, and 0-5-0

It was the Gators fourteenth season with the South-Eastern Conference (SEC). They placed twelve of twelve teams in the SEC conference standings. They won not even one game v SEC teams, where the tough football is played. This was the first time ever that a Gators team was shut out and last in any conference.

1947 Florida Gators Football Coach Raymond "Bear" Wolf

The 1947 Florida Gators football team was the forty-first season for Florida. It was the second of four seasons for Raymond "Bear" Wolf as the Football Gators head coach. This year Wolf finally began to win some games, but not right away.

It was the Gators fifteenth season with the South-Eastern Conference (SEC). The overall record was 4-5-1, and 0-3-1 in the SEC. They placed twelve of twelve teams in the SEC conference standings. For the second year in a row, the Gators were last in the conference. They won no games v SEC teams, where the tough football is played.

1948 Florida Gators Football Coach Raymond "Bear" Wolf

The 1948 Florida Gators football team was the forty-second season for Florida. It was the third of four seasons for Raymond "Bear" Wolf as the Football Gators head coach. This year Wolf's record finally broke even.

It was the Gators sixteenth season with the South-Eastern Conference (SEC). The overall record was 5-5-0, and 1-5-0 in the SEC. The Gators were still having trouble winning games against the tough members of the SEC. They placed tenth of twelve teams in the SEC conference standings. They won just one game in the SEC, where the tough football is played.

1949 Florida Gators Football Coach Raymond "Bear" Wolf

The 1949 Florida Gators football team was the forty-third season for Florida. It was the fourth and last of four seasons for Raymond "Bear" Wolf as the Football Gators head coach. After a 500 season in the prior year, this year the Gators lost ground again.

It was the Gators seventeenth season with the South-Eastern Conference (SEC). The overall record was 4-5-1, and 1-4-1 in the SEC. The Gators were still having trouble winning games against the tough members of the SEC. They placed tenth of twelve teams in the SEC conference standings. They won just one game in the SEC, where the tough football is played.

After Bear Wolf left Gainesville, he returned to his alma mater, Texas Christian University, where he became a longtime administrator. As a former professor at several colleges myself, I am sure the Bear felt like he was still part of a tradition when he went to work every day on the TCU campus.

<< Chuck Hunsinger Tailback 1946-1949 had a brilliant career at UF rushing for over 2,000 yards. He was the 3rd overall selection in the 1950 NFL draft. Vs Georgia in 1949 rushed for 174 yards on 18 carries and scored 3 TDs leading the Gators to victory.

Chapter 12 Bob Woodruff Era 1950-1959

Coach # 13 **George Robert Woodruff**

Year	Coach	Record	Conference	Record
1950	Bob Woodruff	5–5-0	SEC	2–4-0
1951	Bob Woodruff	5–5-0	SEC	2–4-0
1952	Bob Woodruff	8–3-0	SEC	3–3-0
1953	Bob Woodruff	3–5–2	SEC	1–3–2
1954	Bob Woodruff	5–5-0	SEC	5–2-0
1955	Bob Woodruff	4–6	SEC	3–5-0
1956	Bob Woodruff	6–3–1	SEC	5–2-0
1957	Bob Woodruff	6–2–1	SEC	4–2–1
1958	Bob Woodruff	6–4–1	SEC	2–3–1
1959	Bob Woodruff	5–4–1	SEC	2–4-0

1953 Florida Gators Coach Bob Woodruff

1950 Florida Gators Football Coach Bob Woodruff

The 1950 Florida Gators football team was the forty-fourth season for Florida. It was the first of ten seasons for Bob Woodruff as the Football Gators head coach. After a lackluster 1949 season, the Gators showed signs of life with a 500 season.

It was the Gators eighteenth season with the South-Eastern Conference (SEC). The overall record was 5-5-0, and 2-4-0 in the SEC. The Gators were still having trouble winning games against the tough members of the SEC. Even with one more win they still placed tenth of twelve teams in the SEC conference standings. They won just two games in the SEC, but this was twice as many as all seasons from 1941 to 1949.

On Oct 14 at home, Florida beat Auburn W (27-7).

Gators v Auburn

1951 Florida Gators Football Coach Bob Woodruff

The 1951 Florida Gators football team was the forty-fifth season for Florida. It was the second of ten seasons for Bob Woodruff as the Football Gators head coach. After a 500 season, the 1951 Gators followed it up with another 500.

It was the Gators nineteenth season with the South-Eastern Conference (SEC). Just like the prior year, the overall record was 5-5-0, and 2-4-0 in the SEC. The Gators were still having trouble winning games against the tough members of the SEC. With the same record as last year, they placed ninth of twelve teams in the SEC conference standings. They won just two games in the SEC, but this was twice as many as each season from 1941 to 1949.

1952 Florida Gators Football Coach Bob Woodruff

The 1952 Florida Gators football team was the forty-sixth season for Florida. It was the third of ten seasons for Bob Woodruff as the Football Gators head coach. After a 500 season, the 1951 Gators followed it up with another 500.

It was the Gators twentieth season with the South-Eastern Conference (SEC). It was a big year—Woodruff's best overall record. The team record was 8-3-0, and 3-3-0- in the SEC. The Gators were solving their problem of winning games against the tough members of the SEC. They placed sixth of twelve teams in the SEC conference standings. They won three games in the SEC. This mark had been achieved last in 1937 with Josh Cody's team.

1953 Florida Gators Football Coach Bob Woodruff

The 1953Florida Gators football team was the forty-seventh season for Florida. It was the fourth of ten seasons for Bob Woodruff as the Football Gators head coach. After a great season, the 1953 Gators were well below 500.

It was the Gators twenty-first season with the South-Eastern Conference (SEC). It was a poor showing —Woodruff's worst overall record and just his first of two losing seasons. The team record was 3-5-2, and 1-3-2 in the SEC. The Gators were slipping back from having improved in tough SEC games. The 1953 season was in fact a year of rebuilding and backsliding after the graduation of All-American Charlie LaPradd and the loss of fullback Rick Casares to the U.S. Army. They placed ninth of twelve teams in the SEC conference standings. They won just one game in the SEC.

1954 Florida Gators Football Coach Bob Woodruff

The 1954 Florida Gators football team was the forty-eighth season for Florida. It was the fifth of ten seasons for Bob Woodruff as the Football Gators head coach. The 1954 Gators brought in their third 5-5 season out of five.

It was the Gators twenty-second season with the South-Eastern Conference (SEC). It was a so-so showing but a powerful showing in the SEC. The team record was 5-5-0, and 5-2-0 in the SEC. Best showing ever in the SEC. They had really improved in the tough SEC games. The 1954 season was another rebuilding year and it looked like it was working.

They placed third (tie for third) of twelve teams in the SEC conference standings. They won just one game in the SEC.

1955 Florida Gators Football Coach Bob Woodruff

The 1955Florida Gators football team was the forty-ninth season for Florida. It was the sixth of ten seasons for Bob Woodruff as the Football Gators head coach. 1955 was another losing season for the Gators – the second and last losing season for coach Bob Woodruff.

<<< Don Chandler Kicker/Punter 1954-1955. Transferred into UF from tiny Bacone College in Oklahoma. Played 12 years in the NFL including the first two overtime games (the 1958 classic between the Colts and Giants being one of them) and was named to the NFL's all-decade team for the 60's. It was the Gators twenty-third with the South-Eastern Conference (SEC). It was a medsa meds showing but a powerful showing in the SEC. The team record was 4-6-0, and 3-5-0 in the SEC. They placed tenth of twelve teams in

the SEC conference standings. They had won just three games in the SEC.

On Oct 1, the Gators traveled to Cliff Gare Stadium in Auburn Alabama and lost to the Tigers L (0-13).

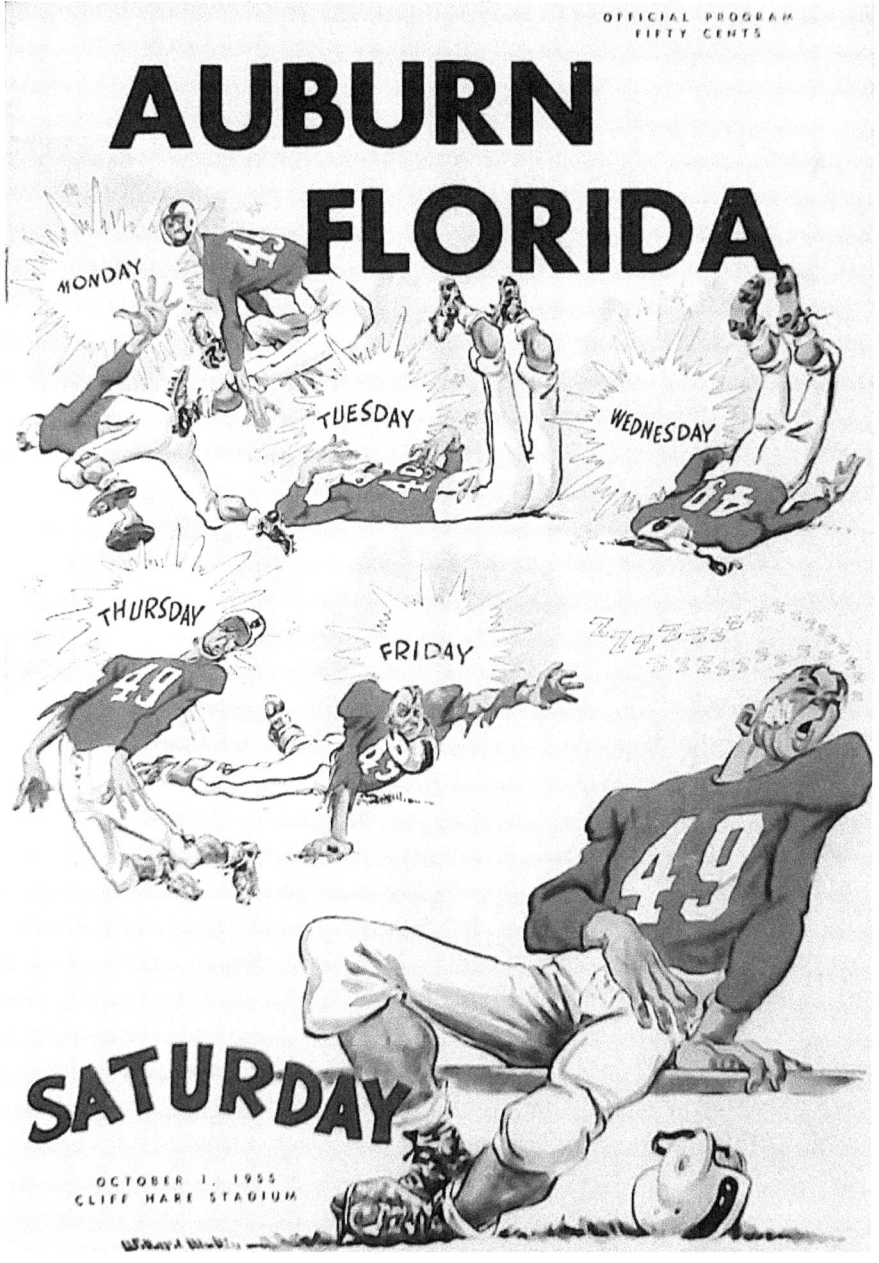

1956 Florida Gators Football Coach Bob Woodruff
3rd place in the SEC

The 1956 Florida Gators football team was the fiftieth season for Florida. It was the seventh of ten seasons for Bob Woodruff as the Football Gators head coach. The 1956 Gators climbed back over 500 and kept a winning percentage for the duration of Woodruff's tenure as head coach. However, the team achieved no more than 6 wins per season during this period.

It was the Gators twenty-fourth season with the South-Eastern Conference (SEC). It was a very nice showing and an excellent showing in the SEC. The team record was 6-3-1, and 5-2-0 in the SEC. They placed third in the SEC conference standings after winning 5 SEC games.

This Gators team was led by All-American tackle John Barrow, quarterback Jimmy Dunn, two-way halfbacks Joe Brodsky, Bernie Parrish, Jim Rountree and Jackie Simpson, and defensive back John Symank.

1957 Florida Gators Football Coach Bob Woodruff
Tied for 3rd place in the SEC

The 1957 Florida Gators football team was the fifty-first season for Florida. It was the eighth of ten seasons for Bob Woodruff as the Football Gators head coach. The 1957 Gators were again over 500 for the year.

It was the Gators twenty-fifth season with the South-Eastern Conference (SEC). It was a fine showing and a nice showing in the SEC. The team record was 6-2-1, and 4-2-1 in the SEC. They tied for third place in the SEC conference standings among the twelve SEC team after winning 4 SEC games.

On Oct 26, the next week at home again, the Gators beat #10 LSU in a nice game W (22-14). The squad enjoyed upsetting Billy Cannon and his 10th-ranked LSU Tigers.

Gators v LSU 1957

1958 Florida Gators Football Coach Bob Woodruff
<u>Gator Bowl Participant</u>

The 1958 Florida Gators football team was the fifty-second season for Florida. It was the ninth of ten seasons for Bob Woodruff as the Football Gators head coach. The 1958 Gators were again over 500 for the year.

It was the Gators twenty-sixth season with the South-Eastern Conference (SEC). It was a fine showing and a nice showing in the SEC. The team record was 6-4-1, and 2-3-1 in the SEC. They were eight in the SEC conference standings among the twelve SEC team after winning just 2 SEC games.

Jimmy Dunn Florida QB

Jimmy Dunn, above was a Florida QB from 1956-1958 Despite the protests by FSU that Dunn had committed to them, he signed with the Gators and although a pint-sized 5'10' 147 pounds, Dunn was nonetheless an effective runner due to his excellent quickness

Gator Bowl

On December 27, playing in the 1958 Gator Bowl, eleventh ranked Ole Miss beat the Gators in a defensive struggle at Gator Bowl Stadium in Jacksonville L (3-7).

1958 Gator Bowl v Ole Miss

1959 Florida Gators Football Coach Bob Woodruff

The 1959 Florida Gators football team was the fifty-third season for Florida. It was the tenth and last of ten seasons for Bob Woodruff as the Football Gators head coach. The 1959 Gators were once again over 500 for the year.

It was the Gators twenty-seventh season with the South-Eastern Conference (SEC). It was an OK showing and a poor showing in the SEC. The team record was 5-4-1, and 2-4-0 in the SEC. They were ninth in the SEC conference standings among the twelve SEC team after winning just 2 SEC games.

The Gators did not have many conference wins so getting one was a cause for celebration. Florida celebrated a blowout conference shutout over Tulane W (30-0) and a close conference win over the Mississippi State Bulldogs (14–13), and then suffered close conference defeats to the Vanderbilt Commodores (6–13), the top-ranked LSU Tigers (0–9) and the eighth-ranked Auburn Tigers (0–6).

Woodruff finished his ten-year tenure on a high note, with the Gators' victories over Florida rivals Florida State Seminoles (18–8) and the twelfth-ranked Miami Hurricanes (23–14).

Wrap-Up on Coach Woodruff

The Woodruff years were not bad comparatively. He brought a level of competitive respectability to Florida within the Southeastern Conference (SEC) in his ten seasons as the Gators' coach and athletic director. It was not enough to prompt University of Florida president J. Wayne Reitz to renew Woodruff's contract in 1959 after two previous contract extensions. Woodruff landed on his feet as he returned to the University of Tennessee, his alma mater, in 1963. He became athletic director of the Tennessee Volunteers sports program for the long-haul. During the 1950s, the Gators compiled an overall record of 53–42–6 (.555) during his tenure.

Chapter 13 Ray Graves Era 1960-1969

Coach # 14 Ray Graves

Year	Coach	Record	Conference	Record
1960	Ray Graves	9–2-0	SEC	5–1-0
1961	Ray Graves	4–5-1	SEC	3–3-0
1962	Ray Graves	7–4-0	SEC	4–2-0
1963	Ray Graves	6–3-1	SEC	3–3-1
1964	Ray Graves	7–3-0	SEC	4–2-0
1965	Ray Graves	7–4-0	SEC	4–2-0
1966	Ray Graves	9–2-0	SEC	5–1-0
1967	Ray Graves	6–4-0	SEC	4–2-0
1968	Ray Graves	6–3–1	SEC	3–2–1
1969	Ray Graves	9–1–1	SEC	3–1–1

Ray Graves 1960 – 1969 Florida Gators Coach

1960 Florida Gators Football Coach Ray Graves
2nd place of 12 teams; Gator Bowl Champions

The 1960 Florida Gators football team was the fifty-fourth season for Florida. It was the first of ten seasons for Ray Graves as the Football Gators head coach. The 1960 Gators had a great year – well over 500 for the year. It was Graves' first of three very successful seasons in his ten years.

It was the Gators twenty-eighth season with the South-Eastern Conference (SEC). It was a very good showing and a very good showing in the SEC. The team record was 9-2-0, and 5-1-0 in the SEC. The Gators days of sucking wind were behind them. They were second in the SEC conference standings among the twelve SEC team after winning 5 SEC games. This was the Gators best season yet in the SEC.

Before the season, of course coach Woodruff had not received a contract renewal. Somehow, they found Graves who was a great coach and he made the program much better than it had ever been.

Graves was a former Tennessee Volunteers lineman and assistant coach under the legendary coach Robert Neyland. He then became a long-time Georgia Tech Yellow Jackets defensive assistant for coach Bobby Dodd. When Graves' came to Gainesville, it was a big change in the Gators' football outlook. No longer would the Gators espouse Bob Woodruff's conservative, ball control, "go for the tie" philosophy. Graves was interested in winning games even if there was some risk.

On Sept 17, the Gators began this new season with its new coach with a nice win over George Washington at Florida Field W (30-7). Florida State was getting tougher every year since they'd been added to the schedule and this year, it was a close call but on Sept 24, the Gators beat the 'Noles by a Field Goal W (3-0). Georgia Tech played Florida at Florida Field on Oct 1 and the Gators picked up a hard fought one W (18-17 showing the desire of the new coach to win and not to tie. Rice was next on Oct 8 at Orange Bowl Stadium in Miami Fl. The Gators let this one get away L (0-10). At home again on Oct 15, the Gators beat Vanderbilt W (12-0).

Florida traveled to Louisiana State on Oct 22 to beat the Tigers at Tiger Stadium in Baton Rouge, LA W (13–10) Auburn came to Florida on Oct 29 and beat the Gators in a tight match L (7-10)

Georgia was next on Nov 5 again at Jacksonville for a Gator win W (22-14) The Gators beat Tulane the next week at home W 921-6) with two games left having a good year so far, the Gators beat Miami at Miami W 918-0) They followed this nice win up with another against Baylor in a nail biter at the Jacksonville Venue W (13-12)

This was the Florida Gators first-ever nine-win season when they got this hard-fought 13–12 victory over the twelfth-ranked Baylor Bears in the Gator Bowl on New Year's Eve 1960. In the Gator Bowl, the Gators defense halted a 75-yard drive by Baylor on the half-yard line in the first quarter, then set the stage for two second quarter touchdowns. Baylor dropped a pass for the two-point conversion and the win, and quarterback Libertore was voted game MVP. Great year for the Gators.

1961 Florida Gators Football Coach Ray Graves
Sugar Bowl Participant

The 1961 Florida Gators football team was the fifty-fifth season for Florida. It was the second of ten seasons for Ray Graves as the Football Gators head coach. The 1961 Gators had a rebuilding year below 500 for the first time in about five years. It was Graves' worst season as Gators coach.

It was the Gators twenty-ninth season with the South-Eastern Conference (SEC). It was a poor showing but not as bad in the SEC. The team record was 4-5-1, and 3-3-0 in the SEC. They were sixth in the SEC conference standings among the twelve SEC team after winning 3 SEC games.

1962 Florida Gators Football Coach Ray Graves
Gator Bowl Champions

The 1962 Florida Gators football team was the fifty-sixth season for Florida. It was the third of ten seasons for Ray Graves as the Football Gators head coach. The 1962 Gators had a nice year well above 500 for the season and they had a better than usual year in the SEC.

It was the Gators thirtieth season with the South-Eastern Conference (SEC). It was a reasonable showing. The team record was 7-4-0, and 4-2-0 in the SEC. They were fifth in the SEC conference standings among the twelve SEC team after winning 4 SEC games.

The Gators won the Gator Bowl again in 1962, upsetting ninth-ranked Penn State. They wore the Confederate Battle Flag on the side of their helmets to pump up the southern team facing a favored northern school.

In the Gator Bowl Game on the day before New Year's Eve, The Gators beat #9 ranked Penn State W (17-7).

1963 Florida Gators Football Coach Ray Graves

The 1963 Florida Gators football team was the fifty-seventh season for Florida. It was the fourth of ten seasons for Ray Graves as the Football Gators head coach. The 1963 Gators had a nice year well above below 500 for the season and they had an OK year in the SEC.

It was the Gators thirty-first season with the South-Eastern Conference (SEC). It was another reasonable showing. The team record was 6-3-1, and 3-2-1 in the SEC. They were seventh in the SEC conference standings among the twelve SEC team after winning 3 SEC games.

1964 Florida Gators Football Coach Ray Graves
2nd place in the SEC

The 1964 Florida Gators football team was the fifty-eighth season for Florida. It was the fifth of ten seasons for Ray Graves as the Football Gators head coach. The 1964 Gators had a nice year well above below 500 for the season and they had an OK year in the SEC.

It was the Gators thirty-second season with the South-Eastern Conference (SEC). It was another reasonable showing. The team record was 7-3-0, and 4-2-0. They tied for second in the SEC conference standings among the eleven SEC teams after winning 4 SEC games.

This was the first season with sophomore Steve Spurrier in his first season as QB. Freshman were not yet eligible to play varsity football. In fact, it was not until 1972 -- the first in which freshmen were eligible to play varsity football in the University Division.

On Sept 19, the Gators beat So. Methodist to kick off the 1964 season with a win. W (24-8). After quarterback Tom Shannon led the Gators to a 10–8 halftime lead, Spurrier entered the contest and threw a 56-yard pass to Jack Harper. On September 26 Mississippi State played Florida at Veterans Memorial Stadium • Jackson, MS. The Gators won the game W 16–13. On Oct 10, The Gators beat Mississippi at Florida Field on the Gainesville campus. W 30–14.

October 17 found South Carolina at Florida Field to put some smiles on Homecoming fans as the Gators took really good care of business W (37–0). Feeling good at 3-0 in a great season start, the smiles disappeared on October 24 at #3 Alabama's Denny Stadium in Tuscaloosa, AL, as the Gators lost a nail biter to the Crimson Tide L (14–17).

Nothing worth having is easy but the Alabama game could have been the Gators'. Going in to their 1964 homecoming game against Florida, Alabama was ranked very high at #3 and Florida was doing well at #9 in the AP Poll. This was a back and forth game.

Against the Gators, as noted, Alabama grabbed a 17–14 victory. It did not look like it was theirs for the asking but then they scored ten unanswered points in the fourth quarter.

After a scoreless first quarter, Florida got a 7–0 second quarter lead when Steve Spurrier threw a nine-yard touchdown pass to Randy Jackson. Alabama tied it up when Steve Bowman got a one-yard touchdown run later in the quarter. It was 7–7 at halftime. Thee fans were on edge. Fingernails were found all over the stadium by the maintenance crew the next day.

In the third, the Gators got the lead back with a three-yard John Feiber touchdown run but then the Crimson Tide began its fourth quarter rally. It began with a 30-yard Bowman touchdown run, which tied the game, and it was a 21-yard David Ray field goal with just 3:06 left in the game that broke the backs of the Gators. Spurrier did his best by then leading the Gators on a drive that looked like it would reach pay dirt at the Tide's seven-yard line.

The Gators went for the tie and not the win and James Hall (surely, he does not want his name in this book) missed a field goal to tie the game and that single missed opportunity preserved the 17–14 Alabama win.

Putting their winning ways back in gear after the heartbreaking Alabama loss, the Gators beat Auburn on Oct 31 at Florida Field on the Gainesville Campus W (14–0). The Gators beat the favored Tigers by picking off four passes, returning one for an 84-yard touchdown, and by recovering three fumbles. QB Steve Spurrier ran in the final score from 5 yards out. For so many turnovers, the score was low.

Tommy Tolleson and David Ray rattle the Gator kicker to send a fourth down field goal wide at the end of the game and ensure Alabama's 17-14 victory

On Nov 7, Georgia kept its annual date in Jacksonville FL to defeat UF at the Gator Bowl Stadium L 7–14. Georgia's had a major overall advantage in the series, However, in recent years as the Gators began to play better football, the Gators enjoyed a 10–2 streak from 1952 to 1963 under head coaches Bob Woodruff and Ray Graves.

Vince Dooley, the infamous and great Georgia coach would permit none of that without a big fight. He became the new head coach of the underdog 1964 Georgia Bulldogs. In a game where the Bulldogs' quarterback failed to complete a single pass and was intercepted twice, "Dooley's Dogs," somehow were able to rely on their running game, a staunch second-half defense, and a little bit of luck to beat Coach Graves' tenth-ranked Gators and Sophomore sensation Steve Spurrier.

With the game tied at 7–7 in the fourth quarter, Bulldogs placekicker Bob Etter lined up for a potential game-winning field goal. Instead, in a poorly executed broken play, the Bulldogs' center and placeholder mishandled the snap, but the kicker picked up the bobbled ball and ran it for a touchdown to win the game 14–7. The sound of a deflated Gator permeated the stadium.

On Nov 21, Florida lost its second in a row. This loss was to the Florida State Seminoles and since they are in-state-rivals, it was a tough battle but the Seminoles prevailed at Doak Campbell Stadium in Tallahassee, FL L (7-16. It was the Seminoles to win and they did.

Nobody likes to talk about it but it was the first time that the Florida State Seminoles had ever defeated the Gators. Even though many of the early games in the series were close (and the 1961 contest actually ended in a 3–3 tie), Florida State had yet to beat their in-state rivals in a full six attempts.

The 1964 game would change that dynamic as the Gators would journey to Doak Campbell Stadium, and the Seminoles under coach Bill Peterson were at the end of having enjoyed their best season since joining the ranks of major college football programs. Nonetheless, the Gators looked at the Seminoles as the scrubs. Florida felt very confident that another victory was coming their way. In fact, the signage coming out onto the playing field boasted "Never, FSU, Never!" It was attached to their helmets. The game proved otherwise.

Florida State quarterback Steve Tensi hit Fred Biletnikoff with a first-half touchdown, helping the Seminoles to a 13–0 lead at the half. The Gators had a hard time holding on to the ball as the offense fumbled four times, including once at the FSU one-yard line. Florida was led by the inspirational quarterback Steve Spurrier, and the Gators finally scored in the 3rd quarter to cut the lead to 13–7. But, that was it. They were unable to find the end zone again. Les Murdock kicked a

42-yard field goal to secure the win for FSU, 16–7. Somethings happen because of destiny and others because of hard work. In this game, it looked like the Seminoles were willing to work harder for the win.

On Nov. 28. The Gators beat Miami at home W (12-10). On Dec 5, the Gators won a big one against a tough LSU squad at Tiger Stadium in Baton Rouge, LA W (20-6).

During the buildup to this classic 1964 game in Baton Rouge, all signs pointed to an exciting game. LSU was playing great football at the time Florida, though unranked, was moving and looking good. It had an exciting up-and-coming young player (and future Heisman Trophy winner) named Steve Spurrier.

God had interfered with the original schedule of this game, but of course we all defer to his judgment. But, after being delayed several weeks to the season finale due to Hurricane Hilda, the game did not have the same meaning and was anti-climactic. Florida rolled to a surprisingly easy 20–6 win over the No. 7 Tigers. Particularly noteworthy is the fact that this game was Steve Spurrier's first win over LSU. He was just a sophomore. This was the first of a long win streak that player and ultimately Coach Spurrier would have over the LSU Tigers.

Though it was not a championship season, there were lots of nice wins and a nice season for the Gators. Nobody was complaining about the team or the coach. Hopefully, those days were behind the Gators and the future was looking bright.

1965 Florida Gators Football Coach Ray Graves

The 1965 Florida Gators football team was the fifty-ninth season for Florida. It was the sixth of ten seasons for Ray Graves as the Football Gators head coach. The 1965 Gators had a nice year—well above 500 for the season and they had another fine year against the tougher SEC teams.

It was the Gators thirty-third season with the South-Eastern Conference (SEC). It was another reasonable showing. The team record was 7-4-0, and 4-2-0. They placed third in the SEC conference standings among the eleven SEC teams after winning 4 SEC games. Heisman winner Steve Spurrier was a junior this year and the team looked very good. Nothing in life, however, comes easy.

Coach Ray Graves

The Sugar Bowl

Finishing off the post season #6 Missouri, played the Gators at Tulane Stadium in New Orleans, LA in the (Sugar Bowl). The Gators almost won L (18–20) but got no cigars to pass-out to admiring fans.

Following the game, Gators quarterback Steve Spurrier, a name most Gators recognize, was recognized as the game's Most Valuable Player—the only MVP selected from the losing team in the history of the Sugar Bowl. Spurrier is quite a guy!

1966 Florida Gators Football Coach Ray Graves

The 1966 Florida Gators football team was the sixtieth season for Florida. It was the seventh of ten seasons for Ray Graves as the Football Gators head coach. The 1965 Gators had a nice year—well above 500 for the season and they had another fine year against the tougher SEC teams.

It was the Gators thirty-fourth-ninth season with the South-Eastern Conference (SEC). It was another reasonable showing. The team record was 9-2-0, and 5-1-0. They placed third in the SEC conference standings among the ten SEC teams after winning 5 SEC games.

Heisman winner Steve Spurrier was a senior this year and the team looked very good. Spurrier made a big difference in his three years. But, nothing in life, even if SS is on your team comes easy.

1966 Florida Gators Team Picture

This team and the team for the last two seasons before were led by quarterback Steve Spurrier. The Spurrier Gators outscored their opponents by a combined total of 265 to 147 and concluded their 1966 season with a 27-to-12 victory over the Georgia Tech Yellow Jackets in the 1967 Orange Bowl. The Gators were not a favorite of the AP, but nonetheless, they were ranked # 11 final UPI Coaches Poll. The Gators-- Steve Spurrier and Ray Graves had a great year.

Player Steve Spurrier

You can literally write forever about Steve Spurrier, the multi-talented and extremely successful Heisman Trophy Winner and great college football coach. Spurrier played from 1994 to 1966 when Freshman were not permitted on the active varsity teams. The most noteworthy achievements for this Tennessee native as a player was that he helped revolutionize the Florida Gators offense by breaking every school and SEC passing record while in Gainesville. Though he had many great moments, pundits have credited his breaking of six Sugar Bowl records during an attempted comeback against Missouri in 1966 as his crown jewel. Spurrier led Florida to three fourth-quarter touchdowns to nearly overcome a 20-0 deficit.

Spurrier receives the coveted Heisman Trophy for his 1966 season

Spurrier established himself as one of the best passers in SEC history on his way to winning Florida's first Heisman Trophy in 1966.

Steve Spurrier was born in Miami, Fla. And attended Science Hill High in Johnson City, Tenn., where he was a three-sport letterman starring in high school football, basketball and baseball. In three years as the starting pitcher for Science Hill, he never lost a game and led his team to two consecutive state baseball championships. He was an all-state selection in football, basketball and baseball, and a high school All-American quarterback in 1962. His accomplishments seem to never end.

Spurrier was recruited by several top college programs but he was not seriously recruited by Tennessee because the Volunteers ran a wing-T offense that featured a running quarterback while Spurrier was an excellent passer. He ultimately chose to accept a scholarship offer from Florida in 1963 because of "the passing, the SEC, the weather, and coach Ray Graves."

The 6-2, 203-pound, Spurrier became the Gators' starting quarterback in 1964 and he had a solid debut season by throwing for 943 yards and six touchdowns while leading Florida to a 7-3 record. As a 1965 junior, he passed for 1,893 yards and 14 touchdowns as the Gators went 7-4. Spurrier finished ninth in that year's Heisman vote.

His senior year was a special one. Spurrier threw for 2,012 yards and 16 touchdowns as Florida finished the regular season with an 8-2 record and a No. 11 ranking in the polls. Spurrier closed out his three-year, thirty-one-game college career with 4,848 passing yards and 37 touchdowns, breaking numerous school and conference records. In addition to winning the Heisman Trophy and the Walter Camp Award as a senior, he was also a unanimous All-American.

Spurrier was the third overall pick in the 1967 draft by the San Francisco 49ers, where he played for nine years, spelling John Brodie as quarterback in 1972 and leading the '49ers to a third-consecutive NFC West Title.

A head coach at the collegiate level since 1987, he was 20-13-1 at Duke and won the ACC Championship in 1989. While head coach at Florida, his team won the SEC Championship in 1990, '91, '93-'96, 2000 and the National Championship in 1996. He became the first Heisman winner to coach another Heisman winner when Florida quarterback Danny Wuerffel won the award in 1996. After Florida, he coached the Washington Redskins in the NFL before returning to coach South Carolina.

Spurrier is a member of the Orange Bowl Hall of Fame and the Tennessee Sports Hall of Fame. He was elected to the National Football Foundation and College Hall of Fame in 1986.

Steve Spurrier was so noticeable that he won the 1966 Heisman Trophy and he was the unanimous first-team quarterback on the 1966 All-America Team. That is quite a bit of plaudits for a guy from a team that the AP did not even see as competitive.

Spurrier completed every pass he threw. Well, not exactly! He was so accurate; however, he actually did complete 179 of 291 passes for 2,012 yards and 16 touchdowns with just eight interceptions.

Teammate and tailback Larry Smith took pressure of Spurrier as a QB as he was the team's leading rusher with 742 yards and nine touchdowns on 162 carries. Smith got his own accolades. He was selected as the most valuable player in the 1967 Orange Bowl after setting two Orange Bowl records with 187 rushing yards and a 94-yard touchdown run.

Looking for other greats on the team, it is not difficult. Actually, QB Spurrier helped all players play better than they might have been inclined. For example, flanker Richard Trapp set a new team record with 63 catches during the 1966 season.

More than just Spurrier created the difference for this team. In addition to the QB, center Bill Carr was the team's only other first-team All-American, receiving first-team honors from Time magazine and The Sporting News. Five Gators received first-team honors from either the Associated Press (AP) or United Press International (UPI) on the 1966 All-SEC football team.

Carr, Smith, Spurrier and Trapp were consensus first-team picks by both the AP and UPI, while guard Jim Benson took first-team honors from the UPI and second-team honors from the AP. The Gators of 1966, but for their overall record were one of a kind in football that year.

The season began with everybody knowing that Quarterback Steve Spurrier was returning to the 1966 team. However, nothing comes in football without some buts. But, Spurrier's two leading receivers, Charles Casey (58 catches in 1965) and Barry Brown (33 catches in 1965), had graduated and other receivers needed to be discovered.

This predicament was not lost on Coach Graves who is quoted: "This team has to be a question mark. I don't know what type of football team we have." Yet, Coach Graves was pleased to have the talent, including QB Spurrier that he had. He used the players to extract a toll from every opponent the Gators faced. Bravo to the 1966 team.

On Sept 17 in the season opener against a Big-10 Northwestern team, at Florida Field on the Gainesville Campus, the Gators won a nice game W 43–7. In this 1966 season and home opener over the Northwestern Wildcats at Florida Field, Quarterback Steve Spurrier passed for 219 yards and three touchdowns and he kicked two field goals in the game. Receiver Richard Trapp caught two touchdown passes (19 and 53 yards) and Elsden caught another (10 yards). Back-up quarterback Harmon Wages also scored on a 25-yard run. Preston also scored on a 15-yard pass from Kay Stephenson. In all, Florida gained 506 yards of total offense, 206 rushing and 302 passing. Great start!

On Sept 24, Mississippi State played at Florida Stadium and succumbed to the Gators W (28-7). Florida became two and 0. It was a record home crowd of 49,333 at Florida Field. When the first half ended, the teams were knotted 7–7; but the Gators had not yet gone into high gear. UF scored three touchdowns in a seven-minute span in the third quarter.

Quarterback Steve Spurrier threw two TD passes, a 16-yard pass to Jack Coons and a 13-yard pass to end Paul Ewaldsen. Florida's other touchdowns came on runs by Larry Smith and Harmon Wages. Three of Florida's four touchdowns were set up by interceptions of passes thrown by Mississippi State quarterback Don Saget. Good "D!"

On Oct 1, the Florida Squad traveled to Dudley Field in Nashville, TN to beat Vanderbilt W (13-0). Then, on Oct 1, Florida State played extremely tough in their home game against their in-state rivals but lost nonetheless to the Gators W (22-19) in a definite nail biter. Both Florida touchdowns were the result of passes thrown by Steve Spurrier, a 22-yarder to Jack Coons in the second quarter and a five-yarder to Larry Smith in the third quarter.

In the fourth quarter, Spurrier took charge and threw a 41-yard touchdown pass to Larry Smith and then completed a pass to Richard Trapp for the two-point conversion. This gave the Gators a three-point lead. Late in the game, a Florida State receiver was ruled out of bounds when he caught a pass in the end zone. The Seminoles kept battling but scored no more points. They missed a 48-yard field goal attempt as time expired. Senior QB Spurrier completed 16 of 24 passes for 219 yards and three touchdowns

On Oct 15, NC State took on a *riding high doing well* Florida team at Carter–Finley Stadium in Raleigh, NC, but lost to the Gators W (17-1). This was the Gators' fifth game and they were ranked #8 in the AP Poll. This victory marked the first time since 1928 that the Gators had won the first five games in any season.

It was a close game all the way. Early in the fourth quarter, North Carolina State kicked a field goal and grabbed the lead 10–3. The Gators then sustained a 74-yard drive and tied the game on a short touchdown run by Larry Smith. Shortly thereafter, linebacker Steve Heidt intercepted a pass on Florida's 23-yard line. Quarterback Steve Spurrier then led a 77-yard drive capped by a 31-yard touchdown pass to Richard Trapp.

Then, on Oct 22, an always tough LSU SEC team played the Gators at Tiger Stadium in Baton Rouge, LA but were defeated by the Gators W (28-7). Florida took a 21–0 lead at halftime on an eight-yard touchdown pass from Steve Spurrier to Larry Smith, a two-yard touchdown run by Smith, and a 13-yard touchdown pass from Spurrier to Richard Trapp. Fullback Graham McKeel also scored a touchdown on a short run in the third quarter. Louisiana State did not score until the fourth quarter. Steve Spurrier had another great game completing 17 of 25 passes for 208 yards and two touchdowns.

On Oct 29, Auburn played at Florida Field in a Gators Homecoming Game on the Gainesville Campus and were beaten by the Gators for a great HC celebration W (30–27).

This was the University of Florida's seventh straight winning game, defeating coach Shug Jordan's Auburn Tigers before a record homecoming crowd at Florida Field. In the game, the teams traded the lead back and forth all day.

When Auburn fumbled the opening kickoff, quarterback Steve Spurrier got right in gear and threw a touchdown pass to Richard Trapp on the third play of the game. On the day, Spurrier completed 27 of 40 passes for 259 yards. Other touchdowns came on short runs from backs Graham McKeel and Larry Smith. Smith finished the day with 102 rushing yards on twenty-two carries, including a 53-yard run. It was a great overall effort.

In the fourth quarter, Spurrier did what was necessary and scored a touchdown on a quarterback sneak after a 71-yard drive. Now the game as tied at 27, and Spurrier had the daunting task of engineering another late drive for the win. But, Florida was stopped at Auburn's 39-yard-line following an intentional grounding penalty.

The distance was outside the usual range of the Gators regular placekicker Wayne "Shade tree" Barfield, but Spurrier had kicked 40-yard field goals in practice. Fans still remember Steve Spurrier waving off the kicker and booting the game-winning, 40-yard field goal. That is the very definition of a real not faux superstar. There was no fake news reporting on Steve Spurrier when he was just about twenty years old. He's been that good for that long.

This was super exceptional play for the Florida Field General. Most believe this play eventually was responsible for Spurrier winning the Heisman. "Steve Spurrier may own the patent for thrills in football after the 1966 season. Indeed, Spurrier proved he was every bit the calm, collected candidate for the Heisman Trophy." said Pat Parrish of the All Florida News. What a player! What a team!

On Nov 5, as usual Georgia traveled to the Gator Bowl Stadium in Jacksonville, FL and as always played the Gators. Florida lost this one L (10–27). It was the first loss of the 1966 season, falling to the rival Georgia Bulldogs. Florida had been ranked #7 in the AP Poll prior to the game. With the loss, the Gators, dropped out of the AP top 10 after the loss. Bulldogs running back Ron Jenkins led the attack for Georgia with 88 rushing yards and a touchdown on 20 carries.

Florida got off to a fine start in the game. On the squad's first possession, the Gators put forth an 86-yard scoring drive with fullback Graham McKeel going over for the touchdown. Thereafter, the Gators were limited to a field goal, as Georgia was successful in repeatedly blitzing Florida quarterback Steve Spurrier, holding him to 16 of 29 passes for 133 yards.

Then, on Nov 12, Tulane played at Florida Field who lost to the Gators W (31-10). Florida rebounded with this fine victory over the Tulane Green Wave at Florida Field. Quarterback Steve Spurrier gained 282 yards of total offense in the game, breaking the SEC career total offense record. At the end of the game, Spurrier had a three-year total of 5,082 yards, surpassing Zeke Bratkowski's prior record of 4,824 yards from 1951 to 1953. Spurrier also set a new Florida single-season record with his 15th touchdown pass of the season. The game included an 83-yard punt return in the fourth quarter by Florida's George Grandy. Running back Larry Smith rushed for 93 yards on 26 carries. Everybody plays well when Steve Spurrier is playing or coaching or rooting on their side.

As the season closed, it was Miami playing against # 9 Florida at home. Miami won the game in a squeaker, L (16-21) Florida had a great season. This regular season ending loss at Florida Field was played before 59,211. It stung for sure.

Miami had led 21–3 at one point in the third quarter. Quarterback Steve Spurrier, who was playing in his last home game, engineered and executed a "desperate surge" that brought the Gators to within five points. He completed ten straight passes in one stretch and threw a touchdown pass to end Paul Ewaldsen late in the third quarter. Spurrier led another long drive in the fourth quarter that was capped by a touchdown run by Larry Smith.

As time ran out, the Gators had advanced the ball to the Miami 30-yard line. In all, Spurrier completed 26 of 49 passes for 224 yards. Flanker Richard Trapp caught 11 passes and set a team record with 63 receptions during the 1966 season. After the game, coach Ray Graves announced that Spurrier's number 11 jersey would be permanently retired. Tough game! Great player; Great regular season. Great team!

The Gators accepted an invitation for January 2, 1967 to play the Georgia Tech Yellow Jackets in the Orange Bowl. With Steve Spurrier as a senior QB at the helm in his last college game as a player, the Gators prevailed and won the Bowl Game W (27-12). It was great!

This was the 33rd Orange Bowl game. Florida tailback Larry Smith carried the ball 23 times for 187 yards in the game for a super yeoman effort. His game included a 94-yard touchdown run in the third quarter while he had a personal issue. His pants kept falling causing him to take time from running to keep his pants up. No kidding! He set Orange Bowl records for the most rushing yards in a game and for the longest run from scrimmage, and he was selected as the game's most valuable player.

Fullback Graham McKeel also got two nice touchdowns, and the Florida defense intercepted four passes and recovered a fumble. It was a great all-over effort. Quarterback Steve Spurrier was Mr. Inspiration though he saw limited action due to a sore throwing arm. Even in pain, the great QB still completed 14 of 30 passes for 160 yards. Backup QB Harmon Wages was tickled to get some time and he did very well. He threw a touchdown pass to end Jack Coons. What a nice story and the best part is that it is true. Florida coach Ray Graves called the game "the sweetest victory of my coaching career." For readers of this book, it surely was a season long overdue.

1966 Heisman Trophy winner Steve Spurrier.

There were a lot of post-season awards for this fine Florida team. Florida quarterback Steve Spurrier received many awards for his one-of-a-kind efforts, including the following:

On November 23, 1966, Spurrier was announced as the winner of the 1966 Heisman Trophy. The QB received 433 of 869 first place votes and 1,679 points, outpacing Purdue quarterback Bob Griese who garnered 184 first place votes and 816 points.

Spurrier was also recognized by the NCAA as the unanimous first-team quarterback on the 1966 All-America Team, having received first-team honors from the Associated Press (AP), United Press International (UPI), Newspaper Enterprise Association, Central Press Association, American Football Coaches Association, Football Writers Association of America, Time magazine, and The Sporting News.

Spurrier in the Middle

On December 3, 1966, Spurrier was selected by UPI as for its "back of the year" award. Spurrier received 137 of 327 possible votes, outpacing Bob Griese who finished second with 48 votes. In any other year, Bob Griese an outstanding back, would have gotten the nod.

On December 4, 1966, Spurrier was named the Sporting News College Football Player of the Year based on the votes of professional football scouts.

Florida center Bill Carr was Florida's other first-team All-American. He received first-team honors from Time magazine and the Sporting News. The team honors were not finished yet.

Five Gators received first-team All-SEC honors from either the AP or UPI on the 1966 All-SEC football team. Spurrier, Carr, running back Larry Smith, and flanker Richard Trapp were consensus first-team picks by both the AP and UPI, while guard Jim Benson took first-team honors from UPI and second-team honors from the AP.

The NFL Draft Favored the Gators

The 1966 Florida Team provided ten players to the NFL. They are: Steve Spurrier - selected by the San Francisco 49ers with third overall pick, played for the 49ers (1967–1975) and Tampa Bay Bucs, (1976).

The challenges of American football make it the most exciting sport in the world. The folks at home and those on the college game sidelines seem to like college football the best because there is no guarantee of million-dollar lives. Yet, when some of our college favorites make it to the pros, we love it and we root for them almost for eternity. My case in point of course among others is the master, Steve Spurrier.

1967 Florida Gators Football Coach Ray Graves

The 1967 Florida Gators football team was the sixty-first season for Florida. It was the eighth of ten seasons for Ray Graves as the Football Gators head coach. The 1967 Gators had a nice year—well above 500 for the season and they had another fine year against the tougher SEC teams.

It was the Gators thirty-fifth season with the South-Eastern Conference (SEC). It was another reasonable showing. The team record was 6-4-0, and 4-2-0. They placed third in the SEC conference standings among the ten SEC teams after winning 4 SEC games. Heisman winner QB Steve Spurrier was not available this year and it made a difference for sure.

1968 Florida Gators Football Coach Ray Graves

The 1968 Florida Gators football team was the sixty-second season for Florida. It was the ninth of ten seasons for Ray Graves as the Football Gators head coach. The 1968 Gators had a nice year—well above 500 for the season and they had another fine year against the tougher SEC teams.

It was the Gators thirty-sixth season with the South-Eastern Conference (SEC). It was another reasonable showing. The team record was quite respectable at 6-3-1, and 3-2-0 in the SEC. They tied for sixth in the SEC conference standings among the ten SEC teams after winning 3 SEC games.

Senior tailback Larry Smith led Florida's offense. He was a first-team All-American.

1969 Florida Gators Football Coach Ray Graves

The 1969 Florida Gators football team was the sixty-third season for Florida. It was the tenth and last of ten seasons and the most successful for Ray Graves as the Football Gators head coach. The 1969 Gators had a very nice year—almost undefeated. they had a great year against the tougher SEC teams.

It was the Gators thirty-seventh season with the South-Eastern Conference (SEC). It was another reasonable showing. The team record was quite respectable at 9-1-1, and 3-1-1 in the SEC. They placed fourth in the SEC conference standings among the ten SEC teams after winning 3 SEC games.

Graves' final Gators squad was an outstanding team, led by a surprising group of second-year offensive players known as the "Super Sophs." The group included quarterback John Reaves, wide receiver Carlos Alvarez and tailback Tommy Durrance.

In what some consider a strange twist, the Gators were invited to play coach Doug Dickey's SEC champion Tennessee Volunteers in the December 1969 Gator Bowl. The Florida defense dominated the game. With linebacker Mike Kelley (the game's MVP), defensive back Steve Tannen and defensive end Jack Youngblood, the Gators upset the Volunteers 14–13 to cap their 9–1–1 season.

This was the Gators' best ever single-season record to that time. After the Gator Bowl, Ray Graves was ready to go and he resigned as the head coach of the Gators football team. He chose to continue as the athletic director of the Florida Gators sports program until 1979.

Graves was the best overall coach to date at Florida. During the 1960s, Graves compiled an overall record of 70–31–4 (.686) during the decade, making him the winningest coach in the history of the Gators football program to that time.

Chapter 14 Doug Dickey Era 1970-1978

Coach # 15 Doug Dickey

Year	Coach	Record	Conference	Record
1970	Doug Dickey	7-4-0	SEC	3-3-0
1971	Doug Dickey	4-7-0	SEC	1-6-0
1972	Doug Dickey	5-5-1	SEC	3-3-1
1973	Doug Dickey	7-5-0	SEC	3-4-0
1974	Doug Dickey	8-4-0	SEC	3-3-0
1975	Doug Dickey	9-3-0	SEC	5-1-0
1976	Doug Dickey	8-4-0	SEC	4-2-0
1977	Doug Dickey	6-4-1	SEC	3-3-0
1978	Doug Dickey	4-7-0	SEC	3-3-0

Doug Dickey spent 15 seasons as the head coach at Tennessee and Florida, winning two SEC titles and playing in nine bowl games during that time. He was later inducted into the College Football Hall of Fame.

1970 Florida Gators Football Coach Doug Dickey

The 1970 Florida Gators football team was the sixty-fourth season for Florida. It was the first of nine seasons for Doug Dickey as the Football Gators head coach. The 1970 Gators had a nice year in the overall season and they were so-so in the SEC.

It was the Gators thirty-eighth season with the South-Eastern Conference (SEC). It was another reasonable showing. The team record was respectable at 7-4-0, and 3-3-0 in the SEC. They placed fourth in the SEC conference standings among the ten SEC teams after winning 3 SEC games.

Doug Dickey has retired from college football where he was head coach for both the Florida Gators and the Tennessee Volunteers.

Dickey had been the starting quarterback for the Gators under coach Bob Woodruff in 1952 and 1953, and had previously served as the head coach of the Tennessee Volunteers before returning to his alma mater in 1970.

Player Jack Youngblood

Monticello Native Jack Youngblood played for Florida from 1968 to 1970. He entered college at UF, where he could not play as Freshman and he wanted to be stronger. So, he put on 10 pounds a year through weight-lifting, finishing around 245 pounds when he graduated. He weht on to be NFL Defensive Player of the Year after his career as the most dangerous pass rusher in Gator history. He played 14 seasons with the Los Angeles Rams and was inducted into the Pro Football Hall of Fame in 2001. With Florida down seven,

Youngblood is remembered for having stopped a Georgia running back on the 1-yard line, forced a fumble and recovered it to begin a come-from-behind 24-17 victory in 1970.

Jack Youngblood

Also known to his parents as Herbert Jackson Youngblood III, he was born January 26, 1950 in Jacksonville, Florida. He graduated from the University of Florida as an All-America selection and he is considered among the best players the school has ever produced, having been named to the Gator Football Ring of Honor and having been voted to the College Football Hall of Fame.

He had a great NFL career and then spent time in the front-office for the Rams and other teams until about 2002. He's been a busy guy who made overtures into broadcasting (both radio and television), acting, business, and he even penned an autobiography.

Youngblood was named to Florida's All-Time High school football team by Sports Illustrated in 1989. In November 2007, he was voted to the Florida High School Athletic Association's All-Century High School football team. Jack Youngblood was never an also-ran

1971 Florida Gators Football Coach Doug Dickey

The 1971 Florida Gators football team was the sixty-fifth season for Florida. It was the second of nine seasons for Doug Dickey as the Football Gators head coach. The 1971 Gators had a miserable year in the overall season and they were terrible in the SEC.

It was the Gators thirty-ninth season with the South-Eastern Conference (SEC). It was another reasonable showing. The team record was respectable at 4-7-0, and 1-6-0 in the SEC. They placed fourth in the SEC conference standings among the ten SEC tied for eighth after winning just one SEC game. This was one of those rebuilding years for the Gators. They would be coming back but not like in the Graves years.

1972 Florida Gators Football Coach Doug Dickey

The 1972 Florida Gators football team was the sixty-sixth season for Florida. It was the second of nine seasons for Doug Dickey as the Football Gators head coach. The 1972 Gators had a 500 year in the overall season and they had a similar year in the SEC.

It was the Gators fortieth season with the South-Eastern Conference (SEC). It was another reasonable showing. The team record was respectable at 5-5-1, and 3-3-1 in the SEC. They tied for eighth after winning just one SEC game. This was one of those rebuilding years for the Gators. They would be coming back but not like in the Graves years.

1973 Florida Gators Football Coach Doug Dickey
<u>Tangerine Bowl Participants</u>

The 1973 Florida Gators football team was the sixty-seventh season for Florida. It was the fourth of nine seasons for Doug Dickey as the Football Gators head coach. The 1973 Gators had a fine record—the best for a Doug Dickey team. This was better than a 500-percentage year in the overall season and not quite as good in the SEC.

It was the Gators forty-first season with the South-Eastern Conference (SEC). It was another reasonable showing. The team record was getting positive at 7-5-0, and 3-4-0 in the SEC. They placed fifth in the SEC conference standings among the ten SEC teams.

The Gators were invited to the Tangerine Bowl for the Dec 22 game against the Miami Redskins (now RedHawks) of Ohio. The Tangerine Bowl was temporarily moved from Orlando to Gainesville as the completion of the Citrus Bowl expansion was delayed. The fans were greeted by a record cold snap, with game time temperatures at 25 degrees Fahrenheit (minus-4 degrees Celsius); the cold weather benefited the visiting Miami Redskins from Ohio, who won the game in the cold L (16–7).

1974 Florida Gators Football Coach Doug Dickey

The 1974 Florida Gators football team was the sixty-eighth season for Florida. It was the fifth of nine seasons for Doug Dickey as the Football Gators head coach. The 1974 Gators had a better than 500 year in the overall season and not quite as good in the SEC.

It was the Gators forty-second with the South-Eastern Conference (SEC). It was another reasonable showing. The team record was getting positive at 8-4-0, and 3-3-0 in the SEC. They placed fourth in the SEC conference standings among the ten SEC teams.

The 1974 Gators were powered by a strong backfield that included Tony Green and Jimmy DuBose, Dickey employed the wishbone offense for the first season in the Gators' history.

1975 Florida Gators Football Coach Doug Dickey
2nd place SEC Gator Bowl Participant

The 1975 Florida Gators football team was the sixty-ninth season for Florida. It was the sixth of nine seasons for Doug Dickey as the Football Gators head coach. The 1975 Gators had a great record; Dickey's best, and one of the best records for Florida ever in the SEC.

It was the Gators forty-third with the South-Eastern Conference (SEC). It was another nice showing. The team record was getting positive at 9-3-0, and 5-1-0 in the SEC. They tied for second in the SEC conference standings among the ten SEC teams. In Forty-Three seasons, the Gators had yet to win an SEC Championship. That day will come while you are reading this book.

The 1975 team featured consensus All-American linebacker Sammy Green. Sammy sure helped build this fine record.

The Gators played in the Gator Bowl at the Gator Bowl on Dec 29 against #17 Maryland but could not keep up with the Terrapins and wound up losing the encounter L (0-13).

That is it for the University of Florida's 69th season.

1976 Florida Gators Football Coach Doug Dickey

The 1976 Florida Gators football team was the seventieth season for Florida. It was the seventh of nine seasons for Doug Dickey as the Football Gators head coach. The 1976 Gators had a nice record, one of Dickey's best, and a nice record for Florida in the SEC.

It was the Gators forty-fourth with the South-Eastern Conference (SEC). It was another nice showing. The team record was getting positive at 8-4-0, and 4-2-0 in the SEC. They tied for fourth in the SEC conference standings among the ten SEC teams. In forty-four seasons, the Gators had yet to win an SEC Championship. That day will come while you are reading this book. But, it would not be during Dickey's tenure.

1977 Florida Gators Football Coach Doug Dickey

The 1977 Florida Gators football team was the seventy-first season for Florida. It was the eighth of nine seasons for Doug Dickey as the Football Gators head coach. The 1977 Gators were the first of two Dickey slides down (not up) the ladder of success. Things would not get better until the coach was changed in a few years. The SEC record was even but not good.

It was the Gators forty-fifth with the South-Eastern Conference (SEC). It was another nice showing. The team record was getting positive at 6-4-1, and 3-3-0 in the SEC. They placed fifth in the SEC conference standings among the ten SEC teams. In forty-five seasons, the Gators had yet to win one SEC Championship.

With a four-year cycle, Freshmen, Sophomores, Juniors, and Seniors, every four years coming and going, colleges must refresh their lineups or be condemned to forever to losing football games. This year, 1977, Florida had several quarterback candidates with Terry LeCount finally designated to be the starter.

Player Wes Chandler

Wes Chandler played for the Gators shortly after Steve Spurrier played – from 1974 1977. By this time, the Gators had learned how to win. Playing in a run-oriented wishbone offense did not hinder Chandler from posting record receiving numbers with the Gators. Chandler, from New Smyrna Beach, completed 11 seasons in the NFL, compiling 559 catches for 8,966 yards and 56 touchdowns for the New Orleans Saints and San Diego Chargers. In a great football moment. Chandler had 163 receiving yards and two touchdowns in a 24-19 victory against Auburn in 1976.

Whenever Gator fans discuss the most dynamic playmakers in school history, those who are 30-and-younger quickly mention the talented Percy Harvin, and deservedly so. But, there was a Percy Harvin well before Percy Harvin was born, and his name was Wes Chandler. If you ever saw Chandler play you know why.

He was well remembered by the National Football Foundation and they showed their long memory by inducting Chandler into the College Football Hall of Fame as a member of the 2015 class. Chandler arrived at UF in 1974 from New Smyrna Beach (Fla.) High and over the next four seasons, despite playing receiver in a wishbone offense, was a two-time All-American. He finished at UF career with 92 catches for 1,963 yards and 22 touchdowns. He added 353 yards and six touchdowns rushing in his senior season.

His 21.3-yard average per catch remains a school record nearly 40 years after he played his final game at UF.

Chandler when inducted ,joined eight other former UF player to be inducted into the Hall of Fame—Dale van Sickel, Steve Spurrier,

Jack Youngblood, Emmitt Smith, Wilber Marshall, Carlos Alvarez and Danny Wuerffel.

Chandler believes that his most noteworthy game at Florida is a victory over Georgia in 1977 at the old Gator Bowl in Jacksonville. The Bulldogs had won three in a row over the Gators, including a 41-27 win the previous season in which the Gators blew a big lead. In his final opportunity to get a win against Georgia, Chandler split time at receiver and running back. Pundits over the years like to use this to describe the games results: The final score: Wes Chandler 18, Georgia 17.

For the record, the actual score was 22-17, but Chandler scored all three Florida touchdowns while catching three passes for 50 yards and rushing 15 times for 57 yards in an emotional win for the Gators.

1978 Florida Gators Football Coach Doug Dickey

The 1978 Florida Gators football team was the seventy-second season for Florida. It was the ninth and last of nine seasons for Doug Dickey as the Football Gators head coach. The 1978 Gators were a big slide from past Gator seasons. Dickey had climbed down to the bottom of the Gator football success ladder after almost being right at the top. Things would not get better for the Gators until the coach was changed in 1979, the following year. The SEC record was even but still not good.

It was the Gators forty-sixth with the South-Eastern Conference (SEC). It was another meds medsa showing. The team record was no longer positive at 4-7-0. 3-3-0 in the SEC was not so bad. They tied for fourth in the SEC conference standings among the ten SEC teams. In forty-six seasons, the Gators had yet to win one SEC Championship.

Dickey Epitaph

There were worse coaches at Florida before Doug Dickey, and as a young coach, Dickey showed some signs of being a fine coach but in the end, it did not happen. After leaving Florida, Dickey went into private business for several years before becoming the athletic director of the University of Tennessee's Volunteers sports program in 1985. He was a football pioneer for sure when all the moves had yet to be invented. Doug Dickey was inducted into the College Football Hall of Fame as a coach in 2003. After a dozen years spent as an offensive assistant and head coach in college football and the USFL, Steve Spurrier would return to Florida again to become Florida's head coach in 1990. In 1978, as an assistant, Coach Spurrier was thrown out, shall we say, with the baby's bath water. Too bad!

Chapter 15 Charley Pell Era 1979-1984

Coach #16 Charley Pell

Year	Coach	Record	Conference	Record
1979	Charley Pell	0-10-1	SEC	0–6-0
1980	Charley Pell	8–4-0	SEC	4–2-0
1981	Charley Pell	7–5-0	SEC	3–3-0
1982	Charley Pell	8–4-0	SEC	3–3-0
1983	Charley Pell	9–2–1	SEC	4–2-0
1984	Pell/Hall	9–1–1	SEC	5–0–1

Charlie Pell, A Formative Gator Coach

1979 Florida Gators Football Coach Charley Pell

The 1979 Florida Gators football team was the seventy-third season for Florida. It was the first of six seasons for Charley Pell as the Football Gators head coach. The 1979 Gators were an abomination with no wins at all. Pell would do a lot better but his inaugural season cast a doubt on Florida's future and made the folks wish

Doug Dickey were back. But, Pell got his chance in 1980. No wins is no wins even in the SEC.

It was the Gators forty-seventh with the South-Eastern Conference (SEC). It was another terrible showing. The team record was so bad, with a lone tie as the high point that nothing was positive 0-10-1 and 0-6-0 in the SEC. They were dead last in the SEC conference standings among the ten SEC teams. In forty-seven seasons, the Gators had yet to win one SEC Championship. During the Pell Years, I regret to say this dream would still not come true.

1980 Florida Gators Football Coach Charley Pell

The 1980 Florida Gators football team was the seventy-fourth season for Florida. It was the second of six seasons for Charles B. "Charley" Pell as the Football Gators head coach. The 1980 Gators were the comeback kids of the SEC. Pell did lots better than his zippo inaugural season which cast a doubt on Florida's future. After 1980 was in the record books, nobody was wishing for Doug Dickey to make a comeback. Pell got his big chance this year in 1980 and I am pleased to say, he just about hit the ball out of the park.

It was the Gators forty-eighth with the South-Eastern Conference (SEC). It was another fine showing. The team record was a zillion time better than the prior year, and it was simply good, period. The record was 8-4-0 with a 4-2-0 record in the SEC. The Gators finished tied for fourth in the SEC conference standings among the ten SEC teams. In forty-eight, the Gators had yet to win one SEC Championship. During the Pell Years, it seemed like this might change.

Nineteen Eighty marked a remarkable one-year turnaround for the Gators from their 0–10–1 record in 1979. The winless 1979 season caused many in the support base of Florida to lose heart but as they looked at how hard the team was playing against tough teams. There was a lot of forgiveness. Recognizing the injuries and the changes to the game and the talent pool, this year was the make-up year and Gators fans were tickled pink.

Yes, 1979 had been the worst season in Gators history, and yes it was Charley Pell's first campaign as the new head coach of the Gators. But all was not copacetic with the Gators' previous head coach, Doug

Dickey, who had been fired in the aftermath of a poor 4–7 season in 1978.

Pell's 1980 Florida Gators were not looking back, instead they posted an 8–4 overall record and a Southeastern Conference (SEC) record of 4–2, tying for fourth place in the ten-team SEC.

1981 Florida Gators Football Coach Charley Pell

The 1981 Florida Gators football team was the seventy-fifth season for Florida. It was the third of six seasons for Charles B. "Charley" Pell as the Football Gators head coach. The 1981 Gators were the comeback kids of the SEC. Pell had another respectable plus 500 season.

It was the Gators forty-ninth with the South-Eastern Conference (SEC). It was another respectable showing. The record was 7-5-0 with a 3-3-0 record in the SEC. The Gators finished tied for fourth in the SEC conference standings among the ten SEC teams. In forty-nine years, the Gators had yet to win one SEC Championship. During the Pell Years, it seemed like this might change. Not this yr!

1982 Florida Gators Football Coach Charley Pell

The 1982 Florida Gators football team was the seventy-sixth season for Florida. It was the fourth of six seasons for Charles B. "Charley" Pell as the Football Gators head coach. The 1982 Gators performed better than the prior year. Pell had another respectable plus 500 season.

It was the Gators fiftieth with the South-Eastern Conference (SEC). It was another fine showing. The team record was very positive 8-4-0 with a 3-3-0 record in the SEC. The Gators finished tied for sixth place in the SEC conference standings among the ten SEC teams. In fifty years of play, the Gators had yet to win one SEC Championship. During the Pell Years, some of us thought that might change. It did not.

For their 8-3 performance, UF was invited for the Astro-Bluebonnet Bowl on New Year's Eve, 1982 against Arkansas in the Astrodome in Houston. Arkansas had just a little more than the Gators in this encounter and they prevailed L (24-28).

1983 Florida Gators Football Coach Charley Pell
3rd place in SEC

The 1983 Florida Gators football team was the seventy-seventh season for Florida. It was the fifth of six seasons for Charles B. "Charley" Pell as the Football Gators head coach. The 1983 Gators had their best season of the Charley Pell Era so far.

It was the Gators fifty-first with the South-Eastern Conference (SEC). It was a terrific showing. The team record was very positive 9-2-1 with a 4-2-0 record in the SEC. The Gators finished third in the SEC conference standings among the ten SEC teams. In fifty-one years of play, the Gators still had yet to win one SEC Championship. During the Pell Years, including this year, it seemed like this might change soon.

The Pell Gators loved to run the ball and they were darned good at it. Behind a stout defense and a rushing attack led by future pros Neal Anderson, John L. Williams, and Lorenzo Hampton, Pell's 1983 Gators were the first squad in program history to be ranked among the top ten teams in the final Associated Press poll. It was a banner year for the Gators. It was also the second time that the Gators were ranked in every weekly AP Poll throughout the season, (1975 was the first).

In May of 2008, Archie Manning, father of Peyton & Eli and a hall-of-famer himself, chairman of the National Football Foundation and College Hall of Fame, announced that the great Wilbur Marshall would have his name etched in college football history as a member of the College Football Hall of Fame Class of 2008.

Marshall, who played for the Gators from 1980-83, was one of 13 players and two coaches who were selected to the prestigious class. The group was honored at the NFF Awards Dinner then Marshall was formally inducted at the College Hall of Fame Enshrinement Festival, July 18-19, 2009, in South Bend, Ind.

He became just the fifth Florida player to be given this great honor. He is in good company with end Dale Van Sickel (1927-29), quarterback Steve Spurrier (1964-66), defensive end Jack Youngblood (1968-70), and running back Emmitt Smith (1987-89). Three Florida head coaches are members of the Hall of Fame, including Charles Bachman (1928-32), Ray Graves (1960-69) and Doug Dickey (1970-78).

Wilbur Marshall finished his career at Florida as the record holder in four categories. Along with the two single-season records in 1981, his 23 career sacks and 58 career tackles for loss established new school standards. He has since been passed in career sacks (Alex Brown, 33 between 1998-01) and single-season sacks (Brown, 13 in 1999). In 1999, the Gainesville Sun named him the Defensive Player of the Century and prior to a recent Florida-Auburn game, he was the fifth person to be inducted into the prestigious Ring of Honor.

Following his collegiate career, Marshall took his hard-hitting play to the NFL. Selected in the first round (11th overall) of the 1984 NFL Draft by the Chicago Bears, Marshall played for five teams in 12 seasons on the professional level. He was named first-team All-Pro twice (1986, '92) and played in the Pro Bowl three times (1986, '87, '92).

During his dozen NFL seasons, Marshall recorded 45 sacks and intercepted 23 passes, which he returned for 304 yards and three touchdowns. He also recovered 16 fumbles, returning them for 70 yards and one touchdown. Marshall is among the few players who have recorded 20 sacks and 20 interceptions in their career.

Not known for winning bowl games; but having been invited and having played in its share of post season games, Florida chose not to pay heed to its past bowl game results and came out blazing against Iowa at Gator Bowl Stadium in Jacksonville in the Gator Bowl. The Gators won the game by consistent hard playing and relentless pursuit W (14-6) Go Gators!

1984 Florida Gators Football Coach Charley Pell
<u>**SEC Champions**</u> <u>**National Champions (disputed by NCAA)**</u>

The 1984 Florida Gators football team was the seventy-eighth season for Florida. It was the sixth and last six season for Charles B. "Charley" Pell as the Football Gators head coach. After preparing the team for the season, Charley Pell was fired after the third game of the season due to numerous NCAA violations reputedly committed by him and his staff over the previous few years. Consequently, though not on the field during the remainder of the season, Pell shared honors with Coach Hall who took over the season for Pell after game three.

New offensive coordinator Galen Hall served as "interim coach," not co-coach for the remainder of the season. The 1984 Gators had their best season of the Charley Pell Era, period. Just one loss. Galen Hall was a fine coach and he brought in the crops that Pell had planted.

It was the Gators fifty-second with the South-Eastern Conference (SEC). It was a phenomenal showing, often good enough to win a national championship. The team record was very positive at 9-1-1 with a 5-0-1 record in the SEC. The Gators finished first in the SEC conference standings among the ten SEC teams. In fifty-two years of play, this was the Gators first team to win an SEC Championship on the merits of the on-field play. This was a big deal. During the Pell Years, it seemed like this might change soon so it would be a more regular occurrence. In 1984, the Gators won, regardless of the NCAA..

Another look at the season would show that after the Gators began the season as a 1–1–1 team under Pell. You'd have to be there to feel the anguish during the season. I bet Steve Spurrier has an opinion but we'll spare him.

Coach Galen Hall's version of the 1984 Florida Gators posted a 9–1–1 overall record and a Southeastern Conference (SEC) record of 5–0–1 (8–0–0 and 4–0–0, respectively, under Hall), finishing first among ten SEC teams. The Florida Gators were initially and formally recognized as the SEC champions.

The Gators had such a great year that they finished third in the Associated Press National Poll and seventh in the Coaches Poll, and they were so good that they were also named national champions by twenty-two publications including The New York Times and The Sporting News. How about that?

I have been writing about the Gators at this point in this book for seventy-eight seasons. Enough bad stuff had happened naturally in the course of all those seasons that man-made manufactured crap was not necessary for a team that had finally made it. Find another team to pick on!

What a shame that the big power brokers in college football conspired to take this great honor from the Florida Gators.

Somehow, the smoke filled closed rooms had something more in store for the Florida Gators than just telling the team to go get 'em. On May 30, 1985, the presidents of the ten SEC-member universities voted 6–4 to vacate the Gators' 1984 SEC title, the only title ever won by Florida and they declared that the team would be ineligible for the SEC championship during the upcoming 1985 and 1986 seasons because of the rule violations committed under Pell. Boo Hiss Boo!

Some say Charley Pell was responsible but many others say his trust in mankind was his downfall.

What did Charley Pell really do that was so bad?

Let's take a closer look at Charley Pell, the coach who first put Florida on the map. I think you will be impressed. This article about Charley, was written in 2014 after his way-too-soon death.

Charley Pell, the great coach who is credited with bringing the University of Florida to football prominence in the 1980's but, who was fired amid highly publicized violations of N.C.A.A. rules, died in Southside, Ala on May 29, 2001. He was just 60.

He had been suffering from lung cancer.

Pell was a disciplinarian who drove himself, his assistants and his players. Jeff Bostic, who played for him at Clemson before a long professional career, said: "I'm convinced he was the most organized, philosophical, psychological coach I've ever met. He was a master organizer."

http://www.gatorcountry.com/florida-gators-football/legacy-charley-pell/

THE LEGACY OF
CHARLEY PELL
Written by FRANZ BEARD, MAY 12, 2014,

Original article also contains 10 COMMENTS

Charley Pell was angry. It took every ounce of strength, both physical and emotional, to hold back what he was really thinking that December Saturday afternoon in 1980 when he marched into the Florida State dressing room at Doak Campbell Stadium, congratulated Bobby Bowden and the Seminoles for a game well played and a 17-13 victory well earned. It was the march back to the Florida dressing room that the seething emotions began to spill over.

He was barely in the Florida locker room when he told the Gators, still quiet and still smarting from a game in which they had snatched defeat from the jaws of victory, "Gentlemen, I just did the most unpleasant thing I've ever done in my life. I just congratulated Coach Bowden for beating us. I want you to know that as long as I'm the head football coach at the University of Florida, that opportunity will never present itself again."

Bob Hewko remembers that like it was yesterday. Injured in the game, Hewko sat in that tiny, cramped, visitor's locker room with his teammates waiting for what seemed an eternity for Pell to arrive and when he did, there was a look on his face that he and every other Gator knew all too well and understood.

Hewko braced himself.

"What he said wasn't anything like we were expecting," Hewko said on the phone from Las Vegas where he was mixing some business with pleasure. "He was mad. He was really mad and we probably deserved to get chewed out because that's a game we knew we should have won, but if you understand one thing about Coach Pell, he used moments like this. He was a master at turning the worst thing into something good and when he told us we weren't going to lose to them again as long as he was the coach, it was totally believable. It was like, okay, there is never even a shot that we're going to lose to them again … ever.

"Coach Pell always said that his goal was to win the state of Florida. He said once you win the state of Florida, you're in position to win the national championship but that's where it all starts."

Feel free to read the rest about the great Charles Pell at the link above. He was one of the best.

…

Post Script on Charley Pell

This is my fifth "Great Championships" book. My first was about Notre Dame. When I write a book such as this, I get the opportunity to study a football program from beginning to the current moment in time. It is a very enjoyable experience. I don't particularly like writing about the game highlights as they are exhaustive and exhausting but I would not put my name to a book that simply showed box scores without some commentary.

Each school so far that I have studied has a prime mover before the prime mover. At Florida, Steve Spurrier, whose coaching period is coming up soon in this book has been the prime mover with all the credit at Florida. Spurrier deserves the accolades. At Notre Dame, it was Knute Rockne. But, before these legends, there were not so well-known legends who greased the skids for their success. For Florida, it was Charley Pell. What a well-written piece by Frank Beard to get one's heart moving towards a truth that otherwise would not be known. Thank you Frank

At Notre Dame, the Charley Pell Character was played by Coach Jesse Claire Harper. Harper coached ND when QB Gus Dorais and End Knute Rockne became All-Americans. His five-year record was- 34–5–1 To show the unsung similarities between Harper and Pell, let me quote from a great article about Harper: http://www.und.com/sports/m-footbl/spec-rel/082913aad.htm.

"There are six former Notre Dame head coaches in the National Football Foundation Hall of Fame. Five of them are immortalized with sculptures just outside Notre Dame Stadium. Harper is the lone omission. It somewhat defines how he was the man behind the scenes who went relatively unnoticed despite serving the school so well as a coach, administrator, businessman, educator and an example to emulate."

Frank Beard did his best in 2014 to bring Charley Pell to everybody's attention. Both Pell and Harper have great legacies. Both could use just a little more attention from their respective universities. Though I must admit, neither would ever think they deserved extra attention nor would they consider asking for it. But, guys like me and Frank Beard and the great Gator Nation surely can.

Chapter 16 Galen Hall Era 1985-1989

Coach # 17 Galen Hall
Coach # 18 Gary Darnell

Year	Coach	Record	Conference	Record
1985	Galen Hall	9–1–1	SEC	5-1
1986	Galen Hall	6–5	SEC	2-4
1987	Galen Hall	6–6	SEC	3-3
1988	Galen Hall	7–5	SEC	4-3
1989	Galen Hall	7–5	SEC	4-3
1989	Gary Darnell			

Galen Hall with the Gators

1985 Florida Gators Football Coach Galen Hall
SEC Championship Shoulda been championship!

The 1985 Florida Gators football team was the seventy-ninth season for Florida. It was the first official year for Galen Hall as the Football Gators head coach. Former Offensive Coordinator and 1984 "interim coach" had been coaching the Gators for a number of years.

Hall had performed miracles in 1984 taking over for a 1-1-1 team that had been trained by Chrley Pell. There were no more losses and no more ties once Hall took the reins in 1984. This 1985 year would be just as good but it had the same shaky start. So, the 1985 Gators tied their best season of the Charley Pell Era and their best season of the Galen Hall era. Galen Hall was a fine coach and he brought in every crop that Charley Pell had planted, including the perennials.

It was the Gators fifty-third with the South-Eastern Conference (SEC). It was another phenomenal showing, almost good enough to win a national championship. The Galen Hall team record was very positive 9-1-1 with a 5-1-0 record in the SEC. The Gators finished tied for first for their second conference topping performance among ten SEC teams. In fifty-three years of play, this was just the second team to win enough games to win the SEC Championship. This was a big deal. During the Pell Years, the team inched up at the championship and finally snagged it in 1984.

With a similar record to 1984, the Gators came in tied for first and the would not see another Championship in the SEC until Steve Spurrier came in as head coach in 1990 when Galen Hall was replaced. Spurrier wasted no time to grab the SEC in his first year as head coach.

Unfortunate, because the SEC wanted to punish Galen Hall's team for Charley Pell's issue, this fine coach's 1985 Florida Gators were ineligible to win the Southeastern Conference (SEC) title, receive a bowl bid, or appear on live television.

Season Games

Ranked # 5 to begin the season, on Sept 7, to get the season started right, the Gators defeated Miami at Orange Bowl Stadium in Miami, FL W (35–23) before a crowd of 80,227. Ranked #3 with a chance for all the marbles, Sept 14, Rutgers, which finished the season at 2-8, destroyed the Gators hopes of an unblemished record and a shot at the national championship. They totally surprised Florida at Florida Field on the Gainesville campus by tying the Gators in the last minutes of play T (28-28).

Rutgers QB Joe Gagliardi threw a 16-yard touchdown pass to Bruce Campbell with 35 seconds left and then connected perfectly with Curtis Stephens for a 2-point conversion to give Rutgers a surprising and exciting 28-28 tie over highly favored Florida.

It gets even worse. Gagliardi was not even the starting QB. He was the backup for Eric Hochberg. He came off the bench in the fourth quarter with the Scarlet Knights trailing by 14 points in their season opener. He engineered two long touchdown drives of 65 and 86 yards to gain the upset tie. This snapped Florida's 10-game winning streak before 71,708 fans. At one point Rutgers had trailed by 21 points shortly before Gagliardi entered the game. This is a game that would haunt the Gators all season long.

Now ranked #11, on Sept 28, the Gators beat Mississippi State at Scott Field in Starkville, MS W (36–22). Then, on Oct 5, with a much-improved defense, Florida shut out Louisiana State at Tiger Stadium in Baton Rouge, LA W (20-0). On Oct 12, the Gators beat # 14 Tennessee at home by a close margin W (17–10). Now ranked #5, on Oct 18, the Gators whipped Southwestern Louisiana in a blowout at Florida Field W 45–0. On Oct 26, #2 ranked Florida beat Virginia Tech at Gainesville W (35–18)

On November 2, in a close match at against #6 Auburn at Jordan–Hare Stadium in Auburn, AL, Florida won W (14–10) before 75,000 fans. Then on Nov 9, the old nemesis Georgia came into Jacksonville Town for the annual neutral field game just as Florida was reranked at #1 in the national polls. The Gators could not get their act together this game and fell to the #17 Bulldogs for a season crushing first loss L (3-24).

Still feeling the pain again playing in Jacksonville, Florida almost lost another to Kentucky but survived W (15-13). the next big state of Florida match up was won by UF on Nov 30 against #12 Florida State at Florida Field W 38–14. Florida were declared ineligible for post-season Bowl Games by the NCAA.

After the season, the Eck Rating System, an NCAA recognized selector created by Steve Eck, named Florida as the 1985 national champions, though Florida does not claim the title. Florida finished with a 9-1-1 overall record and an SEC record of 5-1, tying for first place in the ten-team SEC.

1986 Florida Gators Football Coach Galen Hall

The 1986 Florida Gators football team was the eightieth season for Florida. It was the second year for Galen Hall as the full-year Football Gators head coach. Hall had performed miracles in 1984 taking over for a 1-1-1 team. The 1986 year would be a rebuilding year after Charley Pell's recruits made 1985 such a success for Galen Hall.

It was the Gators fifty-fourth with the South-Eastern Conference (SEC). It was a so-so showing, just better than 500. Galen Hall's record was 6-5-0 and 2-4-0 in the SEC. Hall was not getting the talent that Charley Pell had brought to the Gators. Florida finished tied for seventh in the SEC Conference among ten SEC teams. In fifty-four years of play, the 1984 and 1985 years were #1 years for the Gators but both championships were taken away after the seasons due to violations and sanctions.

Of course, Gator fans know we got them!

Point of note: This was the last year that Florida lost to the Kentucky Wildcats, as of 2016---the longest annual win streak of any team over another in NCAA history and the longest such streak in Southeastern Conference history.

1987 Florida Gators Football Coach Galen Hall

The 1987 Florida Gators football team was the eighty-first season for Florida. It was the third official year for Galen Hall of five as the Football Gators head coach. Galen Hall was not as successful at recruiting as Charley Pell and could not rebuild the team to the strength of Pell's squads. This year was Hall's worst effort with a flat 500 season.

It was the Gators fifty-fifth with the South-Eastern Conference (SEC). It was mediocre showing at 500. Galen Hall's record was 6-6-0 and 3-3-0 in the SEC. Florida finished sixth in the SEC Conference among ten SEC teams.

The season was the debut of freshman running back Emmitt Smith. Few football fans have not heard of the great Emmett Smith when he played pro for Dallas. Smith went on to break the 1,000-yard barrier in the seventh game of his freshman season, the fastest any running back had ever broken that barrier to begin his college career. He was named SEC and national freshman of the year.

Player Emmitt Smith

Everybody who loves football and has been alive and over the age of ten tears old any time from the late 1980's to the mid 2000's has heard of Emmitt Smith as a great gentleman and a great football player for the Gators and for the Dalls Cowboys. There is just one Emmitt Smith. He played for the Gators from 1987 to 1989, foregoing his senior year at Florida to enter the NFL draft.

A Pensacola native, when he moved on to the NFL he held 58 UF records. His best memory of a great moment occurred in the third game and his first start when he rushed for 224 yards and two touchdowns in a 23-14 upset victory at Alabama. As you can see when they retired his Jersey at his High School, Escambia in Pensacola, those he touches hold him in the highest regard.

Emmitt Smith left his mark on Escambia High School in Pensacola, Fla. He had his jersey retired, the weight room bears his name and the sign outside the school brags "Home of Emmitt Smith." ESPN RISE

Emmitt rushed for over 100 yards in 45 of the 49 games he started for Escambia (including the last 28 in a row) and finished with a 7.8 yards per carry average. Twice, he broke the 2,000-yard rushing mark in a season. In track & field, Smith competed as a sprinter and was a member of the 4x100m (42.16 s) relay squad.

For his efforts, Smith was named the USA Today and Parade magazine high school player of the year for 1986. In 2007, twenty years after Smith graduated from high school, the Florida High School Athletic Association (FHSAA) named Smith to its "All-Century Team," recognizing him as one of the thirty-three greatest Florida high school football players of the last 100 years. As part of its "100 Years of Florida High School Football" awards ceremony, FHSAA named Smith as its "Player of the Century."

At the conclusion of his junior season in 1989, Smith was named a first-team SEC selection for the third year and SEC Player of the Year, was a unanimous first-team All-American, and finished seventh in the Heisman Trophy balloting.

On January 1, 1990, Florida hired Steve Spurrier to coach the Gators. Smith, concerned about his potential role in Spurrier's reportedly pass-first offense, decided to forgo his senior year at Florida and he entered the NFL draft (Smith's school rushing record would be broken by Errict Rhett, Spurrier's first starting running back at Florida, albeit over four seasons instead of three and on 173 more rushing attempts). Smith returned to the university during the NFL off-season and completed his bachelor's degree in 1996.

Emmitt Smith was subsequently inducted into the University of Florida Athletic Hall of Fame as a "Gator Great" in 1999, the Gator Football Ring of Honor and the College Football Hall of Fame in 2006. As part of a series of articles written for The Gainesville Sun in 2006, he was recognized as the No. 3 all-time player among the top 100 from the first 100 years of the Gators football program.

Drafted at 17th in the first round of the 1990 NFL Draft, the Cowboys never regretted that decision.

Smith was the first player in NFL history to rush for 1,400 rushing yards or more in five consecutive seasons. Smith, Jim Brown, and LaDainian Tomlinson are the only players with seven straight ten-touchdown seasons to start their careers. With 1,021 rushing yards in 2001, Smith became the first player in NFL history with 11 consecutive 1,000 yard seasons and the first to post eleven 1,000-yard rushing seasons in a career. He is the NFL's all-time leader in rushing attempts with 4,409. Smith is the only player to post three seasons with nineteen or more touchdowns. He also holds the record for most games in a season with a touchdown and most games in a season with a rushing touchdown (15), set in 1995. And, somebody once said he would fall on his face. I remember that.

-- End of player highlights --

1988 Florida Gators Football Coach Galen Hall

The 1988 Florida Gators football team was the eighty-second season for Florida. It was the fourth official year for Galen Hall of five seasons as the Football Gators head coach. The team record showed one more win than in 1987 but the program was not yet back on track.

It was the Gators fifty-sixth with the South-Eastern Conference (SEC). It was a respectable showing just above 500 but not the type of season to which Florida had become accustomed. Galen Hall's record was 7-5-0 and 4-3-0 in the SEC. Florida finished tied for fourth in the SEC Conference among ten SEC teams.

The Gators started the 1988 season as if they were invincible with five wins in a row. They were ranked as high as No. 14 during this period. Then, some bad things happened. Overall, It was an unremarkable year.

1989 Florida Gators Football Coach Galen Hall / Gary Darnell

The 1989 Florida Gators football team was the eighty-third season for Florida. It was the fifth official year for Galen Hall of five /six seasons as the Football Gators head coach. It was Hall's last year and it would end abruptly. Galen Hall was replaced as the Gators head coach after five games by his defensive coordinator, Gary Darnell. The team record was the same as in 1988 but the program had not come back in the last four years of Galen Hall.

It was the Gators fifty-seventh with the South-Eastern Conference (SEC). It was again a respectable showing just above 500 but not the type of season to which Florida fans and alums had become accustomed. Galen Hall and Gary Darnell's combined record was 7-5-0 and 4-3-0 in the SEC. Florida again finished tied for fourth in the SEC Conference among ten SEC teams.

Galen Hall had come in to finish Charley Pell's 1984 season after three games and was replaced after the fifth game of this season. Overall, we can say that Hall coached for five seasons plus two games. Gary Darnell would not be retained in 1990. Instead Steve Spurrier took the reins.

Galen Hall Epilogue

As you can see by reviewing the game results, Galen Hall had the Gators moving well during the 1989 season. With the team record at 4-1, It looked like another Charley Pell-like year was on the way. Then, the boom fell on Galen Hall.

It seemed like all coaches of the day were shaving corners and doing their best to get the best recruits and some practices. Charley Pell knew that but was mostly above it but he had a few assistants who stretched the rules.

Hall therefore inherited a probation-wracked program when he replaced Pell in 1984. He was pressured to resign himself less than 24 hours after a dramatic 16-13 victory at Louisiana State that brought the Gators record to 4-1. I

<<< Gary Darnell the administration accepted the resignation, effective that day, of head football coach Galen Hall,' said AD Bryan. 'The detailed reasons for this resignation are set forth in his letter to me. In short, Coach Hall has conceded to me his personal involvement in 1987 in helping to solve the problems of a player, the details of which assistance are outlined in his letter; and the personal payment of unauthorized salary supplements to assistant coaches from 1986-89. All of these actions are in direct violation of NCAA rules; they were also clearly in breach of the responsibilities imposed upon him by his contract with the university.

'This resignation results from an investigation jointly conducted by the NCAA and the university which began a number of months ago. Our cooperation with the NCAA made sending a preliminary notice of inquiry unnecessary. That investigation continues. It involves both the football program and the basketball program. My mandate is that it be both searching and fearless, and that as it proceeds, verified violations will be brought to my attention for immediate action.'

In his letter of resignation, Hall outlined the reasons for his departure. Hall received a vote of confidence from the university last fall amid rumors of his imminent firing. Gator boosters have been vocal in their displeasure with Florida's play in recent years, but this year's team has won four straight after opening with a home loss to Mississippi.

'Dear Dr. Bryan, recently special council for the university together with investigative representatives of the NCAA discussed with me and my council various allegations relating to my actions as head coach,' said the university president, reading from Hall's letter. 'I acknowledge that I made the payments to both of the assistant coaches in question and further concede that the $4,000 payment was made in currency. Although these payments were entirely derived from my own funds, I acknowledge that I failed to report these matters to the athletic director or to secure his approval as required by my employment agreement and in apparent violation of NCAA rules.'

Darnell, 40, was head coach at Tennessee Tech from 1983-85 before serving as inside linebacker coach and defensive coordinator at Wake Forest. He joined the Gators in 1988 and directed a defensive unit that ranked third nationally. This year's Gator defense was rated No. 1 in the nation entering the LSU game.

Chapter 17 Steve Spurrier Era 1990 to 2001

Coach # 19

Year	Coach	Record	Conference	Record
1990	Steve Spurrier	9–2–0	SEC	6–1–0
1991	Steve Spurrier	10–2–0	SEC	7–0–0
1992	Steve Spurrier	9–4–0	SEC	6–2–0
1993	Steve Spurrier	11–2–0	SEC	7–1–0
1994	Steve Spurrier	10-2-1	SEC	7–1–0
1995	Steve Spurrier	12–1–0	SEC	8–0–0
1996	Steve Spurrier	12–1–0	SEC	8–0–0
1997	Steve Spurrier	10–2–0	SEC	6–2–0
1998	Steve Spurrier	10–2–0	SEC	7–1–0
1999	Steve Spurrier	9–4–0	SEC	7–1–0
2000	Steve Spurrier	10–3–0	SEC	7–1–0
2001	Steve Spurrier	10–2–0	SEC	6–2–0

Nothing wrong with that record. Right?

Steve Spurrier, Leading the Gators

1990 Florida Gators Football Coach Steve Spurrier
SEC Championship

The 1990 Florida Gators football team was the eighty-fourth season for Florida. It was the first year for Steve Spurrier, Gator's Heisman Trophy-winning quarterback to return to his alma mater for twelve seasons as the new Football Gators head coach. The team record was immediately the best since Galen Hall's first official year as coach.

It was the Gators fifty-eighth with the South-Eastern Conference (SEC). It was again a fine showing with just two losses. It was just the kind of season for which Florida fans and alums were hoping. Spurrier had a fine record of 9-2-0 and 6-1-0 in the SEC. Florida again finished first in the SEC Conference among ten SEC teams. But, unfortunately, the great win did not count.

From Galen Hall's supposedly major infractions, Spurrier's 1990 Florida Gators, were ineligible to win the SEC title or receive a bowl bid because of lingering NCAA probation. Why can't the NCAA pick on other teams?

Nonetheless, as noted above, the Spurrier-led Gators posted a best-in-the-SEC record of 6–1 to accompany a stellar 9–2 overall record. This season laid the foundation for the Gators' run of six SEC championships and a national title during the next decade. Florida finished thirteenth in the season's final AP Poll.

When fans and alums consider that this was the third time that the Gators had won the SEC Championship on the field and the third time that the NCAA had taken away their earned championship, one must ask if Florida would vote to remove the NCAA from College Football if given the opportunity. You already know how I feel.

Just before Coach Spurrier's Gator coaching debut, the Gainesville campus was stunned by the Danny Rolling murders. You may recall that Rolling was 36 when he showed up in Gainesville shortly before the fall semester began at the University of Florida. He had been a drifter with a criminal past.

He lived in a tent pitched in some woods near campus. He followed two freshman roommates, Sonja Larson, 18, and Christina Powell, 17, to their off-campus apartment, killed both of them with a hunting knife and desecrated their bodies. He's gone but his deeds are not forgotten.

On Oct 25, 2006, about six years after their deaths, this savage serial killer who murdered five college students in total here in 1990 was executed by lethal injection. The relatives of his victims said afterward that they could finally feel the beginnings of relief. The world in Florida breathed a collective sigh of relief.

During Steve Spurrier's first season, he was able to build on the strong talent recruited by coach Galen Hall.

The Spurrier first loss did not come until the sixth game when the # 5 Tennessee Volunteers whipped the Gators L (3-45).

This 3-45 road loss to the fifth-ranked Tennessee Volunteers was very disappointing 3–45 road loss in Knoxville, Tennessee. There was a link between Spurrier and Tennessee. He had been a star quarterback at Science Hill High School in Johnson City, Tennessee during the early 1960s. Although Knoxville is nearby, the coach did not seriously consider attending UT because he was an excellent passer and the Vols ran a single-wing offense at the time which featured a running quarterback. Instead, he choose to come back to Florida, the state of his birth (Miami Beach). Eventually Steve Spurrier became the Gators' first Heisman Trophy winner in 1966.

This first Gator squad of the master coach was 5–0 and ranked No. 9 coming into the game with Johnny Majors' 3–0–2 and #5 Vols. This was the first time in their series history that both rivals were ranked in the AP top-10 when they faced off.

The 1990 game began as a defensive struggle, with UT holding a slim 7–3 lead at the half. However, the Vols' Dale Carter returned the second half kickoff 91 yards for a touchdown, igniting the home crowd at Neyland Stadium.

On their ensuing possession, the Gators fumbled for what would be the first of six UF turnovers in the second half. The opportunistic Vols took full advantage, turning Spurrier's homecoming (and, coincidentally, UT's homecoming game) into a dominating 45–3 rout, the largest margin of victory for either team in the series.

Florida came right back the next week against Akron at home in a blowout shutout W (59-0). Florida was ready again the next week against #4 Auburn as the Gators devoured the Tigers on the home field W (48-7). Coach Pat Dye's Auburn Tigers were the defending three-time SEC champions. By game time, they came in with a ranked 4th in the nation, undefeated with a 6–0–1 record.

Spurrier's fifteenth-ranked Gators were three-point favorites for this game. Opposing coach Dye had been publicly dismissive of Spurrier's pass-oriented offense when interviewed prior to the game. The game started slow like it was anybody's game. The Gators and Tigers were tied 7–7 after the first quarter, but Spurrier's Gators exploded for twenty-seven points in the second quarter, resulting in a 34–7 halftime lead and a 48–7 victory for the Gators. This was the Gators' biggest margin of victory in the series, and the worst loss of Coach Dye's career.

Georgia had been very successful for years playing the Gators in Jacksonville. Not this season, Florida pounded the Bulldogs W (38-7) on Nov 10. Still ready to roll the #6 ranked Gators kept rolling right over Kentucky at Commonwealth Stadium in Lexington, Kentucky W (47–15).

Shane Matthews ready throwt

On Dec 1, the #6 ranked Florida Gators suffered a bitter bill defeat to #8 ranked in-state rival Florida State in a give and take game L (30-45) played at Doak Campbell Stadium in Tallahassee, Florida. The

NCAA sanctions prevented the Gators from engaging in a post-season bowl game so this game was the last of the season.

Shane Matthews finished the season with 2,952 passing yards and twenty-three touchdowns—then the most passing yards in Gators history. He was SEC Player of the Year.

Before Coach Spurrier returned to Gainesville, the Gators had never won an officially sanctioned Southeastern Conference (SEC) or national football championship (Florida's first SEC championship was in 1984, but was retroactively vacated by the SEC for infractions incurred by former head coach Charley Pell). Before Spurrier resigned to seek a coaching position in the National Football League in January 2002, the Gators would win six official SEC titles, play for two national championships, and win one in 1996. What a difference a great coach makes.

1991 Florida Gators Football Coach Steve Spurrier

The 1991 Florida Gators football team was the eighty-fifth season for Florida.

Brad Culpepper is a Florida great who deserves recognition. He played from 1988-1991. He was a defensive Tackle. Brad is both the son, grandson and nephew of former Gator players; he was named as a first team All-American in 1991, Culpepper set a school record for tackles for loss by an interior Defensive Lineman that year (21.5) and for his career (47.5). In this, his Senior season he was also elected as the student body vice president. He enjoyed a productive 9 year career in the NFL and is currently an attorney residing in Tampa.

It was the second year for Steve Spurrier of twelve seasons as the Football Gators head coach. The team record was better than 1990, the first time the Gators had achieved a ten-game win-season.

It was the Gators fifty-ninth with the South-Eastern Conference (SEC). It was again a fine showing with just two losses. It was a better season than the last and just the kind of season for which Florida fans and alums were hoping. Spurrier had a fine record of 10-

2-0 and 7-0-0 in the SEC. Florida again finished first in the SEC Conference among ten SEC teams. This time it counted.

The Gators were led by quarterback Shane Matthews and first-team All-American defensive tackle Brad Culpepper. Spurrier's 1991 Florida Gators compiled the first-ever ten-win season in program history, and a perfect SEC record of 7–0. There was reason on campus to celebrate.

In a matchup of the two teams with the Florida name, the Gators beat the Seminoles in a defensive battle at home W (14-9). That was the end of the regular season and a great win streak of eight games. Among the Gators' 1991 victories, this sweet 14–9 defensive upset of the Florida State Seminoles was a particularly memorable victory played in front of an overflow home crowd at Ben Hill Griffin Stadium. The Gators loved to beat "State."

They scored touchdowns on a first-quarter run by tailback Errict Rhett, and a 72-yard bomb from Shane Matthews to wide receiver Harrison Houston in the third quarter, and held on to win. Gators defensive ends Darren Mickell and Harvey Thomas kept Seminoles quarterback Casey Weldon off balance and on the run in the second half, and, in the fourth quarter, Gators safeties Will White and Del Speer combined to break up a fourth-down pass in the end zone by Weldon, thus preserving the victory for Florida.

Sugar Bowl v Notre Dame

#3 ranked Florida was invited to the Sugar Bowl to play #18 Notre Dame at the Superdome in New Orleans, Louisiana. Notre Dame got the best of the Gators L (28-39). This was the Gators first New Year's Day bowl appearance since 1974. The defeat by Notre Dame brought the team in at a rank of seventh in the final Associated Press Poll. Florida won the team's first official SEC championship, 59 seasons after joining the conference as a charter member. Quarterback Shane Matthews repeated as SEC Player of the Year in 1991.

1992 Florida Gators Football Coach Steve Spurrier
SEC Championship

The 1992 Florida Gators football team was the eighty-sixth season for Florida. It was the third year for Steve Spurrier of twelve seasons as the Football Gators head coach. The team record was very good but not as good as 1991.

It was the Gators sixtieth with the South-Eastern Conference (SEC). It was again a fine showing with just four losses in a thirteen-game season. Spurrier led the Gators to another fine record of 11-2-0 and 6-2-0 in the SEC. Florida again finished first in the SEC Conference Eastern Division among six division teams.

The SEC showing gave the Gators a berth in the first-ever SEC Championship Game in Birmingham, Alabama. Spurrier's scrappy young Gators, however, fell short against the SEC Western Division champion. The Alabama Crimson Tide squeezed out the victory L (21–28). The Crimson Tide would later defeat the Miami Hurricanes in the Sugar Bowl to win the 1992 national championship.

As noted previously, Spurrier's 1992 Florida Gators posted a 9–4 overall record, concluding their season with a victory over the twelfth-ranked North Carolina State Wolfpack (27–10) in the Gator Bowl, and ranking tenth in the final AP Poll.

1993 Florida Gators Football Coach Steve Spurrier

The1993 Florida Gators football team was the eighty-seventh season for Florida. It was the fourth year for Steve Spurrier of twelve seasons as the Football Gators head coach. The team record was very good. It was the first season with 11 wins, counting the bowl wins.

It was the Gators sixty-first with the South-Eastern Conference (SEC). It was again a fine showing with just four losses in a thirteen-game season. Spurrier led the Gators to another fine regular season record of 11-2-0 and 7-1-0 in the SEC. Florida again finished first in the SEC Conference Eastern Division among six division teams.

The Gators continued to use coach Spurrier's pass-heavy "fun 'n gun" offense. The 1993 Gators fell short of their hopes for a national championship. The Gators legacy is one of continual improvement This season, for example, marked the first time that they were ranked in the top ten of the Associated Press Poll during every week of the season, and they were ranked fifth in the final AP Poll, following their 41–7 Sugar Bowl victory over the West Virginia Mountaineers.

Before the season even began, instead of being speculative as in years past, the players' and fans and alumni had their preseason expectations for the Gators' fourth season under Spurrier set at very high. Some commentators began to speak openly about the possibility of the Gators making a run for the national title. It was a nice time to be a Florida fan.

Then, on Oct. 2, #5 UF defeated Mississippi State at Ben Hill Griffin Stadium W (38–24). Wuerffel and Doering teamed up for three touchdown passes. Down 21–17, Jack Jackson had a 100-yard kickoff return to put the Gators up 24–21. It was a big play.

On Oct 9, Louisiana State was walloped by Florida at Tiger Stadium in Baton Rouge, Louisiana W (58–3). Florida scored 58 unanswered to beat the LSU Tigers 58–3. Wuerffel, who was destined for a Heisman Trophy completed 14 passes for 221 yards and four touchdowns. It was the largest margin of victory over a road opponent under Spurrier and the worst loss in LSU football history.

On Oct 16, an always-tough nationally ranked #19 Auburn squad beat # 4 ranked Florida at Jordan-Hare Stadium in Auburn, AL L (35–38). Coach Terry Bowden's undefeated Auburn Tigers barely upset the Gators 38–35. It was a miserable day -- cold, drizzling, and dreary—not even fit for a mailman.

The fourth-ranked Gators amassed 560 yards of total offense, including 386 yards passing by quarterback Danny Wuerffel and 196 yards rushing by tailback Errict Rhett. Though close to record-breaking, the Gators' offensive fireworks were not enough for the win, as Auburn's defense sacked Wuerffel four times and made two key interceptions. The game could have gone either way. The two teams were tied at 35 with 1:21 left in the game, when Tigers placekicker Scott Etheridge booted a 41-yard field to beat the Gators, 38–35. Auburn dropped the Gators to their lowest ranking (10th) of the season.

On Oct 30, Georgia lost to Florida at Jacksonville in a tough game W (33-26). The rain just would not stop. It affected the usually accurate passing game of coach Steve Spurrier's Gators. The Gators were stymied. SO, they relied on tailback Errict Rhett to amass 183 yards and two touchdowns, building a 33–26 fourth-quarter lead.

Led by quarterback Eric Zeier, the Georgia Bulldogs mounted a potentially killer drive into Florida territory in the final minute and a half. Zeier completed what appeared to be the game-tying touchdown to Jerry Jerman with just five seconds remaining in the game.

However, it would not stand. Gators cornerback Anthone Lott had called a timeout just before the ball was snapped, forcing the Bulldogs to play the down again. Lott was called for pass interference on the ensuing play, giving Georgia one last untimed chance to score. Zeier's final pass was launched but it fell incomplete. The Gators won a hard-fought, but controversial 33–26 victory. There is always an element of luck in a football game.

On Nov 6, Southwestern Louisiana were mauled by # 9 Florida at home in a great Homecoming win W 61–14. On Nov 13, Florida beat South Carolina W (37-26) at Williams-Brice Stadium in

Columbia, South Carolina W 37–26. The Gamecocks had jumped out to a 17–0 lead, but the Gators cut the lead to 23–20 by halftime. Down 26–23, Jack Jackson avoided a safety and ran free for 76 yards. After a roughing the passer penalty, Errict Rhett scored and the Gators never relinquished the lead.

Then, on Nov 20, the Gators trounced Vanderbilt at home W (52-0) in a lop-sided shutout. In the second-last game, on Nov 27, a tough #1 ranked Florida State team pulled out all the stops and beat Florida at home L (21-33). The Florida offense was stymied early, and Dean subbed for Wuerffel by the second half. The Gators never led, although they had cut the score to 27–21 late in the game.

With just under six minutes left and the crowd roaring, the Seminoles faced third down at its 21-yard-line. Heisman Trophy-winning quarterback Charlie Ward hit freshman running back Warrick Dunn on a drag route, who turned up the sideline for a 79-yard touchdown and a 33–21 FSU win.

Florida won the Eastern SEC Championship and played Alabama for the total SEC prize. The game was played at Legion Field on December 4. #17 Alabama played hard but not good enough. The Gators again won the SEC Championship by beating Alabama W (28-13).

The Gators had finished the regular season with a conference record of 7–1, and they held first place among the six teams of the SEC Eastern Division. This had earned them an automatic berth in the second SEC Championship Game in Birmingham, Alabama.

The Gators were paired against the Alabama Crimson Tide in the championship game, which was seen as a rematch of the 1992 SEC Championship Game. The Gators defeated the Crimson Tide 28–13, winning their first SEC Championship Game and their second SEC football championship in three seasons. It was celebration time in Gainesville.

Florida made it to another January 1, 1994 Bowl Game. The Sugar Bowl was played at the Superdome in New Orleans. Florida's very worthy opponent was #3 ranked West Virginia. The Gators won the game handily by a score of W (41-7).

Yes, with a crowd of 75,437, the Gators handed it to the third-ranked West Virginia Mountaineers 41–7 in the Sugar Bowl, thereby finishing fifth in the AP Poll. The Gators were hot. After a quick touchdown from Jake Kelchner to Jay Kearney to put West Virginia up 7–0 early, the Gators came right back and answered with a touchdown by Errict Rhett to tie the score at 7.

The fans expected the half would end that way, but just before halftime, Gator defensive back Lawrence Wright picked off an errant pass from West Virginia QB Darren Studstill right on the midfield logo. He first made his way to his right side, but when he ran out of blocking help just inside the WVU 40, he turned around and backtracked, circling back to the 45 before finding some running room, and he sprinted into the end zone from there to cap a 51-yard interception return touchdown.

That put Florida up 14–7, and it simply seemed to crush the Mountaineers' competitive spirit, as Florida's defense proceeded to force a quick three and out. This short amount of free time gave Terry Dean time to connect with Jack Jackson for a 39-yard touchdown to make it 21–7 at halftime. The game was over but for the motions after that.

From there, the Gators cruised in the second half. Errict Rhett ran in two more touchdowns and Judd Davis added two insurance field goals in the fourth quarter to make the final score a convincing 41–7.

Steve Spurrier's 1993 team set a then-record for wins in a season. Halfback Errict Rhett, offensive tackle Reggie Green, and defensive tackle William Gaines made first-team All-SEC. Placekicker Judd Davis won the Lou Groza Award. Florida was more than back. They were inching up to lead the whole pack.

1994 Florida Gators Football Coach Steve Spurrier
<u>SEC Championship</u>

The 1994 Florida Gators football team was the eighty-eighth season for Florida. It was the fifth year for Steve Spurrier of twelve great seasons as the Football Gators head coach. The team record was again very good. It was almost as good as the 1993 season but for a tie.

It was the Gators sixty-second with the South-Eastern Conference (SEC). It was again a fine showing with just two losses and a tie in a thirteen-game season. Spurrier led the Gators to another fine regular season record of 10-2-1 and 8-1-0 in the SEC. Florida again finished first in the SEC Conference Eastern Division among six division teams and the Gators won the SEC Championship game.

Before the season, with Steve Spurrier as a most capable coach, the The Gators were eyeing a national title and more and more they believed it would come from the hands of Steve Spurrier and one of his great Florida teams.

On Dec 3, in the SEC Championship Game, Florida would not give up and beat the #3 Alabama Crimson Tide at the Georgia Dome, winning the SEC Championship by a score of W 24–23.

On New Year's Day, Florida was getting accustomed to playing football. After the twenty-eight-day layover from the SEC Championship game. Florida was not as crisp as Florida State and the Gators could not hold on, losing to Bobby Bowden's Seminoles L (17-23). Florida in-state losses stung Steve Spurrier more than any others.

1995 Florida Gators Football Coach Steve Spurrier

The1995 Florida Gators football team was the eighty-ninth season for Florida. It was the sixth year for Steve Spurrier of twelve great seasons as the Football Gators head coach. The team record was the best ever with twelve wins. It was one of the most successful years in school history. the Gators finished the regular season unbeaten and untied for the first time. Even the 1911 team went 5–0–1.

It was the Gators sixty-third with the South-Eastern Conference (SEC). It was again a fine showing with just one loss in a thirteen-game season. Spurrier led the Gators to another fine regular season record of 12-1-0 and 8-0-0 in the SEC. Florida again finished first in the SEC Conference Eastern Division among six division teams and the Gators again won the SEC Championship game.

The Gators used coach Spurrier's pass-heavy "fun 'n gun" offense". Led by Heisman Trophy finalist quarterback Danny Wuerffel, the offense set many school and conference offensive records, including passing touchdowns, passing yards per game, total yards per game, and points per game, among others.

After finishing the regular season 12-0 (8-0 in the SEC), Florida defeated the Arkansas Razorbacks 34-3 in the 1995 SEC Championship Game.

As the No. 2 ranked team, the Gators were invited to play in the 1996 Fiesta Bowl, which was the Bowl Alliance national championship game. In Tempe, Florida lost 24-62 to the No. 1 ranked Nebraska Cornhuskers but remained No. 2 in the final AP poll. So, Spurrier's squad got to the National Championship game but lost—this time!

It is never acceptable to lose a National Championship. However, the 1995 Gators played one of the best teams ever. The 1995 Nebraska squad has been voted as the greatest college football team of all-time in many surveys, including the all-time Sagarin ratings. An ESPN poll put them at #3, just only behind the 1971 Huskers and the 1972 USC Trojans.

1996 Florida Gators Football Coach Steve Spurrier
<u>**SEC Champions;**</u> <u>**National Championship**</u>

The1996 Florida Gators football team was the ninetieth season for Florida. It was the seventh year for Steve Spurrier of twelve great seasons as the Football Gators head coach. The team record was tied for the best ever with twelve wins. It was the most successful year in school history. the Gators finished the year as National Champions. Let me say that again. Steve Spurrier had directed the Florida Gators great 1996 team to a national chammpionship. **No kidding!**

It was the Gators sixty-fourth with the South-Eastern Conference (SEC). It was again a great showing with just one loss in a thirteen-game season. Spurrier led the Gators to another fine regular season record of 12-1-0 and 8-0-0 in the SEC. Florida finished first in the SEC Conference Eastern Division among six division teams for the fifth consecutive season. Additionally, the Gators again won the SEC Championship game for the fourth straight year. Of course, we must reiterate that this great team was designated consensus National Champions. Bravo Florida!

This was the first national championship for Florida in team history. It came from a 52–20 Sugar Bowl rout of their in-state rivals, the Florida State Seminoles.

All season long, the Gators used coach Spurrier's pass-heavy "fun 'n gun" offense". Quarterback Danny Wuerffel won the Heisman Trophy. Wuerffel as well as his wide receivers Ike Hilliard and Reidel Anthony were consensus All-Americans. It was a very good year for the Florida team, Florida fans, Florida alums, and of course their great coach Steve Spurrier.

Player Danny Wuerffel

Danny Wuerffel is a Fort Walton Beach native. He played football for the Florida Gators from 1993 to 1996 for Coach Steve Spurrier, another Heisman winner. Wuerffel rewrote the Florida passing record book while leading the Gators to their first national championship in 1996. His great moment some say was when he threw for 306 yards and three touchdowns in the Gators' 52-20 victory over Florida State in the 1997 Sugar Bowl, which led to Florida's first national title.

Danny Wuerffel became the second player from the University of Florida to win the Heisman, joining his coach, Steve Spurrier. It marked the first time that a Heisman winner came from a school coached by another former Heisman winner.

Wuerffel was his class valedictorian and led his HS football team to the state championship. He was widely considered the top player in the state of Florida as a 1991 senior. He was highly recruited. He let nobody down who helped him be discovered.

The 6-1, 210-pound Wuerffel was average size for a great Quarterback in those days. Coach Spurrier is 6'2" and 204 pounds. He signed with Florida the following spring and, after redshirting his first season in Gainesville, made a big impact as a freshman in 1993. He played as part of a platoon with Terry Dean. Wuerffel threw for 2,230 yards and 22 touchdowns. In 1994, he started again in a platoon role but eventually took over the starting job, throwing for 1,754 yards and 18 scores.

Wuerffel had a breakout All-American season in 1995, throwing for 3,266 yards and 35 touchdowns while leading Florida to the national championship game against Nebraska. For his efforts, Wuerffel finished a strong third in the Heisman vote behind Eddie George and Tommie Frazier.

Wuerffel bounced back in 1996 with another stellar season, throwing for 3,625 yards and 36 touchdowns as he guided the Gators to an 11-1 record and another shot at the national title. After winning the Heisman, he threw for 306 yards and three TDs to lead Florida to a 52-20 victory over rival Florida State as the Gators claimed their first national title.

He finished his Gator career by throwing for 10,875 yards and 114 touchdown passes, the best in SEC history and second-most in major college history (at the time). He graduated with a bachelor's degree in public relations.

Wuerffel was selected in the fourth round of the 1997 NFL draft (99th overall) by the New Orleans Saints. He spent six years in the NFL with the Saints, Packers, Bears and Redskins before retiring.

After football, Wuerffel began work at Desire Street Ministries, a non-profit, faith-based, organization focusing on spiritual and community development in areas of New Orleans.

Wuerffel in action

The game was decided on Florida's first drive. Spurrier called off the punt team on a 4th and 10 from the UT 35, and Wuerffel connected with Reidel Anthony for a touchdown to put the Gators up 7–0. Teako Brown then intercepted Manning on the Volunteers' first drive, and it took Wuerffel only one play to find the end zone again, hitting Terry Jackson to extend the lead to 14–0.

Florida doubled its lead in a 52-second stretch early in the 2nd quarter, as Ike Hilliard and Jacquez Green became the third and fourth different receivers with touchdown receptions on the afternoon. Their TDs were the bread sandwiched around a James Bates interception of Manning. Anthone Lott's fumble return stretched the lead to 35–0, before Manning finally got the Vols moving before halftime with a perfect strike to Peerless Price.

Florida switched to a more conservative offensive game plan in the second half. Because of this, Manning was able to cut the lead to 35–22 with 8 minutes left. These came on touchdown passes. Manning clicked again to Andy McCellough, which brought the score to 35–29 with 10 seconds to play. Florida recovered the ensuing onside kick to hang on for a six-point win on a rainy Knoxville afternoon.

On September 28 as Florida was ranked #1 for this first time this year, the Gators beat the Wildcats of Kentucky at home in a shutout blowout W (65–0) before 85,422. The rest of the year followed a similar pattern.

In what was expected to be one of the greatest games in history, on Nov 30, #1 Florida and #2 Florida State met at Doak Campbell Stadium in Tallahassee, Florida. The Seminoles beat the Gators by a field goal L (21-24) spoiling the Gators season and knocking Florida out of first place. FSU took over as the #1 team in the country.

The arch rival Florida State Seminoles did their best to hold back the Gators, winning 24–21. Both squads were an undefeated 10–0 before game time. The Seminoles scored 17 straight points in the first quarter and Warrick Dunn rushed for a career-best 185 yards in the game.

"We just hit to the echo" said FSU coach Bobby Bowden. Nobody got many chances against FSU as the Seminoles had one of the best defenses in the nation. The 'Noles had a ferocious pass rush, which included All-Americans Peter Boulware and Reinard Wilson. They did not mind roughing it up a bit, hoping not to get caught. The

Seminoles had been flagged for roughing the passer twice during the game, and Spurrier had the UF video staff compile footage which he claimed showed FSU players tackling Wuerffel late a half-dozen additional times. The 'Noles were nasty for sure.

Despite the constant pressure. Gator receiver Reidel Anthony still managed career bests in receptions (11) and yards gained (193). "If Danny would have had more time, we would have killed them. I was getting past them all the time with all kinds of routes."

Florida had 443 yards of offense, but with all the pressure, Wuerffel threw three interceptions and despite the defense doing its best to protect him for the big gainers, he was sacked six times.

In 3Q, nobody scored as both teams played their best on defense. FSU's "Pooh Bear" Williams managed to get the ball into the end zone to put the Seminoles up 24–14 midway through the fourth quarter. Down late in the game but never retreating, Florida went 80 yards in eight plays, including a 31-yard pass to Anthony, down to the 3-yard line with little time left. A short pass to Anthony brought Florida within a field goal with just over a minute remaining.

The subsequent Florida onside kick went out of bounds, and the game was sealed when FSU ran a play and Dunn ran for a first down. Spurrier sees it how it is. He continued to complain to the press about the late hits while FSU coach Bobby Bowden responded that he thought the hits in question were clean while admitting that "we just hit to the echo (of the whistle), instead of the whistle." Think about that. It was the kind of game a team playing to the rules would like to be able to do over. Florida would get its opportunity for a do-over. Just hold on. This season is not over yet.

On Dec 7, #4 Florida whipped #11 Alabama at the Georgia Dome in Atlanta to win the SEC Championship again. What a team. The score was W (45–30). UF always played tough against Alabama, who always had a dominating team. The Gators beat Alabama, the Western Champs but good 45–30 in the SEC Conference Championship game.

Danny Wuerffel got to play the whole game because Alabama did not lay low as they were being shellacked by the Gators. Wuerffel stayed in the game long enough to pass for six touchdowns.

There was a scary 94-yard touchdown pass by Alabama which got the Crimson Tide within 3. But even this was answered by Danny Wuerffel with an 85-yard touchdown to Jacquez Green. Nothing assures that the AP and the UPI polls will grant any team a national Championship so soon in the post-season. But, FSU was the odds-on favorite.

Texas upset Nebraska in the inaugural Big 12 Championship game. This gave the Gators its spot in the Sugar Bowl. To have a shot at a national title, the Gators needed Ohio State to beat second-ranked Arizona State—the only team to go through the regular season in 1996. They had to be undefeated. So, Ohio State did its job in the Rose Bowl, on the final play of the game, setting up the Sugar Bowl as the Bowl Alliance national championship game. But, who would be in this game?

In the rematch of the century, on January 2, #1 FSU and #3 Florida chose to go at each other once again in the Sugar Bowl, played at the Superdome in New Orleans LA. The Gators shellacked the Seminoles. W (52–20). But, before the game there was no such certainty on the day after New Year's Day at the Superdome before 78.344 excited attendees.

The Gators, coached by Steve Spurrier decided to use the shotgun formation to give Danny Wuerffel more time to throw. Florida defeated Florida State in this historically classic rematch 52–20, for the first national football title for the University of Florida.

Ike Hilliard scored once on a "stop and pop." It was perfect. Hilliard stopped on a dime to avoid Seminole defenders. He then ran into the end zone. A 42-yard, Terry Jackson touchdown run sealed the victory. It was a beautiful day in the neighborhood if you were from Gainesville or rooting for Gainesville.

Gators in 1996

The National Championship is simply a big deal. However, along with a national title, quarterback Danny Wuerffel was presented with the coveted Heisman Trophy, annually awarded to college football's top player. Wuerffel was the 1966 winner. He had a phenomenal year and was also awarded the Maxwell Award, Walter Camp Award, Davey O'Brien Award, Johnny Unitas Golden Arm Award, as well as the Draddy Trophy, National Football Foundation and College Hall of Fame Scholar, and College Football Association Scholar-Athlete Team. You can bet Danny Wuerffel got a lot of other honors. As a humble man, he probably would not tell you about them.

Lawrence Wright won the Jim Thorpe Award, and was on the College Football Association Scholar-Athlete Team. Jeff Mitchell was an Outland Trophy semi-finalist. It was a great Florida year. There is more. Danny Wuerffel, Ike Hilliard, and Reidel Anthony all were consensus All-Americans. It was a big year for the Pros, Ike Hilliard was selected 7th overall by the New York Giants, and Reidel Anthony was selected 16th by the Tampa Bay Buccaneers. What a great Florida year for everybody!

1997 Florida Gators Football Coach Steve Spurrier
2nd Place SEC

The 1997 Florida Gators football team was the ninety-first season for Florida. It was the eighth year for Steve Spurrier of twelve great seasons as the Football Gators head coach. The team record was super but not championship quality—but again, Florida was living close to the top of the SEC.

It was the Gators sixty-fifth with the South-Eastern Conference (SEC). It was again a great showing with just two losses in a twelve-game season. Spurrier led the Gators to another fine regular season record of 10-2-0 and 6-2-0 in the SEC. Florida finished tying for second place among the six SEC Eastern Division teams. After a national championship season, often there is rebuilding. Nonetheless, the Gators had a great double-digit winning year.

On Nov 22, the Gators got to take another whack at Florida State, ranked # 1 at the time while the Gators were listed at #10. The game was played in Gainesville, Florida's home field and the Gators got the win in a very close encounter W 32–29 before a mixed crowd of 85,677 from both schools.

FSU was No. 1 and undefeated coming into Gainesville. This was a fantastic game no matter what your allegiance (FSU fans might not remember it fondly, but a neutral party would agree with me).

Lots of stuff was in play Fred Taylor's run; the deep pass from Doug Johnson to Jacquez Green; the way Spurrier rotated QBs on each play: there are many legendary things about this game.

The opening kickoff came to the NE corner of the stadium. The FSU guy received, and got hit so hard it looked like his head exploded. Fans were thinking 'There goes the pregame meal". There were chunks of vomit on the field throughout the game. Sorry!

Secondly, after the famous Johnson-to-Quezzie connection, some guy actually jumped down from the upper ledge (those walls with 'Home of the... Florida Gators' painted on them) and landed right next to another fan uninjured during the celebration.

Lastly, this game was among the- if not the- loudest of all time. Go to any forum and they'll have the argument, but it's definitely the loudest many heard.

#6 ranked Florida agreed to play #11 ranked Penn State in the Citrus Bowl on New Years' Day 1-1-1998 in Orlando, Florida. The Gators could beat everybody and they had no problem with a tough Penn State team, winning W (21–6).

1998 Florida Gators Football Coach Steve Spurrier
2nd place SEC

The1998 Florida Gators football team was the ninety-second season for Florida. It was the ninth year for Steve Spurrier of twelve great seasons as the Football Gators head coach. The team record was super but not championship quality but again, Florida was living close to the top of the SEC.

It was the Gators sixty-sixth with the South-Eastern Conference (SEC). It was again a great showing with just two losses in a twelve-game season. Coach Spurrier led the Gators to another fine regular season record of 10-2-0 and 7-1-0 in the SEC. Florida finished second among the six SEC Eastern Division teams. The Gators had another great double-digit winning year.

In the Spurrier years, no season was complete until the Florida State game, which this year came on Nov 21 at Doak Campbell Stadium in Tallahassee, Florida, and the Seminoles whipped up enough chutzpah to beat Florida 12–23 before 81,614 State of Florida fans.

On the day after New Year's, 1999, #7 Florida got itself into a great Bowl game against #18 Syracuse. It was the Orange Bowl played at Orange Bowl Stadium in Miami. The Spurrier team played tricky and tough enough to defeat Syracuse W 31–10.

1999 Florida Gators Football Coach Steve Spurrier

The 1999 Florida Gators football team was the ninety-third season for Florida. It was the tenth year for Coach Steve Spurrier of twelve great seasons as the Football Gators head coach. The team record was super but not national championship quality. Again, Florida was living close to the top of the SEC, but not as much this year.

It was the Gators sixty-seventh with the South-Eastern Conference (SEC). It was again a great showing with just two losses in a twelve-game regular season. Coach Spurrier led the Gators to another fine total season record of 9-4-0 and 7-1-0 in the SEC. Florida finished first among the six SEC Eastern Division teams. The Gators had another great almost double-digit winning year.

After a two-year hiatus, Florida was again in the SEC Championship Game, but the team did not bring home another SEC Championship trophy. After losing the SEC Championship Game 34–7 to the Alabama Crimson Tide, the Gators ended their season with a last-second 37–34 loss to the Michigan State Spartans in the Citrus Bowl. Sometimes football brings some disappointments.

However, the Spurrier legacy was intact as an OK showing by a Spurrier-led team was substantially better than when Gator fans had presented to them for the many years before there was a Steve Spurrier. Thank you, Coach!

It was a tough end of season for the Gators as they lost their third in a row on New Year's Day 2000, in a Citrus Bowl match with Michigan State in Orlando Fl. The game ended with Michigan State kicking a last-minute field goal. L (34-37)

2000 Florida Gators Football Coach Steve Spurrier
SEC Championship, Sugar Bowl Champions,

The 2000 Florida Gators football team was the ninety-fourth season for Florida. It was the eleventh year for Coach Steve Spurrier of twelve great seasons as the Football Gators head coach. The team record was very good and improved from 1999, but not quite national championship quality. Again, Florida was living so close to the top of the SEC, that this year, again, they claimed another title.

It was the Gators sixty-eighth with the South-Eastern Conference (SEC). It was again a great showing with just two losses in a twelve-game season. Coach Spurrier led the Gators to another fine regular season record of 10-3-0 and 7-1-0 in the SEC. Florida finished first among the six SEC Eastern Division teams. The Gators had another great double-digit winning year.

As noted, they were coached by Steve Spurrier, who led the Gators to their sixth SEC championship, a Sugar Bowl berth, and an overall win-loss record of 10–3 (.769).

There is a thing about losing to Florida teams and the Gators had already lost to Florida State on Nov 18. Nonetheless the Spurrier-led Gators, then ranked at #7 agreed to meet the #2 ranked team in the country, the Butch Davis coached Miami Hurricanes on January 2, in the Sugar Bowl at the Superdome in New Orleans, Louisiana. The last thing the Gators wanted or needed was a loss to in-state rival Miami but they got one nonetheless L (20-37).

2001 Florida Gators Football Coach Steve Spurrier

When I first began writing chapter summaries back when I had researched the 1906 Florida season and all the way to 1990 when Steve Spurrier took over the reins of UF, I was anticipating writing about the Spurrier years. I knew they were very successful seasons and it is a lot more fun writing about successful seasons than struggling seasons.

There were a lot of high points before reaching the Spurrier era and I relished them but there was little consistency in winning. Florida is a much different team post spurrier than in the pre-Spurrier times but right now, as I begin the last year of Coach Spurrier's magical period with the Gators, I miss him already.

For me, it's like he is leaving again. I know we will get by. But, just like the Bryant's, the Rockne's, the Paterno's, the Osborne's, the Shembeckler's, the Leahy's great seasons with their teams, I know something will be missing. But, we'll get by. Go Gators!

Get me by the 2001st Gators season, OK!

The 2001 Florida Gators football team was the ninety-fifth season for Florida. It was the twelfth and last year for Coach Steve Spurrier of twelve great seasons as the Football Gators head coach. The team record was very good again and improved from 2000 with one less loss, but not quite national championship quality. Again, Florida was living close to the top of the SEC where they belong. But, the championship might not be this year.

It was the Gators sixty-ninth with the powerful South-Eastern Conference (SEC). It was again a great showing with just two losses in a twelve-game season. Coach Spurrier led the Gators to another fine total season record of 10-2 and 6-2 in the SEC. Florida finished second among the six SEC Eastern Division teams. The Gators had another great double-digit winning year. How can there be any arguments?

Orange Bowl

Steve Spurrier led the Gators to a 56–23 Orange Bowl victory over the Maryland Terrapins in his final game before moving on to the NFL. A sophomore quarterback really came through this year, throwing for more than 4,000 yards. As a sophomore, Grossman was the Heisman Trophy runner-up. Grossman, wide receiver Jabar Gaffney and defensive end Alex Brown were consensus All-Americans. Brown's 33 sacks are still a school record for a career. OK but what then?

In one of the few times in school history, going into the season, the Gators were ranked preseason # 1.

The season got underway on September 1 with the home opener at Ben Hill Griffin Stadium on the University campus at Gainesville, Florida against Marshall going to the Gators W (49–14). This season opened at night in the "Swamp" with a 49–14 triumph over Marshall who used both quarterbacks Byron Leftwich and the Marshall Thundering Herd. Rex Grossman, Florida's Sophomore QB had a career-high in passing yards by halftime, including a 64-yard touchdown reception by Taylor Jacobs. The defense also played well as Alex Brown and linebacker Andra Davis had two sacks each.

On Sept 8, Louisiana–Monroe played a then-ranked #2 Florida team at home and were beaten W (55–6) before a crowd of 85,011. In this second week of play, the Gators simply overwhelmed the Louisiana-Monroe Warhawks. Grossman passed for 331 yards and three touchdowns, including two TDs to Jabar Gaffney.

Grossman fumbled the game's first exchange from center, and Louisiana-Monroe capitalized on the opportunity when it scored the game's first touchdown. "It was just an awkward start." said Grossman. As usual, the Gators and Tennessee Volunteers were slated to meet on the 3rd Saturday of September. However, the SEC canceled all games on the weekend following the September 11 attacks, and all contests were rescheduled for December 1, 2001, requiring the SEC Championship Game to be pushed back a week as well.

The World Trade Disaster on September 11 had its impact on the world as well as college football. The annual rivalry game with Tennessee scheduled for September 15, was thus rescheduled to the final week of the regular season as a result of the tragic events of September 11, 2001.

On Sept 22, Florida traveled to Kentucky and beat the Wildcats at Commonwealth Stadium in Lexington, Kentucky W (44–10). Grossman passed for 302 yards and four touchdowns. The Gators struggled early and led just 16–3 at the half, but eventually thrashed the Wildcats with four touchdowns in the second half. After Kentucky made a touchdown, Earnest Graham sprung lose for a 50-yard touchdown run in the third period to go up 30–10.

On Sept 29, the #2 Gators beat Mississippi State at home in a blowout W (52–0). Florida avenged last year's loss to the 21st-ranked Mississippi State Bulldogs by shutting them out 52–0. Grossman had 317 yards passing in just the first half. The Gators piled up 640 yards of total offense on the day, the most in school history for an SEC game. Grossman passed for 393 yards and five touchdowns in total, becoming the first Florida quarterback to throw for 300 yards in four straight games. Linebacker Andra Davis, who missed the prior year's game, excelled on the defensive side of the ball with eight tackles and a fumble recovery.

On Oct 6, #2 Florida beat #18 LSU at Tiger Stadium in Baton Rouge, Louisiana W (44–15) before a crowd of 92,010. Grossman threw for 319 yards and four touchdowns in just the first half, and by game's end had a school-record 464 yards. Florida finished with 632 yards of total offense. LSU quarterback Rohan Davey left the game with a hyperextended knee. "I thought [Davey] he was a serious candidate for the Heisman Trophy before we played them," said LSU coach Nick Saban, "Now I'm convinced of it. I think he is a tremendous quarterback" echoed LSU safety Ryan Clark.

On Oct 13, the #1 ranked Florida Gators were upset by a tough Auburn team, L (20-23) in a nail biter at Jordan–Hare Stadium in Auburn, AL L (20–23). The Tigers were 21-point underdogs when they met the Gators at Jordan–Hare Stadium. Gators quarterback

Rex Grossman threw forty-two passes, completing twenty-five. He threw for two touchdowns, but also threw four interceptions.

The Gators dominated statistically, but the Tigers' bend-but-don't-break defense held the Gators rushing game to negative yardage. Tigers back-up quarterback Daniel Cobb played mistake-free football, and the game was tied at 20 late in the fourth quarter. With 10 seconds left, Tigers placekicker Damon Duval nailed a 44-yard field goal and the Tigers upset the Gators.

On Oct 27, at Jacksonville, #6 Florida beat #15 Georgia W (24-10). Grossman passed for 407 yards. Earnest Graham rushed for 131 yards. The Bulldogs missed a field goal and failed to convert three fourth downs in the second half. The lone score of the second half was a 30-yard touchdown pass to Reche Caldwell. Florida moved into a first-place tie with Tennessee.

Then on Nov 3, the Gators had an enjoyable Homecoming defeating Vanderbilt at home W (71-13) in a game in which the scoring would not stop. The Gators never punted, and forced five turnovers. They were up 71–0 in the fourth quarter and still tossing passes, amassing 571 total yards in all. Eleven Gators got receptions, and Taylor Jacobs had a breakout game. Playing just in the first half, Grossman threw for 306 yards and three touchdowns. Backup quarterback Brock Berlin threw three more in the second.

On Nov 10, #4 Florida shellacked South Carolina at Williams-Brice Stadium in Columbia, South Carolina W 54–17. The game started shaky for the Gators as Lito Sheppard fumbled the opening kickoff, leading to an easy Gamecock score. A touchdown pass to Jabar Gaffney late in the first quarter started the scoring barrage. Grossman had his ninth-consecutive 300-yard passing game.

On Nov 17 at home Florida man-handled Florida State W (37-13). During the game, Gators' starting running back Earnest Graham had been controversially injured in Florida's win and was unable the next week to play against Tennessee. Graham and coach Spurrier accused Darnell Dockett of deliberately twisting Graham's knee, as well as stomping on Grossman's hand. Graham even considered a lawsuit. Dockett denied the charges.

Then, in the season finale at home, on Dec 1, The Gators lost a cliffhanger to the Tennessee Volunteers L (32-34). As the season progressed, this postponed game with Tennessee took on more significance each week. Each squad had suffered only one close loss and Florida entered the contest with Tennessee ranked No. 6 and Florida ranked No. 2. The winner was to represent the SEC East and face LSU in the SEC Championship.

Additionally, with a win in that game, the Gators or Vols were likely to receive an invitation to the Rose Bowl to face the undefeated Miami Hurricanes with a national title on the line. The stakes were high. Despite the teams' identical records and much to the chagrin of the Vols, the Gators were 17-and-a-half point favorites at kickoff. It did not work out that way.

The Volunteers went on to dash the Gators' national title hopes with a nail-biter 34–32 upset, ending a 30-year winless drought against Florida at the Swamp. The star of the game was Volunteer running back Travis Stephens, who rushed for 226 yards and two touchdowns on 19 carries to lead the Vols' attack. Without their star running back, Graham, Florida managed only 36 total yards on the ground. Gator quarterback Rex Grossman threw 51 times for 362 yards and two touchdowns, but his pass on a potentially game-tying two-point conversion attempt with just over a minute left in the 4th quarter fell incomplete. Close but not in the win column

#5 Florida was invited to the Orange Bowl Game at Pro Player Stadium in Miami Gardens, Florida to play the Maryland Terrapins. In Steve Spurrier's last game coached for the Gators, the team gave him a sweet victory, rising to the occasion to score 56 points to 23 for the opposition in a great win W (56-23)

Grossman was the Heisman Trophy runner-up to Nebraska QB Eric Crouch, in one of the trophy's closest ballots. Many feel that with his stats and great season, Grossman should have won. Both Crouch and Grossman made AP All-American.

Steve Spurrier's resignation

In early January 2002, Steve Spurrier announced that he was resigning as Florida's head coach after 12 seasons.

Please read this piece from lubbockonline written when Steve Spurrier announced his resignation over fifteen years ago: http://lubbockonline.com/stories/010502/col_0105020022.shtml#.WPeF4dLyvmY

Spurrier quits as UF coach
12 years 'long enough' for Florida coach
Published: Saturday, January 05, 2002

Morris News Service

GAINESVILLE -- University of Florida football coach Steve Spurrier, who built the school into a national power and became one of the most successful coaches in Southeastern Conference history, resigned Friday after 12 seasons to pursue an NFL coaching position. The most likely candidate to replace Spurrier is Oklahoma coach Bob Stoops, according to several sources.

Spurrier's resignation early Friday morning came as a shock to players, coaches, athletic officials, and his closest friends. Only Norm Carlson, UF's assistant athletic director for communications and a close friend since Spurrier arrived in Gainesville as a player in 1964, knew of Spurrier's decision before Friday.

Spurrier told Carlson on Thursday night while the two were at their condos in Crescent Beach.

"I thought he was joking at first," Carlson said.

So did UF Athletics Director Jeremy Foley, who found out he needed a new coach when Spurrier phoned him with his resignation about 9:15 a.m.

"At one point when he was talking to me, he asked me if I was still there," Foley said. "I really thought he was kidding. I think he told Norm [Thursday] evening and I think Norm had the exact same reaction. He [Spurrier] made an indication not to try and talk him out of it."

Spurrier did not attend Friday's news conference -- he was still in Crescent Beach -- but he did release a 10-paragraph statement through the university's sports information department, and he has scheduled a 4:30 p.m. news conference for Monday.

"I'm announcing my retirement today, Jan. 4, 2002, as head football coach at the University of Florida," the statement began. "I simply believe that 12 years as head coach at a major university in the SEC is long enough."

The statement went on to read: "I'm not burned out, stressed out or mentally fatigued from coaching. I just feel my career as a college head coach after 15 years is complete, and if the opportunity and challenge of coaching a NFL team happens it is something I would like to pursue."

Spurrier did not inform his assistant coaches and players of his decision. In fact, wide receiver Jabar Gaffney found out only when a reporter telephoned him. "Oh, man," Gaffney said when told Spurrier had resigned. "He didn't give us any indications he was leaving or [the Orange Bowl] was his last game at all."

...

He returned to his alma mater in 1990, and that's where his reputation as an offensive genius really flourished. He used a wide-open attack to turn around a moribund program that had finished first in the SEC standings just twice in 56 years and had not won more than nine games in its 83-year history.

Since he arrived, the Gators have won six SEC titles (Spurrier claims the 1990 title as well, even though the Gators were not official champs because of NCAA probation) and the 1996 national title. The Gators have ranked in the top 10 in the final Associated Press poll 10 times, have played in eight major bowl games, and have been ranked No. 1 for 29 weeks. He is the only major college coach to win as many as 120 games in his first 12 years at the school (122-26-1), and he's the only coach in SEC history to win at least 10 games for six consecutive seasons (1993-98).

Spurrier's offense changed the way football was played, not only in the SEC, but around the country. His pass-oriented offense forced defensive coordinators to employ, five, six, or even seven defensive backs, but even then, they couldn't catch up. The Gators totaled 500 yards of offense 51 times and averaged more than 500 yards over the course of the 1995, 1996 and 2001 seasons. Gators quarterbacks have thrown for 400 yards 23 times and have thrown for 300 yards 91 times. They also have averaged more than 315 yards per game during his tenure.

Because the program was so starved for success, and because of his bold and brash nature, Gators fans adored him. But his cocky attitude and sometimes biting comments -- he dubbed FSU "Free Shoes University" following the 1993 Foot Locker store scandal -- drew the ire of opposing fans, who derisively called him Steve Superior and ranted about his huge ego.

Spurrier almost left UF in 1995, when Tampa Bay officials nearly convinced him to leave. But after several days of intense debate, Spurrier decided to remain at UF. Foley believed then that Spurrier would never coach anywhere else.

"I thought he'd be here forever," Foley said. "I knew he enjoyed the college game. His whole life he's been wrapped up in college athletics. He's a Heisman Trophy winner. He's coached a Heisman Trophy winner. He's in the National Football Foundation Hall of Fame. He took Duke to an ACC championship.

"I just honestly thought that as long as he coaches, he'd coach at this level and he'd coach here."

Chapter 18 Ron Zook Era 2002 to 2004

Coach # 20 Ron Zook
Coach # 21 Charlie Strong

Year	Coach	Record	Conference	Record
2002	Ron Zook	8–5	SEC	6–2
2003	Ron Zook	8–5	SEC	6–2
2004	Ron Zook	7-5	SEC	4-4
2004	Charlie Strong (interim)			

New Florida head football coach Ron Zook has the formidable task of replacing Steve Spurrier

August 22, 2002 | By Andrew Bagnato, Tribune college football reporter.

GAINESVILLE, Fla. — It's 6 a.m., and 29 Florida freshmen are stretching to the accompaniment of crickets.
An air horn punctures the steamy predawn air. Decked out in blue jerseys and orange helmets, the freshmen break into groups by position. A raspy voice rises from midfield.

"Let's go, running backs, let's go!" coach Ron Zook hollers.

It's 6:07 a.m. on the first allowable practice day. Daylight is an hour away. The first game is 24 days away. And many of these kids won't see action this year, if ever.

That doesn't matter to Zook. On the first official day of his first season as the Florida Gators' coach, he's making every minute count.

"Sleep's overrated," Zook says as he strides off the field about 7:30 a.m., his neck slick with sweat. "We have a lot of work to do."
The new face of Florida football is an alarm clock.

Gone are the days when former coach Steve Spurrier would arrive from the golf course, arranging the team's practice schedule as he removed his spikes. The new boss at this Sunshine State football factory could not be more different from the old one.

Spurrier, a son of the South, is a smooth sip of bourbon. After a big victory over Tennessee or Florida State he would remove his visor, cast his eyes to the heavens and exclaim, "God smiled on the Gators today!"

Zook is a double shot of espresso, with two lumps of sugar.

"He's very energetic," freshman quarterback Gavin Dickey said. "He gets you riled up and makes you want to play for him."

Gators fans were riled up when athletic director Jeremy Foley named Zook to succeed Spurrier shortly after Spurrier left for the Washington Redskins last January.

<<< Ron Zook. Fans pined for Denver Broncos coach Mike Shanahan or Oklahoma Sooners coach Bob Stoops, both of whom were on Foley's wish list.

Many fretted over handing the program to a 26-year assistant coach who most recently had served as the New Orleans Saints' defensive coordinator. They noted Spurrier had demoted Zook from defensive coordinator to special-teams' coordinator in 1993. And rival coaches warned potential recruits that Zook had no track record as a head coach.

"I heard that and I said, `What about Miami?'" Zook said. "They just won the national championship with a first-year head coach [Larry Coker]."

Indeed, several powerhouses have reaped huge rewards after hiring rookie head coaches. Think about Nebraska, which handed the reins to untested assistant coach Tom Osborne, or Penn State, which gave a Nittany Lions assistant named Joe Paterno his first head-coaching job. Stoops' Sooners finished atop the polls in his second year as a head coach.

"Obviously, in none of those situations were they replacing Steve Spurrier," Foley said: "When it's all said and done, it's going to come down to recruiting and coaching."

"I think Ron's the perfect guy to replace Steve because he's so unlike Steve, and I don't mean that in a negative way. He's not trying to be Steve. He's trying to be himself. If there's only one guy who can win here, and that's Steve Spurrier, then we need to shut the doors down.

"The goal is to get better, not to maintain. That may sound sacrilegious."

The contrasts between Spurrier and Zook are striking. Spurrier won the Heisman Trophy as a quarterback here in 1966. Zook was a walk-on defensive back at Miami of Ohio, where he lived in the same dorm as future Northwestern coach Randy Walker.

Spurrier endured recruiting. Zook enjoys it. Spurrier never paid a moment's notice to his defense. Zook has never called an offensive play.

"Coach Zook hates the comparisons," star quarterback Rex Grossman said. "They're completely different."

Raised in football-crazed Loudonville, Ohio, and educated at Miami University, the cradle of college football coaches, the 48-year-old Zook has spent his entire life preparing for this opportunity. No wonder he's in a hurry.

In 13 frenzied days last spring, Zook visited 71 Florida high schools and addressed 12 Gators booster clubs. Zook spent so much time on the road last spring he claimed not to know the address of his new home in Gainesville, even after wife Denise and daughters Jacquelyn and Casey had taken up residence there.

"I don't even know where the light switches are," Zook said.

Over breakfast one recent morning, Zook perhaps unwittingly gave an indication of his priorities.

"I wasn't going to eat, but that's OK," Zook said as he dug into a plate of scrambled eggs and grits.

"Can you imagine how much you could get done if you didn't have to eat or sleep?"

Zook's zeal appeals to the Gators legions. But it will take more than 20-hour workdays to step out of Spurrier's shadow.

"All of that's fine and good," Foley said. "But what matters is wins." Spurrier produced them by the barrel.

2002 Florida Gators Football Coach Ron Zook
<u>**Outback Bowl Participant**</u>

The 2002 Florida Gators football team was the ninety-sixth season for Florida. It was the first year for Coach Ron Zook of three seasons as the Football Gators head coach. The team record was respectable but it was the worst since Galen Hall in 1989. Steve Spurrier had no seasons in which he won less than nine games. Ron Zook, may have been a good coach but he was not a Steve Spurrier.

It was the Gators seventieth season with the powerful South-Eastern Conference (SEC). It was again a great showing with just two losses in a twelve-game season. Coach Zook led the Gators to an OK season record of 8-5 and 6-2 in the SEC Eastern Division. Florida finished second among the six SEC Eastern Division teams.

Player Rex Grossman

Rex, which means King in Latin, played King QB for the UF squad from 2000-02. The Buzz: Ironically, Florida fans felt snubbed when Grossman did not become the first sophomore to win the Heisman Trophy in 2001. Yet, one day soon, they would have their first sophomore Heisman in Tim Tebow. Grossman was taken in the first round of the 2003 NFL draft by the Chicago Bears and he also played for the Houston Texans and the Washington Redskins.

His great Gator moment was when he played in what became known as the "Slingin' in the Rain" game against LSU, where he threw for 464 yards and five touchdowns in a 44-15 victory.

Grossman decided on Florida in 1999 so he could be coached by Steve Spurrier. His other choice was the University of Indiana—his father's and grandfather's Alma Mater. Grossman was redshirted in his freshman year and then he got the dubious role of third string QB on the Gators.

Grossman got to start his first game as a Florida Gator on October 7, 2000 against LSU. He had won the opportunity to start after completing 13 of 16 pass attempts for 232 yards and two touchdowns against Mississippi State the week before in the Gators' only SEC conference loss of the season.

Grossman solidified his position as Florida's starting quarterback during the next two games by throwing for over 500 yards, eight touchdowns and no interceptions in lopsided wins over LSU and Auburn. He led the Gators to the SEC championship and was named Most Valuable Player of the SEC Championship Game. For the season, Grossman completed 61.8 percent of his passes for 1,866 yards, 21 touchdowns, and only seven interceptions. His passer efficiency rating of 161.8 was the third best in NCAA Division I football.

...

End of profile

The scent of change was already in the air.

"The Swamp. Only Gators get out alive."

During his time at Florida, Steve Spurrier turned Ben Hill Griffin Stadium into a death trap for the Gators' opponents. Spurrier only lost five games at home during his entire tenure as head coach of the University of Florida, making "the Swamp" one of college football's most formidable stadiums.

However, Ron Zook managed to diminish the vision of "the Swamp" as a treacherous place to play. Zook lost an unbelievable five games at home and failed to defeat a ranked opponent at Florida Field during his three years at Florida.

Though we can be nice to coaches if we choose, football is about winning and coaches get paid big bucks to accomplish one simple goal-winning. When Bob Davie took over for Lou Holtz at Notre Dame Ara Parseghian offered some advice that applies to Ron Zook in 2002. In 1997 When Davie replaced Lou Holtz as Irish coach in 1997, Parseghian's advice was simple: "There are a lot of things to worry about," Parseghian told Davie, "but worry about one thing, and that's winning."

2003 Florida Gators Football Coach Ron Zook
<u>SEC Co-championship Outback Bowl Participant</u>

The 2003 Florida Gators football team was the ninety-seventh season for Florida. It was the second year for Coach Ron Zook of three seasons as the Football Gators head coach. The team record was respectable; the same as the prior year.

It was the Gators seventy-first with the powerful South-Eastern Conference (SEC). It was again a great SEC showing with just two SEC losses. Coach Zook led the Gators to an OK season record of 8-5 and 6-2 in the SEC Eastern Division. Florida finished tied for first among the six SEC Eastern Division teams. Consensus All-American Keiwan Ratliff set the school single-season interception mark in 2003 with 9.

Outback Bowl

On January 1, 2004, #13 Iowa engaged against #17 Florida in the Outback Bowl at Raymond James Stadium in Tampa, Florida and beat the Gators L (17–37)

2004 Florida Gators Football Coach Ron Zook
<u>Peach Bowl Participant</u>

The 2004 Florida Gators football team was the ninety-eighth season for Florida. It was the third and last year for Coach Ron Zook of three seasons as the Football Gators head coach. The team record was unacceptable for a post-Spurrier Gators team.

It was the Gators seventy-second with the powerful South-Eastern Conference (SEC). It was again a great SEC showing with just two SEC losses. Coach Zook led the Gators to an OK regular season record of 7-4 and 4-4 in the SEC Eastern Division. Florida finished tied for third among the six SEC Eastern Division teams. Florida picked up another loss in the peach Bowl

For the fifth time in school history, Florida played five of its first six games at home. Four of the last five games were on the road.

Florida's record for the two prior seasons under Zook on the road in conference play was an SEC league best 7–1. Eight starters returned and true sophomore Chris Leak would start the first game of the season at QB for the first time.

On Nov 6 at Vanderbilt Stadium •in Nashville, Tennessee, the Gators won W (34–17) before a crowd of 32,716. On Nov 13, the Gators beat South Carolina at home W (48-14). In the final game of the regular season, the Gators put it all together to beat #10 Florida State at Doak Campbell Stadium in Tallahassee, Florida W 20–13. This was Coach Ron Zook's last game as head coach of the Florida Gators. Charlie Strong (prior page) took over the team for the Peach Bowl.

With a 7-4 record, the Gators were invited to the Peach Bowl at the Georgia Dome in Atlanta GA to play in-state rival #14 ranked Miami. The Hurricanes beat the Gators L (10-27). Charley Strong was hired as defensive coordinator for the Florida Gators before the 2003 season. Florida head coach Ron Zook was fired midway through the Gators' 2004 season, but continued to coach until the bowl game; Strong served as interim coach of the Gators for one game, the December 2004 Peach Bowl. Florida lost the game, 27–10, to Miami.

Chapter 19 Urban Meyer Era 2005 - 2010

Coach # 22 Urban Meyer

Year	Coach	Record	Conference	Record
2005	Urban Meyer	9–3	SEC	5–3
2006	Urban Meyer	13–1	SEC	7–1
2007	Urban Meyer	9–4	SEC	5–3
2008	Urban Meyer	13–1	SEC	7–1
2009	Urban Meyer	13–1	SEC	8–0
2010	Urban Meyer	8–5	SEC	4–4

Coach Meyer leading the Gators onto field for the game

Urban Meyer was a known entity

When Florida, a very successful football program sought a head coach after taking a chance for three years with a fine coach with no head coach experience, it had no choice but to pick a great one. They did with Urban Meyer. Like him or not, Meyer is a great coach.

URBAN MEYER NAMED FLORIDA'S HEAD FOOTBALL COACH From Floridagators.com

Saturday, December 4, 2004

Urban Meyer, a two-time National Coach of the Year and one of the nation's top young coaching talents, has been named the 22nd head football coach at the University of Florida, Gator Athletics Director Jeremy Foley announced today.

Meyer, 40, possesses 19 years of college coaching experience, including four as a head coach. Meyer turned around the football program at Bowling Green State University in 2001-02 and engineered a reversal of fortune at the University of Utah in 2003-04. Meyer, who sports a 10-1 record against Bowl Championship Series teams as a head coach, guided the Utes to a perfect 11-0 campaign this season and an expected berth in the BCS. He has an overall mark of 38-8 (.826) and is 24-6 (.800) in conference play as head coach.

"Urban Meyer represents the qualities that we were looking for in our head coach," Foley said. "He is an innovator of the game with proven success as a head coach. He has shown the ability to attract recruits and is a tremendous teacher. Urban's accomplishments speak for themselves. He is a man of high values and principles and we welcome him and his family to the University of Florida family."

"I am certainly excited about the opportunity to be the head coach at the University of Florida," said Meyer. "There were a lot of factors that went into this decision that our entire family had to consider. The opportunity to compete at the highest level at one of the nation's most-respected academic institutions is something that was attractive for us. The passion of Gator fans is legendary in collegiate athletics and I am eager to be a part of that environment.

"The quality of recruits within the state of Florida and the Southeast Region offers a tremendous recruiting base for us," Meyer continued.

"The support from the University's administration is evident in their commitment to my family and I am looking forward to leading the Gator football program."

"Urban Meyer is an outstanding coach with a strong record, great leadership skills and a very promising future," said UF President J. Bernard Machen. "I am very happy to welcome him along with Shelley and the Meyer family to UF and Gainesville."

Meyer recently earned the Mountain West Conference Coach of the Year award for the second straight time as the Utes begin to reap the benefits of an unbeaten regular season. On Friday, he was announced as The Home Depot 2004 Coach of the Year. In addition, Meyer is a semifinalist for both the Maxwell Club's George Munger College Coach of the Year and the Bobby Dodd Coach of the Year awards. Utah finished as the outright 2004 MWC champion to become the only back-to-back outright winners in the league's history.

Meyer began his head coaching career at Bowling Green in 2001, where he engineered the top turnaround in NCAA Division I-A football, showing a six-win improvement from the previous season. The Falcons rebounded from a 2-9 record to post their first winning season since 1994 with an 8-3 finish. For his efforts, he was named the 2001 Mid-American Conference Coach of the Year.

Meyer's 17-6 record at Bowling Green included a 5-0 mark against BCS teams and two wins over ranked opponents. After his first of two wins over Missouri, Meyer was named ESPN.com National Coach of the Week in 2001.

Meyer apprenticed at Ohio State (1986-87), Illinois State (1988-89), Colorado State (1990-95) and Notre Dame (1996-2000) before getting the head job at Bowling Green. The Ashtabula, Ohio, native learned the coaching trade from the likes of Sonny Lubick, Lou Holtz, Earle Bruce and Bob Davie.

A 13th-round pick in the Major-League Baseball Amateur Draft in 1982, an athletically talented Urban Meyer played two years in the Atlanta Braves' organization. He played as a defensive back at the University of Cincinnati before earning his degree in psychology in 1986. He went on to earn a master's degree in sports administration from Ohio State in 1988.

Urban Meyer was a great choice for Florida. I can't wait to get out from the Zook years into something that even if today were July 1, 2005, I know it would be a positive tour of duty for Coach Meyer.

2005 Florida Gators Football Coach Urban Meyer

The 2005 Florida Gators football team was the ninety-ninth season for Florida. It was the first year for Coach Urban Meyer of six great seasons as the Football Gators head coach. The team record immediately began to match the records of the Spurrier years. Good wins, great players and a great coach were back on the agenda for the Florida Gators. Nobody worked harder than Urban Meyer. We'll give Meyer and Spurrier a tie in the work ethic category. Florida could not have made a better choice for head coach other than convincing the legendary Steve Spurrier to come back home. But, that did not happen.

It was the Gators seventy-third season with the powerful South-Eastern Conference (SEC). It was again a great SEC showing with just three SEC losses. Coach Meyer led the Gators to a Spurrier-quality regular season record of 9-3 and 5-3 in the SEC Eastern Division. Florida finished tied for second among the six SEC Eastern Division teams and Meyer brought Florida an Outback Bowl berth.

Before the season began there was a lot of good feelings because the fan base was not happy from day of the administration's decision to hire the prior head coach. The Urban Meyer arrival was well broadcast and those who rooted strongly for Florida were quite pleased.

And, so, the 2005 season would open with high expectations of new head coach Urban Meyer. Fourteen starters, seven from offense and seven from defense, would return for the 2005 season. The Gators would open the season in Gainesville against Wyoming from the Mountain West Conference. This year would also be the first-time former Gator coach Steve Spurrier would coach against his alma mater. The Florida fans will always admire coach Spurrier.

On Sept 3, #10 preseason ranked Florida opened its season with a nice win against Wyoming at Ben Hill Griffin Stadium on the University campus in Gainesville, Florida W (32–14) before a crowd of 90,707. On Sept 10, the Gators beat Louisiana Tech at home W (41–3), On sept 17, #5 Tennessee ready as always to win v the Gators at home were beaten nonetheless W (16–7). Then on Sept 24, a tough Kentucky club were ready to win v the # 5 Gators but did not have enough muscle to pull it off and went down in a tough game at their home stadium in Lexington, Kentucky W 49–28.

On Oct 1, #15 Alabama a nemesis regardless who coached the team played the #5 Gators at Bryant–Denny Stadium • Tuscaloosa, AL, and creamed the Gators with no prisoners permitted L (3–31) On Oct 8, an always tough Mississippi State played the #13 Gators at home and lost to a tougher UF team W (35–9). On Oct 15, #10 Louisiana State expected a win at Tiger Stadium in Baton Rouge, Louisiana, and they got it L (17–21). On Oct 29, #4 Georgia came to Jacksonville's Alltel Stadium to collect some old debts but Georgia's Bulldogs went home barking with nothing to show as the Gators beat the Dogs W (14–10).

On Nov 5, Vanderbilt, always tough at home or away came to Gatorland's Swamp and put up a phenomenal fight until the Gators got the best of them in a shootout W (49–42) before 90,140. On Nov 12 South Carolina, coached by Steve Spurrier beat #12 Florida at Williams-Brice Stadium in Columbia, South Carolina L (22–30).

Pundits have written that with Mike Davis and Daccus Turman both running for two touchdowns, South Carolina defeated the 12th-ranked Gators 30-22 on Saturday, the first time Spurrier had played the school where he won a Heisman Trophy in 1966 as a quarterback and a national championship in 1996 as a coach. It wasn't the kind of blowout Spurrier's Gators perfected during his 12 seasons as their leader from 1990-2001. But it broke Florida's 14-game winning streak in the series -- Spurrier was 10-0 vs. South Carolina -- that had dated to 1939. Urban Meyer would have loved the win. You'll see that Meyer will have his share of wins when his recruited teams begin to play in 2006.

Coach Urban Meyer takes things seriously. He was not going to permit an instate rivalry to dominate a Florida team while he was coach. So, on Nov 26 when #23 Florida State decided to wipe out Florida at home, Meyer had other ideas. His Gators beat the Seminoles but good W (34–7) before 90,669.

Outback Bowl Champions

On January 2–2006, after being invited to play in the Outback Bowl, Meyer's #16 Florida did not shirk its winning duty v # 25 Iowa at Raymond James Stadium in Tampa, Florida as the UF Squad prevailed W (31–24). Finally, UF won itself a bowl game. Already the winds of change were blowing favorably.

2006 Florida Gators Football Coach Urban Meyer
<u>**SEC Championship**</u> <u>**National Championship**</u>

The 2006 Florida Gators football team was the One hundredth season for Florida. It was the second for Coach Urban Meyer of six great seasons as the Football Gators head coach. The team record immediately improved from the prior year and was on its way to matching and exceeding the great records of the Spurrier years. This year it was more of good wins, great players and a great coaching that would help the Florida Gators become recognized again as the Nation's Football power. And, of course this year's National Championship cemented that notion.

It was the Gators seventy-third with the powerful South-Eastern Conference (SEC). It was again a great SEC showing with just one SEC loss. Coach Meyer led the Gators to a Spurrier-quality regular season record of 13-1 and 7-1 in the SEC Eastern Division. Florida finished first among the six SEC Eastern Division teams and won the SEC Championship and the National Championship. Yes, this season was just the second for head coach Urban Meyer. Yet, he took the Gators that had floundered for three years, and he coached the team to an SEC Championship, a BCS National Championship, and an overall win-loss record of 13–1 (.929). Urban Meyer is a fine coach.

Florida had a lot more to overcome than just s second-year coach. The Gators overcame the toughest schedule in the nation by opponent winning percentage and still they pushed forward to become national champions.

The Gators won their seventh SEC title or ninth as Spurrier counts, by defeating the Arkansas Razorbacks 38–28 in the SEC Championship Game on December 2, 2006. They then defeated the Ohio State Buckeyes, a team which Urban Meyer now coaches, 41–14 in the BCS National Championship Game on January 8, 2007. This began the SEC's streak of seven consecutive national championships. It is not good to fool with the toughness of the Southeastern Conference. h

During the 2006 season, the Florida Gators also celebrated two milestones in their history. It was the tenth anniversary of their first national football championship in 1996, brought forth by Coach Spurrier and a fantastic team. and 100 years of Florida football dating to their first season in 1906. What an accomplishment! What a program!

In addition, thought this is a football book, the fact is that the men's basketball team won both the 2006 and 2007 NCAA men's basketball national championships, and so, the University of Florida became the first Division I school to ever win the football and men's basketball titles during the same year. How about that?

Coincidentally, the Gators, who beat Ohio State for the Football Championship, again faced and defeated Ohio State in the 2007 NCAA Basketball Tournament. This marked the first time in college sports history that identical matchups and results have occurred in both football and basketball championships. I would like my voice to be heard in praising both the Gators and the Buckeyes. That is incredible.

Pundits were high on Urban Meyer as a coach because he had produced before and it was expected that he would produce again. That is what great coaches do. Before the season if you choose to check, the polls in 2006 had Florida listed as one of the top 10 teams entering the season. The Gators had their best pre-season ranking from College Football News, which listed them at No. 2, behind only defending champion Texas. Nothing is certain in any sport but hard work always gives the team deploying such a strategy the edge.

Urban Meyer is a good man. He has another life than football thank God. He and the Gators celebrated 100 years of Florida football this year.

Most of the starters had returned from his 2005 team that went 9–3. They were bolstered by a top-rated recruiting class from the previous February. The Florida schedule included a four-game stretch against teams likely to be in the top-15 teams, starting with Alabama on September 30. Nothing in life worth having, comes easy.

Ten-Year National Championship Anniversary

In this book, we reported the 1996 national championship, as Florida's first and the legendary Steve Spurrier's first. Over times such events have great anniversaries. The Gators celebrated the ten-year anniversary of winning their 1996 national championship in football during the opening game against Southern Miss.

Among the attendees was Steve Spurrier, a Florida legend on multiple fronts. He coached the team to its only championship that season. But, he took off from his coaching duties at the University of South Carolina to pay a tribute to his team. Many people had speculated that because of Spurrier's hiring as the South Carolina Gamecocks coach he would be booed, but instead he received a very loud ovation during the ceremony. Steve Spurrier was, is, and seemingly always will be an adored legendary figure for the University of Florida.

It may not appear so special but in 2006, the Gators also celebrated 100 years since the start of its football program in 1906. You and I have weathered the good and the bad as we traversed 100 years of game highlights, great wins, and great positioning for a great football future. Bravo Gators! Go Gators!

On Sept 2 of this championship season. Southern Mississippi challenged the #7 Gators but were overwhelmed W (34–7). Chris Leak's third pass attempt of the game was intercepted by the Golden Eagles, who scored on a 6-yard Damion Carter pass to Jeremy Young 3 plays later. Leak rebounded to finish 21-of-30 for 248 yards and 3 touchdowns. DeShawn Wynn and Tim Tebow each rushed for a touchdown for the Gators.

On Sept 9, a team that has earned its own credentials over the past years, Central Florida, played at Ben Hill Griffin Stadium on the campus of the University at Gainesville, Florida and were soundly defeated in a shutout W (42–0) before 90,210 screaming Gators. Despite giving up four turnovers and forcing none, the Gators easily beat the spread for the second time this season. By forcing a safety in the third quarter, the Gator defense outscored the blanked Golden Knights offense. It was the Gators' first shutout since blanking Mississippi State on September 29, 2001.

Chris Leak Reday to Pass

Florida QB Chris Leak was 19-of-29 for 352 yards and four touchdowns. Freshman receiver Percy Harvin had a super game with a 58-yard touchdown reception to open the scoring, en route to a 4-catch, 99-yards receiving day. Andre Caldwell caught two touchdowns, and Dallas Baker added one more for the Gators. Florida reserve freshman QB Tim Tebow led the game in rushing, with 61 yards.

On Sept 16, #7 Florida challenged the #13 Tennessee Volunteers at Neyland Stadium in Knoxville, Tennessee and won by a hair W 21–20 before a crowd of 106,818. Considering that UF won the National Championship, how close was Tennessee? How close was UF from not achieving its goal? Point is, Great coaching beats great talent any time the talent factor is close. And, so, this week Florida traveled to Knoxville to face the Tennessee Volunteers. The Gators grabbed an early 7–0 lead, but the Volunteers quickly stole the momentum back when wide receiver Lucas Taylor threw a 47-yard touchdown pass to LaMarcus Coker.

Tebow v Tennessee

The Vols shot out of the gate in the second half with an impressive touchdown drive capped by a one-yard touchdown run by Montario Hardesty, giving the Tennessee a 17–7 lead. Chris Leak rallied the Gators to within a field goal when he found Ryan Williams for a four-yard touchdown. Tennessee scored and went ahead by six when James Wilhoit hit a 51-yard field goal early in the fourth. Leak again brought the team back, but it was freshman Tim Tebow who made a huge play when he converted a crucial fourth down inside Tennessee territory.

Leak came back into the game, and continued his strong play, finding Dallas Baker again for a 21-yard touchdown pass which would eventually prove to be the game winning score. The following drive, Junior quarterback Erik Ainge threw an interception to Reggie Nelson to assure a Gator victory.

As the season moved on, Sept 23 came dutifully forth and strong Kentucky team made itself known at Ben Hill Griffin Stadium as the Gators beat the Wildcats again, W 26–7. Kentucky never gives up in any sport. In this game, the Gators quickly jumped out to a 6–0 lead on a trick play that led to a Chris Leak pass to Jemalle Cornelius for a touchdown with just over two minutes played in the game. From there, the Florida offense stagnated for most of the first half. The Wildcats took the lead for just a while with a TD as the half was coming a close. But, with under two minutes to play, the Gators responded with a touchdown of their own on a DeShawn Wynn run to take a 12–7 lead. Both Gator PATs were blocked in the half.

Jemalle Cornelius Celebrates with Teammate

The defense worked over time for both teams in the second half. Yet, the Gators were able to score two more touchdowns (and made both PATs). This made the final score 26–7. Freshman Tim Tebow—the backup quarterback—led the Gators in rushing for the second time in four games with 73 yards on six rushes. Tebow was already establishing his prowess with one side of his game.

On Sept 30, Alabama which had eaten Florida for breakfast for many years could not get a meal and were whooped at Ben Hill Griffin Stadium by a score of W (28–13) before 90,671 fans. Florida decided to have some fun and the team wore throwback uniforms for the game. They were styled like those worn in the mid-1960s. It was all part of the 100-year celebration of Florida Football. Prior to the game, Florida also unveiled its four initial entries into the Gator Football Ring of Honor—Emmitt Smith, Danny Wuerffel, Steve Spurrier, and Jack Youngblood.

The team entered the game hoping to avenge a 31–3 loss in Tuscaloosa, Alabama the previous season, and end a rare three-game losing streak against a conference opponent. Florida trailed for nearly the entire first three quarters. It was looking "iffy." After a botched snap between center Steve Rissler and quarterback Chris Leak, Alabama's Prince Hall returned the fumble for their only touchdown of the game. The Tide added a field goal to take a 10–0 lead that held until just before the half. Late in the first half, Chris Leak had a career-long 45-yard run. Three plays later, a Tim Tebow designed sneak scored from 2 yards out, putting the Gators on the board with 1:45 left in the half.

Florida took its first lead with 2:39 left in the third quarter on a Leak pass to Andre Caldwell, making it 14–10. The Crimson Tide kept it close by kicking a 26-yard field goal to make it a 1-point game in the fourth quarter. Leak found Ryan Williams on a 21-yard touchdown pass to strengthen Florida's lead. Safety Reggie Nelson then picked off Alabama's John Parker Wilson's pass and took it 70 yards for the score to put the game out of reach.

On Oct 7, #9 LSU played the #5 Gators at Ben Hill Griffin Stadium in Gainesville, Florida on Homecoming day and LSU, as great a team as they have always been, were defeated W 23–10 by Florida. After the Tigers muffed a Gator punt, reserve freshman QB Tim

Tebow scored on a QB sneak from one yard out to tie the game. The Gators also scored right before halftime on Tebow's first touchdown pass, where he faked a leap over the pile and threw the ball to a falling Tate Casey. Tebow added another but a more conventional touchdown pass to Louis Murphy early in the third quarter.

LSU v Florida Homecoming

The Tigers' Early Doucet fumbled the second half kickoff into the end zone for a safety. This led to the long Tebow throw on the next drive. An LSU field goal early in the fourth quarter cut the Gator lead to 23-10. The Tigers drove deep into Florida territory on two other occasions in the fourth quarter, but the UF defense intercepted LSU quarterback Jamarcus Russell on both drives to seal the victory. Starting QB Chris Leak, despite going 17-of-26 passing, was held without a touchdown for the first time in this season.

On Oct 14 at #11 Auburn at Jordan–Hare Stadium in Auburn, AL, even Urban Meyer's Gators could not endure their toughness, courage, and the element of luck as Auburn prevailed v the Gators L (17–27). For another coach, the seasonal quest for excellence might have ended but Meyer chose to keep going. Nothing came easy for the number two ranked Gators as the number eleven ranked Auburn Tigers would not give an inch. Both Lee Corso and Kirk Herbstreit at the pregame show had picked the Gators to defeat the Tigers. The game was broadcast on ESPN Full Circle.

The Tigers started the scoring early. They took the opening drive to the Gators' 5-yard-line before being stopped, forcing a field goal. The Gators came back with a field goal, their first of the season for a 3–3 tie at the end of the first quarter. In the second quarter, Chris Leak threw a touchdown pass to Dallas Baker for a Gators' 10–3 lead.

After the Gators stopped a touchdown by stripping the ball from the Tigers at the goal line, it took just one more play in which Jim Tart held a Tiger in the end zone which created a safety, giving Auburn two points plus the Tigers got the ball right back, with 5 minutes left in the 2nd quarter Auburn scored another field goal making the score 10–8. The Gators got a TD on a Tebow run bringing their lead to 17–8. Auburn got another field goal with 30 seconds in the quarter to cut the Gator lead to six points, 17–11 at the half.

The Gators did not show up in the second half. Auburn shut out the Gators in the half and to add insult to injury. They even blocked a punt for a score to take the lead by one point in the third quarter. The Gators mounted just one threat to take the lead midway through the fourth until a controversial Chris Leak fumble caused by Tray Blackmon of the Tigers gave Auburn the ball. A late field goal put Auburn up four points with just over 30 seconds to go in the game. In desperation, Florida responded on the last play of the game with a failed hook and lateral play, which Auburn's defense was able to pick up and return for a score as time expired. It was the first loss of the season and a heartbreaker. But, Urban Meyer's team would not let it go.

On Oct 28, playing against # 25 Georgia, always a great team, now downgraded to a national rank of # 9, after the loss, the Gators played their hearts out at Alltel Stadium in Jacksonville, Florida and beat the Bulldogs W (21–14). The Gators were heavily favored in this annual rivalry game with Georgia. Florida scored on their first possession of the game. They moved the ball very effectively with a blend of running and passing. Wide receiver Andre Caldwell capped off the drive with a 12-yard touchdown run off a reverse. Florida's defense, which had been touted as one of the best in the SEC, lived up to their billing, stifling the Georgia offense for the entire first half.

Florida added another touchdown before halftime. Chris Leak threw a 40-yard touchdown pass to Andre Caldwell for his second touchdown of the game. Florida's defense came up huge in the second half, when on the first play of the half, Georgia tailback Kregg Lumpkin fumbled the ball and defensive tackle Ray McDonald recovered it and went all the way for a touchdown, making the score 21–0.

Florida's defense continued to stifle Georgia throughout the second half, until late in the third quarter, the Bulldogs offense woke up. After a Chris Leak interception, true freshman quarterback Matthew Stafford led Georgia to a touchdown, on a 13-yard touchdown run off a quarterback draw, cutting the deficit to fourteen points. Florida's offense was stuffed on the following drive but got a muffed punt return by Georgia to regain the ball.

However, the Gators again were unable to capitalize on the turnover, as Chris Hetland missed a field goal. Georgia was unable to score on the following drive. Then freshman Tim Tebow fumbled on Florida's 10-yard line, giving Georgia a shot at drawing within seven points. On third down from the 5-yard line, running back Kregg Lumpkin took a draw play and fought his way for a Georgia touchdown to bring the Bulldogs to within seven. The teams then traded possessions. Florida got the ball back with a little over three minutes in the game. They needed a first down on third and five to seal their victory. The play call was for Andre Caldwell to a carry off a reverse. The play was stopped well short, but with good fortune, Georgia was called for a controversial face mask penalty. This gave Florida the first down they needed to retain possession.

Running back DeShawn Wynn was able to pick up another first down to seal Florida's seventh win of the season. After the win, the Gators took stock in having won fifteen of the last eighteen against their arch rivals from Georgia. The win also moved the Gators into fourth place in the BCS rankings. The further back the Auburn loss was pushed, the higher up the Gators would go in the polls

The season continued on Nov 4 at unranked Vanderbilt as the #7 ranked Gators were looking for a win at Vanderbilt Stadium in Nashville, Tennessee and they found that win W 25–19. It was a big win as the Gators were able to clinch their trip to the SEC Championship Game. It was a sloppy win but a win nonetheless.

Chris Leak struggled throughout the game, going 18 of 25 passing for 237 yards and one touchdown. Leak threw three interceptions, all of which came with the Gators controlling the flow of the game. Florida got very strong play from its defense and special teams, as they were able to block two punts and force an interception. With such a close game, the Gators needed most parts of its game to function precisely to make up for the turnovers. Before the game, it was announced that star defensive lineman Marcus Thomas was kicked off the team for the remainder of the year. Coach Urban Meyer stated during the game that "Marcus did not meet his responsibilities and obligations to remain on the team."

Then on Nov 11, Florida played again to its utmost against a tough South Carolina Squad at home and they managed to win in a very close game W (17–16). This was one of the most anticipated games of the season as former Gator head coach and current Florida sports consultant Steve Spurrier returned to The Swamp as South Carolina's head coach. Spurrier had made two well-received public visits to the stadium earlier in the year as a part of the national championship anniversary celebration and to be enshrined in the Gators' Ring of Honor. Florida fans love Steve Spurrier, and with good reason. Spurrier always brought thrilling games to Gator fans as a player and coach for the Gators. On this day, he brought a thrilling game to the Swamp once again as an opposing coach. Defensive lineman Jarvis Moss blocked an extra point and a field goal, including a potential game winning 48-yard field goal with only eight seconds remaining in the game to enshrine a Gator victory. Ray McDonald also notably blocked a field goal earlier in the game. It was a very close game.

Leading the Gators on offense was Chris Leak with 258 yards passing in the game. With this performance, Leak eclipsed Heisman Winner Danny Wuerffel as the All-Time passing yards leader in Gators history. DeShawn Wynn added 86 yards on the ground to help the Gators maintain a steady attack. Freshman Tim Tebow continued his strong season, rushing for a 13-yard touchdown which proved to be the game winning score. Tebow also converted a critical fourth down play inside Gator territory. Kicker Chris Hetland continued to struggle, missing a 28-yard field goal. He did, however, kick a 22-yard field goal which decided the game.

On Nov 18, a new opponent, Western Carolina came to play the #3 ranked Gators at Ben Hill Griffin Stadium but were defeated in a blowout W (62–0). Chris Leak played his final game at The Swamp.

In a fine performance, he was 9–12 for 98 yards and one touchdown in the first half. Freshman Tim Tebow took over for the majority of the second half, going 10–12 passing, for 200 yards, and two touchdowns. Tebow added two touchdowns rushing along with 47 yards. Tebow was already making heads turn.

The Gators used the game to give young players some playing time. A ton of freshmen played in this blowout game, including Jarred Fayson, who saw time at quarterback and wide receiver. Riley Cooper, yet another freshman, added three receiving touchdowns in the game. Freshman Mon Williams rushed for 97 yards on nine carries. Brandon James also added a 77-yard touchdown from a punt return. Overall, the Gators finished with more points (62) than the Catamounts had yards (59), while playing its reserves for at least half the game.

On Nov 25, #4 Florida beat their favorite Florida foe, Florida State at Doak Campbell Stadium in Tallahassee, Florida, 21–14 To beat the struggling Florida State Seminoles, Chris Leak threw for 283 yards and two touchdowns, Percy Harvin ran for a score and the fourth-ranked Gators won 21–14 to stay in the national title hunt. Florida, with a record of 11–1, won its third straight against Florida State and improved to 6–0 against its three main rivals—Tennessee, Georgia and Florida State—in Urban Meyer's two seasons. This particular game did not give Florida a boost in the Bowl Championship Series standings, leaving the Gators looking for some help from the SEC title game, which would come the following weekend.

2006 SEC Championship Game

On Dec 2, # 8 Arkansas was beaten by # 4 Florida in the Georgia Dome in Atlanta for the SEC Championship W (38–28). The fourth ranked Gators took on the eighth ranked Arkansas Razorbacks in the 2006 SEC Championship Game. Both teams were ready to leave behind their respective SEC Championship droughts. Florida had not won the title since 2000, and the Razorbacks lost in their previous two title game appearances.

The Gators were favored by three points. Before the game really started, both teams traded three and outs. Then, like a time bomb.

Florida exploded in the second quarter. Up 3–0, Chris Leak was called for a rare quarterback draw which he converted by fighting into the end zone. This gave the Gators a 10–0 lead. On the next Florida drive, Leak found game MVP Percy Harvin on a perfectly thrown 37-yard touchdown pass. However, the Razorbacks came back with a single touchdown of their own. QB Casey Dick, who had been struggled in the recent Razorback games threw a perfect pass to Marcus Monk who caught the pass for a 47-yard touchdown. The Gators led 17–7 as the whistle blew for the half.

At half time, the Florida team and fans learned that the third ranked USC Trojans lost in a shocking upset to rival UCLA. With this turn of events, Florida had a great shot at overtaking #2 Michigan to play in the BCS National Championship Game. They therefore needed this win and a strong showing.

But Arkansas came out all fired up and firing on target in the second half. Using the unusual "Wildcat Formation", All American tailback Darren McFadden threw a quick two-yard touchdown to fellow tailback Felix Jones. On the next offensive series, Gators quarterback Chris Leak was intercepted on an attempted shovel pass which was returned by Antwain Robinson for a touchdown, giving the Razorbacks a remarkable 21–17 lead. Florida regained the ball, but was stuffed by the Arkansas defense.

Coach Urban Meyer decided he had to do something to break the inertia of the Razorbacks. He ran a fake punt on his own 15-yard line, which proved to be a good call, as receiver Jemalle Cornelius scampered for a 16-yard gain. Even with this swing of momentum, the Gators were still keep moving and opted to punt from midfield.

The momentum then changed yet again, this time in Florida's favor. Punt returner Reggie Fish muffed the punt after trying to field it over his shoulder; the ball was recovered in the end zone by freshman Wondy Pierre-Louis, giving the Gators a 24–21 lead. It could not have been written out any better. The Gators took the three-point lead into the fourth quarter knowing with a win, they would have made their case to play in the BCS.

They got the job done. In the fourth quarter, Percy Harvin scored on a 67-yard run and Chris Hetland got the kick making the score 31 to

21. Then Arkansas' Felix Jones snagged a 29-yard pass from Cedric Washington for a score with the Gators still in the lead. With Jeremy Davis' kick the score was 31-28. With 9:04 left in the game, Tim Tebow came into the game. Tebow appeared to be running yet again, but pitched the ball to wide receiver Andre Caldwell who threw the ball five yards to Tate Casey. Chris Hetland made the kick giving Florida the game W (38-28).

University of Florida
2006 S.E.C. Football Champions - Florida 38 Arkansas 28

BCS Championship Game—A Great Game

The year was so great that the #2 Gators were invited to play on January 8, 2007 v #1 Ohio State at U. of Phoenix Stadium • Glendale, Arizona (BCS Championship). The Gators had their way W (41–14) before a nice crowd of 74,628.

It sounds so good, let me say it again: The Florida Gators ended this phenomenal season with a stunning 41–14 upset of the number one ranked Ohio State Buckeyes, giving them the school's second national championship in ten years. The national championship win also gives the University of Florida the distinction of being the only school to ever hold both the men's basketball national championship and football championship simultaneously.

Though it ended well, the game did not start well for the Gators. Florida won the toss and elected to defer the option to the second half, giving Ohio State the ball first. On the opening kickoff, Ted Ginn Jr sprinted for a 93-yard kickoff return for a touchdown, turning the largely Ohio State crowd into a frenzy and giving the Buckeyes a 7–0 lead just 16 seconds into the game. However, Ginn injured his foot celebrating the touchdown, leaving the Buckeyes without his deep threat for the rest of the game.

Coach Urban Meyer, who was coaching in his first national championship game, took a timeout to compose his team after the discouraging start. It appeared to work, as senior Chris Leak went 5–5 on the first drive of the game. Leak found three different receivers on the drive, which culminated with a lob pass to fellow senior Dallas Baker.

The Gators tied the game at 7-7 when Leak connected with senior wide receiver Dallas Baker for a 14- yard score just 4:13 later. Leak completed 5-of-5 passes for 35 yards on the drive, which was set up by a 33-yard kick return by freshman running back Brandon James and a subsequent 15-yard facemask penalty against the Buckeyes.

The Buckeyes then got their first offensive possession of the game. Led by Heisman Trophy winner Troy Smith, the Buckeye offense was widely considered to be the best offense in college football. The Gators, however, had one of the top defenses in the nation. The Gators blitzed Smith multiple times on the first drive, leading to a three and out, forcing Ohio State to punt.

Florida used a variety of offensive looks to keep the Ohio State defense off balance, which also included using freshman phenom Tim Tebow as a power rusher. On second down and goal, from the Ohio State four-yard line, Florida ran an option play, in which Chris Leak pitched the ball to freshman star Percy Harvin who fought his way in for a four-yard touchdown. Harvin appeared to be down at the one-yard line, but after further review, it was determined that Harvin did reach the end zone. The score gave the Gators a surprising 14–7 lead.

When the Gators got this lead, they would not relinquish it. It was just the 5:51 mark of the first quarter when freshman wide receiver Harvin took this option pitch from Leak and ran four yards for his third touchdown of the season. Senior kicker Chris Hetland converted the point-after attempt to give UF a 14-7 advantage. The Gators could smell a National Championship but needed to continue.

The Buckeyes came back on their next possession, trailing by a touchdown. Still, the Gator defense managed to put quarterback Troy Smith under heavy pressure. On third down, following a sack, the Gators blitzed, hit Smith as he threw the ball, and cornerback Reggie Lewis intercepted the pass.

Following the interception, the Gators continued to use unorthodox formations and plays to keep Ohio State off balance. Chris Leak remained extremely sharp, going four of five passing on the drive, for 44 yards. On the Ohio State 7-yard line, Tim Tebow came into the game and powered his way to the Buckeye 2-yard line. On the following play, running back DeShawn Wynn rumbled in for a two-yard touchdown, giving the Gators a stunning 21–7 lead.

The score was Wynn's sixth of the season and the 25th of his UF career, moving him into a tie with Buford Long for sixth on the all-time school list.

An 18-yard touchdown run by Antonio Pittman cut the Gators' lead to 21-14 with just over 13 minutes left to play in the first half, but Hetland connected on a 43-yard field goal – his longest of the season – to push Florida's advantage to 24-14 with six minutes remaining in the half. Hetland added a 40-yard field goal to increase the Gators' lead to 27-14.

On the first play of Ohio State's ensuing possession, junior defensive end Jarvis Moss sacked Smith, forcing a fumble that sophomore defensive end Derrick Harvey picked up and returned to the Buckeyes' five-yard line. On third-and-goal from the OSU one-yard line, freshman quarterback Tim Tebow hit junior wide receiver Andre Caldwell for a scoring strike that gave the Gators a 34-14 lead at halftime. The Gators were on their way.

After a scoreless third quarter, Tebow put the Gators ahead, 41-14, with a one-yard plunge at the 10:30 mark of the final period. On the play, Tebow tied Jimmy Fisher's single-season school record for touchdown runs by a quarterback, (8) set in 1979. That touchdown would prove to be the final score of the night, propelling the Gators to the 41-14 win.

Just in case, with 8 minutes remaining in the game, the Gators were determined to end the game and give the school a national championship. DeShawn Wynn, who was in Urban Meyer's doghouse early in Meyer's tenure at Florida, carried the ball 8 times on the drive, picking up several key first downs to keep the clock running. However, Wynn was stopped on a 3rd and 8 play, for only 2 yards. Coach Urban Meyer elected to go for it, and Chris Leak passed to Percy Harvin, who barely made the first down. Knowing this had sealed the win, Meyer began pumping his fist, and gesturing the Florida crowd to get noisy. Chris Leak took a final knee on fourth down, ending his illustrious career as a Gator on top of the college football world. Leak would later be named the game's most valuable player.

UF's victory over the Buckeyes improved their mark to 3-1 all-time in BCS bowl games, and stood as their first win over a top-ranked team since defeating Florida State in Gainesville on Nov. 22, 1997. Florida Head Coach Urban Meyer became just the seventh coach in NCAA history to guide a team to a national championship in his first or second year at a school.

By Rob Schumacher, The Arizona Republic

2007 Florida Gators Football Coach Urban Meyer
<u>Participatiion in the Capitol One Bowl</u>

The 2007 Florida Gators football team was the One hundred-first season for Florida. It was the third for Coach Urban Meyer of six great seasons as the Football Gators head coach. This was literally a rebuilding year from 2006's National Championship Team but still nine wins is not too shabby.

It was the Gators seventy-fifth with the powerful South-Eastern Conference (SEC). It was again a great SEC showing with just three SEC losses. Coach Meyer led the Gators to a Capital One Bowl berth and a regular season record of 9-4 and 5-3 in the SEC Eastern Division. Florida finished third among the six SEC Eastern Division teams. The team's quarterback was Tim Tebow, the first sophomore ever to win the Heisman Trophy.

Player Tim Tebow

In terms of Florida Gator greats, most pundits rate Tim Tebow as the #1 Gator in the school's 110 years of football. A Jacksonville native, Tebow owns five NCAA, 14 SEC and 28 Florida records. His greatest accomplishment in college according to many is that he led the Gators to two touchdowns in the final 10 minutes to beat No. 1 Alabama in the 2008 SEC Championship Game. They say it was better than as a sophomore he won the Heisman Trophy in 2007, becoming the first sophomore to ever win the award.

When Tebow gained the Heisman in 2007, he joined Steve Spurrier ('1996) and Danny Wuerffel ('96) as other Gator Heisman winners.

He was known as a tough, physical player, who happened to be a great QB and a great runner. He rushed and passed for 51 touchdowns during the 2007 regular season, becoming the first of the great 'spread' quarterbacks to win the Heisman.

He is the youngest of five children. He hails from Makati City in the Philippines, making him one of three Heisman winners to be born outside of the U.S. (the other two are Robert Griffin III and Frank Sinkwich).

His family later settled in Jacksonville, Fla., where Tebow attended Trinity Christian Academy, playing tight end for the football team. He went to Nease High, where he earned national recognition as a dual-threat quarterback. During his senior season, he led Nease to the state title, earning himself All-State honors and he had the honor of being named Florida's Mr. Football. A humble man, Tebow takes his honors and wears them well.

Tebow was highly recruited and he had lots of choices. He picked Florida in 2006. He spent that fall as a key true freshman backup to Chris Leak as the Gators won the national title. He had nice stats as a freshman totaling 13 touchdowns running and passing and was the team's second-leading rusher.

When Chris Leak graduated, Tebow took over the starting quarterback job in 2007 and proceeded to record one of the finest seasons in NCAA history. He threw for 3,132 yards and 29 touchdowns, with just six interceptions, and he rushed for 828 yards and 22 scores (the last figure an SEC record) as he won the Heisman solidly over Arkansas running back Darren McFadden. Along the way, Tim Tebow shattered a long-held Heisman streak that saw only juniors and seniors win the trophy.

Tebow's sophomore year was not the only year he was in contention for a Heisman. He flirted with history in the his next two seasons, nearly joining Archie Griffin as the only two-time Heisman winner. As a junior in 2008, he led the nation in passing efficiency and finished a close third in the Heisman race despite garnering the most first-place votes. He led the Gators to the National Championship title too. It was another great fine season in 2009 and he returned to New York on Heisman day for a fifth-place Heisman finish.

At the end of his college career, as previously noted Tebow held five NCAA, 14 SEC and 28 Florida statistical records. Among many mentions in the NCAA Division-I record book, Tebow is ranked second in career passing efficiency, third in career yards per attempt (9.33), eighth in career rushing touchdowns, and he also owns the record for most consecutive games in which he both threw at least one touchdown pass and scored at least one rushing touchdown (14).

Tebow was selected in the first round of the 2010 NFL draft, the 25th pick overall, by the Denver Broncos. He played sparingly as a rookie but led Denver to a playoff win over defending Super Bowl champs Pittsburgh in year two. He later had stints with the New York Jets, New England Patriots and Philadelphia Eagles. A gifted athlete, today he playing professional baseball in the NY Mets organization.

-- End of player notes --

Of course, this year, the Gators had to replace Chris Leak at quarterback. Leak's replacement, sophomore Tim Tebow got a lot of playing time as a freshman.

Capital One Bowl

UF was invited to the Citrus Bowl to play Michigan in the Capital One Bowl on January 1 and the Gators lost a close game to the Wolverines L (35-41). This was only the second meeting between the two storied programs with the first having taken place a short five seasons ago in the Outback Bowl. Lloyd Carr coached his Wolverines for the final time with the announcement of his retirement shortly after his final regular season game against rival Ohio State.

Urban Meyer and the Gators were looking to carry their momentum from the second half of the season with Heisman-winning sophomore Tim Tebow into the bowl game. The Gators lost the game 41–35 as

Michigan barraged the Gator defense for over 500 yards of offense. Chad Henne finished his career at the University of Michigan with a victory in a bowl game, the first in five seasons, and finished with a career high in passing yards. The newly named Michigan head coach, Rich Rodriguez, could be seen during the game along the Michigan sidelines.

2008 Florida Gators Football Coach Urban Meyer
SEC Championship National Championship

The 2008 Florida Gators football team was the One hundred-second season for Florida. It was the fourth for Coach Urban Meyer of six great seasons as the Football Gators head coach. This was another great year for the Gators with just one loss.

It was the Gators seventy-sixth with the powerful South-Eastern Conference (SEC). It was again a great SEC showing with just one SEC loss. Coach Meyer led the Gators to a Bowl berth and a regular season record of 13-1 and 7-1 in the SEC Eastern Division. Florida finished first among the six SEC Eastern Division teams and won the SEC Conference Championship and the BCS Championship finishing #1 in the AP and Coach's poll. The team's quarterback was Heisman winner Tim Tebow, playing in his Junior year.

Before the season, coach Urban Meyer suffered the loss of assistant coaches for the first time in his tenure. Co-recruiting coordinator and safeties coach Doc Holliday left to become an assistant at his alma mater, West Virginia, running backs coach Stan Drayton took the same job with the Tennessee Volunteers, and co-defensive coordinator and defensive line coach Greg Mattison joined the new coaching staff of the Baltimore Ravens. Offensive coordinator Dan Mullen left to become the head coach of the Mississippi State Bulldogs at the end of the 2008 season.

Player Percy Harvin

Percy Harvin played football for the Gators under coach Urban Meyer from 2006-08. Harvin, from Virginia, was the top high school prospect in America in 2006 and he soon became the most dangerous weapon on the Gators' roster by his sophomore season. Some say his greatest moment as when he rushed nine times for 122 yards and caught five passes for 49 yards in Florida's victory over Oklahoma in the team's 2009 BCS National Championship game.

Harvin is still revered as one of the most electrifying players of the BCS era. He is the best wide receiver, ever, from the University of Florida.

And for the doubters: whether you think Harvin is the Gators' best all-time receiver or not, there's no denying he was UF's most versatile and dynamic playmaker ever.

Before we break down Harvin's incredible numbers and overall game, let's take a trip down memory lane to briefly mention a few others high on the list. Carlos Alvarez, the 1969 All-American, and Chris Doering, tied for the most touchdown receptions in SEC history, were big-time talents at the university, and of the two, Alvarez would likely be the most highly regarded in school history. Ike Hilliard, Jabar Gaffney and Jack Jackson were receivers in the golden era of the Gators' passing attack in Steve Spurrier's Fun N' Gun. All five put up incredible numbers, and we haven't even mentioned Reidel Anthony or Wes Chandler yet. Hilliard and

Anthony were the two key cogs that made Florida's 1996 receivers the best in SEC history.

Harvin is the best. He is highly regarded as one of the top high school athletes from the Virginia Beach area ever, joining Ronald Curry and Allen Iverson. Harvin's abilities were obvious, but he had a bad rap in the area. He was suspended twice in high school, once for making contact with an official and using inappropriate language and the other for unsportsmanlike conduct. He was eventually suspended from all high school sports by the VHSL, stemming from a basketball altercation.

Yet, the Gators' coach felt that he was good enough a player to take a chance on. Urban Meyer knew it. He scored 77 total touchdowns, and he scored more points than any player in South Hampton Roads history. He led his team to three consecutive state championship games.

But, the discipline questions lingered, but Meyer believed in Harvin, and ultimately, Harvin's recruitment came down to Florida, Southern Cal and FSU. Harvin's impact didn't take long in 2006. After he hauled in a 58-yard touchdown grab against UCF, Meyer and fans knew he would be something special. He caught 34 passes for 427 yards and two touchdowns, while adding 41 carries for 428 yards and three rushing touchdowns his freshman season. Talk about balance. Some of his biggest and best plays came on the biggest stage, too. Harvin was named the SEC Championship Game MVP, and he was dynamic against Ohio State in the BCS Championship Game. He also won the SEC's Freshman of the Year award, despite having an injury-riddled season.

There was no sophomore slump for Harvin in 2007, either. He combined for 1,622 yards and 10 touchdowns. He led the team with 858 receiving yards and finished second in rushing behind Tim Tebow with 764 yards. He became the first receiver in Florida history to record 1,000 yards receiving and 1,000 yards rushing during his career, and he had another season to add to those numbers. He was named the SEC's first-team All-Purpose player, while being named a second-team receiver in the same year. That year, Tim Tebow won the Heisman Trophy thanks a lot to Harvin's help running and catching the football.

Everybody expected even more from Harvin in 2008. He was even named a Preseason All-American and was featured among the biggest Heisman Trophy candidates in the country. He had a banner year with over 1,300 yards and 17 touchdowns even though he had missed two games due to injury, including the first game of the year against Hawaii and the SEC Championship Game.

Percy Harvin saved his best performance for last. He torched Oklahoma in the BCS National Championship Game while enduring on a high ankle sprain and a hairline fracture. He rushed for 122 yards on nine carries and one touchdown, while making five catches for 49 yards. He flipped field position in a hurry against OU, and other than the incredible defensive performance, Harvin was the biggest reason Florida won the game.

Percy Harvin finished his career with 1,929 receiving yards and 13 receiving touchdowns, while rushing for 1,852 yards and 19 touchdowns. He combined for 3,781 yards and 32 touchdowns during his three-year career.

During Harvin's stay at Florida, the Gators won two national championships and two SEC Championships.

Many define the wide receiver position differently, but Florida never had a player as diverse or electric as Percy Harvin. That's how it was. Harvin has a permanent place in Florida Gators history. The lore can never be a big as the reality.

-- End of player notes --

The season started with a visit from Hawaii to Ben Hill Griffin Stadium on the University campus in Gainesville. The preseason ranked #5 Gators defeated the Rainbow Warriors W (56-10) before a crowd of 90,575.

Brandon Spikes and Ryan Stamper stop Graig Cooper from getting 1st down during 3Q

Beating Miami is really a big deal for Florida

On Sept 6, Florida beat cross-state rival Miami at home W (26-3). It was sweet. This was the first match between the two rivals since the 2004 Peach Bowl where the Gators lost to Miami 27-10. This game is also the first regular season meeting between the two teams since 2003 where the then #18 Gators nearly upset the #3 Miami Hurricanes at the Orange Bowl. The last time the Gators defeated the Hurricanes was in 1985 where the Gators defeated Miami in Miami with a score of 35-23.

Miami was ready as the Hurricanes entered this game with a six-game winning streak and they came in leading the series 28-25. The winner of this game would receive the War Canoe Trophy. Florida fans love watching Florida teams battle it out. This game set an attendance record at Ben Hill Griffin Stadium with 90,833.

The Hurricanes received the ball first with Florida deferring to the second half. Florida's D held Miami to one net yard on their opening drive and forced a quick three and out. The resulting punt netted only 14 yards. This gave Florida excellent field position at the Miami 35-yard line. The Gators, led by third-year junior-year quarterback Tim Tebow, put together a 5-play drive ending in a touchdown pass to TE Aaron Hernandez. The drive took just 1:44 off the clock. The Gators did not mount another drive in the first half.

Miami was able to put together a 42-yard drive with 16 plays consuming 8:42 of the second quarter resulting in a 50-yard field goal. This would end up being the only points of the game Miami scored as well as the closest the Florida defense would allow Miami to get to the end zone. Florida's special teams were able to block a Miami punt attempt resulting in a safety as the ball went out of bounds with 47 seconds left in the half. This brought the halftime score to 9-3.

The Gators received the ball in the second half and did not get anywhere. Offenses were flat on both teams at the end of the third quarter, Florida's defense had forced five Miami punts and allowed only one field goal. In the fourth quarter the Gators offense got some life and scored 17 total points. A drive starting near the end of the 3rd quarter went 86 yards down the field and ended with a fourth quarter 2-yard rushing touchdown by Percy Harvin.

After Florida's defense stopped Miami once again, the UF offense was able to put together another long scoring drive; this one was a 95-yarder that took only 1:34 ending on a 19-yard Tim Tebow touchdown pass to Louis Murphy. The Gator defense forced three fourth quarter Miami punts, 8 in total for the game.

The final score came from a field goal by the Gators, bringing the score to 26-3. Florida's offense was not heralded after the game as it was only able to rush for 89 yards and pass for 256. Neither team had turnovers, but the Gators' defense held Miami to 140 total yards (79 passing, 61 rushing) and the greatest measure of success was that the UF defense kept Miami out of the red zone the entire game.

After a bye week, the Gators beat the Vols of Tennessee in a rivalry game on Sept 20 at Neyland Stadium in Knoxville, Tennessee W (30–6) before a nice crowd of 106,138.

Ole Miss Defeats the Gators

What could have been a big season-changer came next as a determined but unranked Ole Miss defeated #4 UF on Sept 27 at home in a one-point battle L (30–31). From this point on, Florida won every game they played for the rest of the year including the championships and the bowl game.

In the Ole Miss Game, it was back and forth as the score would indicate. This is the first time the Gators had played the Rebels at home since their loss in 2003 against the Eli Manning-led Rebels squad. Entering this game, Urban Meyer was 21-1 at home in Gainesville and Houston Nutt was 0-3 against the Gators. Ole Miss's starting quarterback Jevan Snead, a transfer from the University of Texas, had committed to play for the Gators prior to the 2006 season before decommitting.

The game started with Ole Miss on offense, which didn't stay on the field long after a quick 3-and-out forced punt. The Gators then took over on offense and entered Ole Miss territory, where they were unable to score on their first drive.

Ole Miss got a TD after an immediate 70-yard drive. In response, the Gators drove into Ole Miss territory where they were forced to settle for a 38-yard field goal, narrowing the lead 7-3. With just two offensive plays on Ole Miss's next possession, Florida safety Major Wright picked off a Jevan Snead pass and set up the Gators in Ole Miss territory. Tim Tebow connected with WR Percy Harvin on a 43-yard touchdown pass giving the Gators a 10-7 lead with 12:26 remaining in the second quarter.

After another 3 and out by the Rebels, Florida, regained possession, but quickly turned it over. Tight end Aaron Hernandez of the Gators fumbled the ball. Ole Miss recovered on their 35-yard line. This was the first Gator turnover of the season. Ole Miss's offense did little for the rest of the half and ended their next two possession with punts and a third with a turnover on downs. The Gators did get a score with a nice 81-yard drive capped off with a Tim Tebow 1-yard rushing touchdown, his first of the season. This brought the score to 17-7 at the half.

The third quarter was not as good for the Gators. As they saw their 10-point lead turn into a 7-point deficit. On their first drive of the second half, Percy Harvin fumbled while rushing up the middle. This set up the Rebels and they scored shortly with a 33-yard field goal. Florida's turnover woes continued shortly after the Rebels' kickoff when. Tebow fumbled on the Gators' 18-yard line. This set Ole Miss up for the go-ahead touchdown, a pass which took just 18 seconds off the clock.

With the game was at 17-17 at the 10:30 mark in the third quarter. Florida's next two possessions on offense were negative 3 and the other was for just 19 yards. The Gators punted both times. After having regaining possession with 4:34 left in the third, Jevan Snead and Ole Miss put together a 3:42 drive that went 72 yards down the field resulting in a rushing touchdown by RB Dexter McCluster. This brought Ole Miss's lead back up to 7—same as it was early in the 1st quarter.

After a 25-yard kickoff return by Brandon James, Florida put together a 49-yard drive ending with touchdown from a Tim Tebow rush, tying the game at 24 apiece. Florida's defense could not stop Ole Miss. The Rebels scored again on an 86-yard touchdown reception by Shay Hodge, thereby taking a 31-24 lead with only 5:26 left to play.

Would Florida come back again? Starting on their own 32, a full 68 yards away from the end zone, the Gators scored a touchdown in less than 2 minutes. Percy Harvin took the honors running in from 15 yards for the score. The Gators only needed the extra point to tie the game. Ole Miss was ready and Kentrell Lockett blocked the attempt.

Tim Tebow gets stopped by the Ole Miss defense on fourth down and one in 2008

Florida regained possession with 2:05 left in the game and were able to get to the Ole Miss 32-yard line. On 4th and 1 with 41 seconds left in the game, Tim Tebow rushed the ball but was stopped by an alert Rebels defense--short of the first down marker. Ole Miss got the ball back and ran the clock out upsetting the higher ranked Gators at home.

The stats suggest that Ole Miss should not have won this game, yet, they did and nobody whined about it. The Gators would end the game with more yards, 443 to 325, as well as with more first downs, 24 to 10. The Gators, however, had three turnovers, which was uncharacteristic given that they had zero in the first three games of the season. Ole Miss only had just one turnover in the game as well as double the number of penalties (10 to 5).

After the game, an emotional Florida quarterback Tim Tebow addressed the media on the loss to Ole Miss:

"I'm sorry. I'm extremely sorry. We were hoping for an undefeated season. That was my goal, something Florida's never done here. But I promise you one thing: a lot of good will come out of this. You have never seen any player in the entire country play as hard as I will play the rest of this season and you'll never see someone push the rest

of the team as hard as I will push everybody the rest of this season, and you'll never see a team play harder than we will the rest of this season. God Bless."
— Tim Tebow,

This speech was not a whine. It was the truth about how this team leader felt and it was a promise—win or lose it was a promise to play as well as the team could play. It was very encouraging. It went on to be engraved on a plaque that was placed outside the entrance to the new Gators football facilities. The Florida Gators won the National Championship.

On Oct 4, at Razorback Stadium in Fayetteville, Arkansas, the Gators beat the Razorbacks W (38–7).

Then, they beat #4 LSU at home on Oct 11 W (51-21). This annual rivalry had some other significance. It marked the 10th time in college football history that back-to-back champions played in the following regular season with the home team never losing. The last time this occurred was on October 20, 1990, when the 1989 champions University of Miami played the 1988 champions Notre Dame. Notre Dame beat Miami at South Bend with a score of 29-20.

This game marked the 55th meeting between the Gators and Tigers with Florida leading the series 28-23-3 entering the game. Florida head coach Urban Meyer's record against LSU head coach Les Miles was 1-2 entering the game with the home team winning in each of those three games. This game marked the second of four regular season games where the Gators faced a coach that had won a national championship. Urban Meyer had taken the Gators to the championship in 2006, and things looked like despite the Ole Miss loss, there was still hope.

The Gators opened the game on offense and set the pace early. The first drive of the game only took 1:38 for an early score with a Percy Harvin touchdown off a tipped pass on the third play of the game. Florida's defense stopped LSU on their first possession with a quick three and out and turned the change of possession into a Gator field goal extending their lead 10-0. Their momentum continued finishing the first quarter 17-0 after a second touchdown by Percy Harvin, a career first for receiving TDs in a game.

The Gators defense continued to hound LSU and LSU QB Jarrett Lee threw a picked to Florida linebacker Brandon Spikes. Although Florida did not take advantage of the turnover, LSU turned the ball over again their next possession. Charles Scott's fumble was recovered by Gator AJ Jones. Florida again did not score with its second gained turnover. Having scored 17 points in the first quarter, the Gators could add only 3 points to the board in the second quarter, extending their lead 20-0.

With less than a minute in the first half and down 20-0, LSU put together a 60-yard drive in less than one minute scoring a touchdown with 5 seconds remaining in the half, bringing the halftime score to 20-7. It ain't over 'til it's over!

LSU opened the second half with another TD. This one was very quick off a 3-yard rush by backup QB Andrew Hatch creating a 14-0 run after a 20-0 Florida run. Florida woke up quickly and responded with a 67-yard drive of its won in 8 play. Tim Tebow took the ball in for a rushing touchdown. Then, the Gators' lead was back to 13. The next offensive possession for Florida produced a long touchdown run by true freshman Jeffery Demps. His 42-yard rushing touchdown was his fourth of the season with all four having been over 30 yards. The Gators scored on defense with a Brandon Spikes interception-returned touchdown 12 seconds into the fourth quarter. The Gators had a commanding 41-14 lead.

Spikes then punted the ball into the southeast corner of the stands in celebration. This was not part of the game plan and it was spontaneous and thoughtless, resulting in a 15-yard unsportsmanlike conduct penalty on the ensuing kickoff. This was Spikes second interception of the game and of his career. After a failed fourth down attempt by LSU, Florida turned the ball over to LSU on a forced fumble on Tim Tebow. LSU scored a touchdown shortly thereafter cutting the lead to 20 with 11 minutes left in regulation. This was followed by a failed onside kick off. The following Florida drive resulted in a field goal from 25 yards.

After another failed fourth down attempt on the following LSU drive, Florida romped down the field and scored their 50th point of the game with a touchdown by senior running back Kestahn Moore. The extra point brought the Gators lead to 30 points and that is how it would up – W (51-21.) This was the first time since 1996 that the Gators scored over 50 points on LSU. The Gators ended the game with over 475 yards of offense. Overall, it was a fine game against a tough team.

Then the Gators beat Kentucky on Oct 25, at home W (63-5). On Nov 1, UF beat Georgia at Jacksonville W (49-10) and then Vanderbilt fell to the Gators on Nov 8 at Nashville W (42-14).

The Gators had the magic. Even when Steve Spurrier's Gamecocks came to town, this tough UF squad beat South Carolina on Nov 15 at home W (56-6). This game marked the 12th time the Gamecocks had traveled to Gainesville where they were winless on the road (0-11) coming into this game. The last time the two teams met in Gainesville, the Gamecocks nearly earned their first victory against the Gators in the Swamp, but fell short with a field goal attempt blocked by Jarvis Moss with only a few seconds left in the game.

History was also made in this game with it being the first college football game where a Heisman-winning coach (Steve Spurrier) coached against a Heisman-winning player (Tim Tebow). Both Heisman winners also earned their Heisman trophies at the University of Florida. This was only the fourth time in college football history that two Heisman winners faced one another. South Carolina is the third team of the season the Gators have played against that was coached by a previous championship-winning head coach (Phil Fulmer of Tennessee and Les Miles of LSU being the other two).

It was a rainy day and the afternoon showers rolling through Gainesville, did not make conditions ideal for either team early in the game. The Gamecocks got the ball first and their first drive ended after just four plays resulting in a punt. Florida drove down the field on the following possession, but true freshman Jeff Demps fumbled the ball near the South Carolina 40-yard line. Carolina's and Florida's offensives woes continued in each of their next drives with a South Carolina QB Chris Smelley pass being intercepted and returned for a touchdown by Brandon Spikes. Similar to the prior week, South Carolina head coach and Florida alum Steve Spurrier rotated quarterbacks after nearly every offensive snap.

On the following South Carolina offensive possession, Gator DB Ahmad Black intercepted another Chris Smelley pass after it was deflected by Gator linebacker Brandon Hicks. This was Black's sixth, and team-leading, interception of the season. It only took one offensive play for the Gators to capitalize on the Carolina turnover. Percy Harvin then took off for 26 yards resulting in a UF. The Gators then held a 14-0 late in the first quarter.

South Carolina continued to make mistakes. On the following kickoff, the South Carolina returner threw a lateral pass to his teammate who fumbled the catch. Florida senior long snapper James Smith grabbed the ball and almost ran it into the end zone but he was down at the one-foot line. Tim Tebow took in in with little effort.

After a South Carolina forced-fumble in the first quarter, their defense picked up their second fumble when Tebow coughed up an option-pass to Chris Rainey near the South Carolina redzone. Although South Carolina's defense had spent little time on the field, they were quite productive in collecting two early Florida fumbles.

The SC offense continued to struggle and failed to put up any points. Florida regained possession after a punt and quickly scored with a Tebow touchdown pass to redshirt freshman Deonte Thompson. After failed offensive drives for both teams, South Carolina was able to put together enough of an offense to make a field goal. This made the 28-3 at half-time.

Florida got the ball first in the second half and on the first offensive play for the Gators, Percy Harvin ran it 80 yards for a touchdown. This was Harvin's second rushing TD of the game. The Gators crossed the 30-point mark on this score, which was the first time in Gator history that the Gators scored 30+ points in every regular season SEC game.

On the following offensive drive for South Carolina, Steve Spurrier did not switch QBs. Instead, he left Chris Smelley in to take all snaps on the drive. South Carolina moved down the field effectively compared to its performance in the first half. SC then made a 44-yard field goal with 10:17 remaining in the third quarter. Florida responded with a drive that took less than four minutes ending nicely with a 38-yard Jeff Demps rushing touchdown. This was Jeff Demps' fifth rushing touchdown of the season. All had been runs of more than 35 yards.

On the first play of the fourth quarter, Tim Tebow threw a TD pass to TE Aaron Hernandez, who grabbed the catch with one hand in a great play. The lead was now 49-6. On the following offensive possession, redshirt freshman QB John Brantley took over for Tim Tebow to close out the game. Florida's defense still played its 100% game. True freshman Gator Will Hill picked off a Stephen Garcia pass attempt making it the third Gator interception of the game.

This turnover led to another Gator score when true freshman Chris Rainey put together two runs with the second being the touchdown score that put the Gators over the 50-point mark. The Gators finished the game holding South Carolina's offense to 173 yards while the Gator offense amassed over 519 yards with 346 of those yards coming on the ground.

UF shellacked the Citadel at home W (70-19) on November 22. Even Florida State seemed easy this year on Nov 29 at Doak Campbell Stadium W (45-15).

The final game of the regular season for the Florida Gators featured a matchup against in-state rival Florida State in Tallahassee, Florida. The last meeting between these two teams took place in the Swamp in 2007 with the Gators defeating the Seminoles 45-12. This game was the 53rd meeting between the two teams with the Gators leading the series 31-19-2 entering the game. Bobby Bowden's teams had lined up thirty-five times against the Gators. This would be #36.

Coach Bowden at 17-16-2 had a better record v Florida than his team's overall record against UF squads of the past. The Gators last loss to the Seminoles was during the 2003 season at home on senior day. Home losses are bad but senior day losses are even worse. This game marked the fourth and final regular season contest in which the Gators faced a team led by a national championship-winning head coach. The Gators were about to face two more great coaches in the SEC and BCS championship games.

Florida received the opening kickoff and preceded to score. This made nobody from Seminole Country happy. It was a 65-yard drive with WR Percy Harvin taking it over from the 11. It was a good feeling. This TD completed Harvin's magic of having scored a TD in every game of the regular season. FSU did not toll over. Instead, it quickly established excellent field position by returning a Caleb Sturgis kickoff to the Florida 24-yard line. Florida's defense was able to prevent the Seminoles from scoring a TD and forced them to settle for a field goal. The Gators then led 7-3.

After forcing a punt, the Seminoles regained possession, but QB Christian Ponder threw an interception to Florida safety Major Wright. It was Wright's third of the season. Florida then capitalized on this turnover and scored with an on-target Tebow TD pass to TE Aaron Hernandez. At the end of Q1, the Gators were ahead 14-3. Soon into Q2, Florida punted and true freshman RB Jeffery Demps coughed up the ball during a run play. The miscue was gathered in by Florida State's Neefy Moffett. This put the Seminoles in the red zone having the ball at the Florida 14-yard line. Just as in the first quarter, the Gators defense was able to prevent the Seminoles from pay dirt and the snagged another field goal. The lead was cut to 14-6.

In response to the FG, UF put together a 10 play drive covering 86 yards, capped off by a 4-yard rushing TD by Tim Tebow over a pile of FSU defenders. With the score now 21-6 and an offense that was not clicking, the Seminoles again settled for a field goal on their following possession, their third of the game. With just 2:04 left in the half, the Tebow-led Florida offense connected on 5 consecutive pass plays, culminating in a 24-yard TD pass to TE Aaron Hernandez, the score took just 1:07. This brought the tally at half-time to 28-9. The Gators had amassed 284 yards of offense in the first half.

The second half opened with a Florida State turnover as the woes of the Seminoles continued on offense. They could not do anything right. Florida's defense continued to force big mistakes. In fact, Florida middle linebacker intercepted a Ponder pass on the first play of the half. This set up the Gators' at the FSU 20-yard line. With three plays in just 40 seconds, the Gators added on another TD as hard-working Tim Tebow lofted a 23-yard TD strike to senior WR Louis Murphy. This brought the Gators' lead to 26 with a score of 35 to 9. If the bus were parked at the tunnel, it would have been a good time for the Seminoles to leave.

After the Florida defense held its ground and forced a *three and out*, the Gators scored again. This time it was their first field goal of the game. On the next Florida State drive, former starting FSU QB Drew Weatherford got the nod to see if he could do better than Christian Ponder. He did, for a while at least as he led his team on a touchdown drive capped off with a Jermaine Thomas 4-yard touchdown run.

The Gators D played havoc all day and this time they blocked the FSU extra point to make the score 38-15. Despite the UF lead, the Seminoles were not laying down. Neither team was able to score any additional points in the third quarter and the Gators took their 23-point lead to the fourth quarter. Less than three minutes into 4Q, Gators' true freshman Janoris Jenkins picked off his third interception of the season. The pundits write it like Jenkins was reading QB D'Vontrey Richardson's pass intended for Bert Reed at the FSU 38-yard line, and he closed in and made the grab.

As done earlier in the game, the Gators capitalized off the turnover and scored a TD—this time in only three plays ending with a Jeffery Demps two-yard touchdown run. This would be the final score of the game with the Gators leading 45-15 with a little less than 12 minutes remaining.

Always concerned about building his whole team into champions, when the game was no longer in question, Meyer substituted Redshirt freshman QB John Brantley for Tim Tebow to close out the game while the Florida defense continued to stop Florida State with sacks on the final two FSU offensive possessions. Carols Dunlap and Jaye Howard combined to keep the Seminoles on their side of the goal line. The final sack of the game by Jaye Howard also caused a fumble by Drew Weatherford, which Howard was able to recover.

The Gators had great stats in the game with over 502 yards of offense; more than double FSU's 242 yards. The Gator defense had 4 turnovers gained with three of them were from interceptions. This win extended Florida's winning streak over the Seminoles to five dating back to the 2004 win in Tallahassee.

Some bad news came among all the good. In this game, WR Percy Harvin suffered an injury that would prevent him from playing the SEC Championship Game the following week. Tebow kept his promise and delivered all victories from the Ole Miss game until the FSU game. Two more games were to be played in the post-season.

Tebow had a "Bloody" Jersey in this game. Not that he was looking for anything but things happen. Tim Tebow created an iconic image of himself and the Gators for 2008. Because of the rainy conditions in Tallahassee that day, the field was extremely wet and very slippery. It affected play on both sides.

At one point, on a 4-yard TD run into the end zone, Tebow slid in on the wet turf, causing the front of his white Away jersey to get wet red paint on it. The paint also got on his face and helmet and it stayed on for the majority of the game. The red paint resembled blood to many people, which was all the fans needed to prove that Tebow had a great bravado of bravery and passion. The "bloodiness" also highlighted his intense sideline celebrations and enthusiasm. The image of Tebow's paint-stained Jersey became one of the lasting and memorable images in sports for 2008 and for the decade at large. What a great man and a great Florida Gator—Tim Tebow!

SEC Championship Game

Florida played #1 Alabama on Dec 6 for the SEC Championship and won W (31-20). It was fortuitous as it gave the Gators a head to head win v #1 Alabama for the national rankings and with both teams having just one loss—well, you know!

The Florida Gators came back to the Georgia Dome after two years from when they last won the Championship in 2006 to play against #1 Alabama for the SEC title. This was the Gators' second visit to the SEC Championship Game since the 2006 game where they faced the SEC West champion Arkansas. The 2007 season SEC East representative in the title game was the Tennessee Volunteers. Alabama returned to the SEC Championship Game after a nine-year appearance drought.

In the 1999 SEC Championship Game, the Crimson Tide defeated the Gators with a score of 34 to 7. Florida's last win over the Tide in the title game occurred in the 1996 SEC Championship Game where the Gators would end up playing Florida State in the Sugar Bowl and Steve Spurrier's team would go on to win a first national championship for the Gators.

This game was Florida's ninth appearance in the game and they have a great record of 6-2 before kickoff. Alabama was 2-3 entering the game with their two wins over the Florida Gators in 1992—the first year of the championship game—and 1999.

Alabama had a great year and the Crimson Tide entered the game having been ranked #1 in the AP and USA Today Coaches poll for five consecutive weeks while the Gators entered the game ranked #2 in the AP Poll. This was the first time that the AP #1 and #2 teams ever faced each other in the SEC title game.

This was Urban Meyer's first time coaching against Nick Saban as well as the first meeting between the two legendary programs since their regular season meeting in 2006 season where the Gators defeated the Tide and then went on to win the BCS National Championship. This was the fifth game of the season, in which the Gators faced a team coached by a national championship winning head coach. Alabama entered the game with a 21-13 series lead over the Gators.

It's nice to win the coin toss

After winning the coin toss, the Gators elected to defer to the second half and the Alabama offense took the field after the touchback kickoff. With just three plays and one net yard, the Gators defense had forced Alabama to punt early. The Gators were handicapped because leading Gator WR Percy Harvin had sustained an injury during the Florida State game. Despite not having the talented Harvin in the game, the Gators fired off quickly and put together a nine-play drive that finished with a Tim Tebow touchdown pass to first year Gator WR Carl Moore. This was Carl Moore's first career touchdown reception as a Gator.

Though working hard, it was the vaunted Alabama offense on the other side of the ball and so, the Florida defense was not quite as effective on the second Alabama possession. Alabama had a true freshman WR Julio Jones, who would distinguish himself in his college career and his pro career. Jones made a 64-yard reception and took the ball to the Florida 18-yard line. The next play, Glen Coffee took off and scored a TD.

There was concern on the Gator side for the quickness of the comeback but Florida was nobody's pushover. It had taken just two plays and 54 seconds for the Tide to tie the game at 7-7. After the Crimson Tide forced a 3 and out on the Florida offense, Alabama's offense led by senior QB John Parker Wilson stalled and was unable to score another touchdown. The Tide settled for a field goal after getting into Florida territory with Javier Arenas' punt return. The Gators had enough time to soak it all in and remember Tim Tebow's promise. This had given the Tide its first lead of the game, 10-7, and this was the Gators' first time trailing in the first quarter since their loss at home to Ole Miss earlier in the season. Bad remembrances about past events sometimes conjure up calls to greatness.

After another 3 and out for the Florida offense, the first quarter finally came to a close. The Tide seemed comfortable maintaining their lead on the backs of their defense. Alabama opened the second quarter on offense and were able to move the ball 40 yards to the Florida 32; and elected to go for the first down on 4th and 9. It was not a bad call either way.

Alabama's P.J. Fitzgerald was supposed to get the Crimson Tide a first down. He did not. Fitzgerald was only able to gain one yard and the Gator population were elated.

The Gators gained possession of the ball on downs. On the ensuing drive, Florida tied the game with a 19-yard field goal after getting as close as the 2-yard line. This tied the game at 10-10. Florida's defense dug in and made themselves stop Alabama on the following drive after only three plays and the Gators regained possession with just a bit less than half of 2Q remaining. The Gators were able to regain the lead after a Tim Tebow touchdown pass to junior WR David Nelson. This brought the score at the break to 17-10.

The Gators had deferred and so they got the ball to start the second half. They were unable to move the ball and had to punt after just three plays on offense. If it were the Tide, we would have said, three and out.

The third quarter would turn out to be difficult for the Gator defense and the Tide scored too frequently on their first two possessions on offense in the half. Their first offensive possession totaled 91 yards and consumed nearly 7 minutes off of the game clock. John Parker Wilson was 4 of 6 passing in the drive with 3 of his passes connecting with freshman to-be-great WR Julio Jones. Alabama RB Mark Ingram finished the drive with a 2-yard rushing touchdown tying the game at 17-17.

Florida's offense struggled on its next possession as they were forced to attempt a field goal. Florida kicker Jonathan Phillips had the opportunity to give the lead back to the Gators, but not all definites are definite and so he missed a 42-yard field goal. To close out the third quarter, Alabama was able to get the ball into Florida territory where they attempted, and made, a 27-yard field goal. This gave the Tide a three-point lead—20–17—entering the fourth quarter.

This had to conjure up thoughts of the inevitable Tide overpowering the Gators for the win. But, UF's stalwart squad would have nothing to do with negative thoughts. Tim Tebow had promised that only the best would come from the Gators and it did. The Gators started on offense in the fourth quarter and drove deep into Alabama territory. Florida ran the ball 8 times out of 11 plays, with the final rush being a touchdown from 1 yard out run in by true freshman Jeffery Demps. The Gators would take the lead following the extra point and would not give it back. It wasn't over unless the Gators would continually stop the Crimson Tide, which they did.

Florida's defense dug in for pride and proved to be more effective in the fourth quarter than they were in the third. Florida defensive lineman Jermaine Cunningham sacked Alabama's John Parker Wilson for 11 yards forcing Alabama to punt the ball. With the ball in the hands of the Florida offense, the Gators had the opportunity to take a two-score lead with a touchdown.

It all looked good but.... They were able to get to the 1-yard line setting a 2nd and Goal situation, **but** Florida received a 5-yard penalty for sideline interference. Nonetheless, on the second play following the penalty, who else but Tim Tebow stepped in to fulfill his promise to the Gator Nation. Heisman winner Tebow threw a touchdown pass to Riley Cooper to extend the Gators' lead and final score margin by 11–31 to 20. Alabama's response on the following drive was quickly quiesced. On a 1st and 10, senior QB John Parker Wilson was intercepted by sophomore DB Joe Haden. The Gators ran out the clock after regaining possession and defeated the Crimson Tide by a score of 31-20 for the SEC Championship. Bravo Gators!

This was the Gators' seventh victory in the SEC championship game and Urban Meyer's second SEC title since becoming the head coach of the team in 2005. The teams clearly played great. But, Meyer must be acknowledged as a great coach who led these great athletes to victory.

This was the Florida Gator's eighth officially recognized SEC title with the first occurring in 1991 before the formation of the Championship Game. With the win over #1 Alabama, the Gators were selected to play in the BCS National Championship Game, where they would face destiny against the tough Oklahoma Sooners.

Yes, just two years after the last big celebration, the Gators were back for all the marbles, on January 8. It was now #1 ranked Florida playing #2 ranked Oklahoma at Dolphin Stadium in Miami Gardens, Florida for the BCS Championship. The Gators defeated the Crimson Tide in a fine game W (24–14). Alabama was not going to be the National Champions but the Gators at this point were looking to take it all the way.

A Look at the BCS Championship Game

The Gators closed out the 2008 season against the Oklahoma Sooners for the 2008 BCS National Championship in Miami, Florida. Although this was the first time the two teams had played one another, there was already familiarity between the two programs. Oklahoma head coach Bob Stoops had played a critical role as defensive coordinator for the Florida Gators during the first national championship run in 1996. In addition, Florida Gators quarterback Tim Tebow and Oklahoma Sooners quarterback Sam Bradford met the previous month in New York for the Heisman Award ceremony where Sam Bradford took home the honors.

Even though Tim Tebow received the most first-place votes, 309, to Sam Bradford's 300, he finished third in the final balloting, being surpassed by both Sam Bradford and Texas' quarterback Colt McCoy. Florida's staff also suffered an employment change when offensive coordinator Dan Mullen accepted the head coaching position at Mississippi State University replacing Sylvester Croom who resigned. Urban Meyer had a lot more than coaching to worry about. He picked Steve Addazio as the offensive coordinator shortly thereafter, but Dan Mullen would still coach in this championship game.

Ready for a great game, Florida head coach Urban Meyer was 2–0 in BCS bowl games with his win as head coach at Utah in the 2005 Fiesta Bowl and his second win coming two years ago to the day against Ohio State in the 2007 BCS National Championship Game. Meyer knew how to win. Oklahoma head coach Bob Stoops also knew how to win as this was his fourth appearance in the BCS national championship game.

Stoops first visit was to the same stadium where his Sooners defeated the Florida State Seminoles 13–2 in the 2001 Orange Bowl. However, the Sooners' last two appearances in the title game ended in defeat, losing at the hands of LSU in the 2004 Sugar Bowl and USC in the 2005 Orange Bowl. In addition, the Sooners lost two more BCS bowl games following their loss to USC. Those were to the Boise State Broncos in the 2007 Fiesta Bowl and the West Virginia Mountaineers in the 2008 Fiesta Bowl. Bob Stoops and the Sooners looked to snap a four-game BCS bowl losing streak and Urban Meyer and the Gators aimed to add their third national championship in school history, and their second in three years. There was a lot on the line.

When the game was about to begin. The coin toss favored the Oklahoma Sooners, who elected to receive the ball and put the Gators on defense to start the game. Oklahoma was confident for a win and they began their offense at the Sooner 24-yard line. They were able to scratch out just 31 yards on 8 plays before having to punt the ball to the Gators. The Sooners were not accustomed to punting.

Yes, this was a rare punt by the Sooners, with the team breaking an NCAA record for most points scored in a season with over 700. The Gators' did not do better than the Sooners in their first offensive possession, which ended in just 8 plays, with this possession ending in a miscue as the Sooners intercepted Tim Tebow in this series.

Tebow was not known for interceptions. He had had thrown two interceptions all year. Fortunately for the Gators, the Sooners could not get anywhere with the rare Florida turnover. Florida's second offensive possession was more productive as the Gators got to the Oklahoma 21-yard line before the first quarter ended. The score was 0-0. This was the first time in the Sooners' season where they were unable to score in the first quarter.

The Sooners had scored an average of over 50 points per game and the Gators over 40 points per game, but neither was able to put points on the board as they faced each other on the gridiron. However, the Gators scored a touchdown with a pass from Tim Tebow to senior WR Louis Murphy in just three plays. This gave the Gators the lead, a major psychological advantage at this point in the game.

Not laying down. In response, the Sooners put together a drive initiated with three running plays by RB Chris Brown that got them 45 yards. The next two plays delivered a Sooner touchdown which tied the game at 7-7. It had taken just 2:13 to respond. The time to respond matters psychologically.

The Gators then received the kickoff with 11:49 left in the half and they moved the ball 21 yards to the Florida 36 where Tim Tebow saw something but it resulted in his second interception of the game and this one was to Sooners' defensive standout Gerald McCoy—Big 12 defensive player of the year.

The Sooners' next drive called out four running plays by RB Chris Brown who was able to take the ball one yard shy of the goal line on a 4th and goal. The Sooners elected to go for the touchdown, but were stopped at the 3-yard line by Florida DT Torrey Davis. The Gators took over on the three.

Florida's offense stuttered on their next possession and eventually punted the ball back to Oklahoma who had 2:32 left in the first half.

Sam Bradford led his team down the field and in scoring position with a 1st and Goal at the Florida 6-yard line. Bradford's following pass was tipped by Florida DB Joe Haden and intercepted by Florida safety Major Wright. This was the third interception of the game; the first for Sam Bradford in the game. The Gators were happy to take a knee to close out the half with a 7-7 tie.

The UF squad opened the second half on offense, but struggled to move the ball at all and were forced to punt back to Oklahoma after a quick 3 and out. The Sooners didn't do much better. After just nine plays, Oklahoma punted the ball back to Florida where the Gators would start a drive that worked. It took over 5 minutes to complete. It started at the Florida 25-yard line. The Gators moved the ball effectively. They needed just three plays to get to midfield.

On a 2nd and 4 at the Oklahoma 13, true freshman RB Jeffery Demps took off and ran the ball to the 2-yard line before Oklahoma was called for a facemask while tackling Demps. This infraction put the ball at the 1-yard line and the Gators had a fresh set of downs on which to score.

This was typical Tebow run territory After failing to run the ball in from one yard, Tim Tebow attempted a pass to TE Aaron Hernandez, which was almost caught for a TD. On third down, the next play called was a direct snap to WR Percy Harvin, who made his first appearance since getting injured against Florida State two games earlier. Harvin was able to rush from two yards out and score the TD, which put the Gators up 14–7.

Oklahoma's following drive did not move well. On the first play of the drive, Dustin Doe and Carlos Dunlap sacked Sam Bradford, dropping him for a four-yard loss. After getting to the Florida 32-yard line, the Sooners tried a field goal, which was blocked by the Gators.

After a change of possession, the Gators went 3 and out to close the third quarter. Both teams were tiring but both had a lot of fight left. The Gators entered the fourth quarter with a lead of 14-7. Florida's defense had been able to shut out Oklahoma's offense in two of the three quarters played up to that point.

Oklahoma got the ball to open the fourth quarter after forcing a punt by Florida at the end of the third quarter. The Sooners were able to put together another quick scoring drive. This one took just 2:36 off the clock and 8 plays for the 77 yards necessary to go down the field. The Sooners tied the game at 14–14 after a Sam Bradford pass to Jermaine Gresham, who lost his shoe after catching the ball on the play.

With 12:13 left in the game and the score tied at 14-14, the Gators' first play of their next possession was a hand-off to Percy Harvin who ran the ball 52 yards before being pushed out of bounds. Although the Gators were able to get into the red zone—the Oklahoma 10-yard line—they were unable to score a TD and they settled for a 27-yard field goal, putting them back in the lead.

The Sooners mounted a comeback. They began their drive after the kickoff at the Oklahoma 35-yard line with 10:45 remaining. On the fourth play of the drive from midfield, Sam Bradford threw a deep pass intended for teammate Juaquin Iglesias, but just as Iglesias got his hands on the ball, Gator DB Ahmad Black pulled it away for the interception. This was Black's seventh interception of the season; tying him for first in the NCAA with most interceptions. This was a back-breaker for the Sooners.

At this point, both starting quarterbacks had thrown for two interceptions each. The Gators capitalized on this turnover by a drive that took nearly 7 minutes off the game clock. On a 2nd and Goal at the Oklahoma 4-yard line, Tim Tebow threw for his second TD pass of the game—this time to junior WR David Nelson. The Gators lead was extended 10 as it brought the score to 24–14.

Oklahoma did its best to try to respond on their following drive, but when faced with a 4th and 4, Gator DB Joe Haden broke up a pass that would have been for a first down. After the turnover on downs, the Gators ran out the clock, thus winning the BCS Championship Game, and claiming the BCS Championship.

The statistics said the Gators should have won by more. Bu having ended the game with 480 yards of offense to Oklahoma's 363. Percy Harvin led the Gators on the ground with 122 rushing yards followed by Tim Tebow with 109. The Gators had used seven wide receivers to complete 18 passes for a total of 231 yards.

Gatorade How sweet it is!

Florida defensive lineman Carlos Dunlap was named defensive player of the game and Florida quarterback Tim Tebow was named offensive player of the game.

During the championship celebration three days after the game, quarterback Tim Tebow announced he would return to the University of Florida for his senior season. What a great man and a great player for Florida. Even if an early pro career may have helped him, Tim Tebow was Gators first. Loyalty first! It seems from my vantage point that the Gators have always been Tebow first, along with Wuerffel and Spurrier of course

Bob Stoops and the Sooners extended their BCS bowl losing streak to five games and have lost two national championships at Dolphin Stadium after winning his only championship in the same stadium in 2001.

Urban Meyer's BCS bowl record extended to 3-0 with the first won as head coach of the Utah Utes. He has a bowl game record at Florida of 3-1 with his only bowl loss coming in the previous season. This was the Gators' 3ʳᵈ national champion ship in school history and their second in the last three seasons.

Gator celebration after the BCS win

**2009 Florida Gators Football Coach Urban Meyer   Sugar Bowl CHamps
SEC Eastern Division Champions   Lost BCS Championship Game**

The 2009 Florida Gators football team was the One hundred-third season for Florida. It was the fifth for Coach Urban Meyer of six great seasons as the Football Gators head coach. This was another fine year for the Gators with just one loss.

The Gators competed in the Football Bowl Subdivision (FBS) of the National Collegiate Athletic Association (NCAA) and the Eastern Division of the Southeastern Conference (SEC). It was the Gators seventy-seventh season with the powerful South-Eastern Conference (SEC). It was again a great SEC showing with no SEC losses. Coach Meyer led the Gators to a Bowl berth and a regular season record of 13-1 and 8-0 in the SEC Eastern Division. Florida finished first among the six SEC Eastern Division teams and lost the SEC Conference Championship and played in the BCS Championship finishing #3 in the AP and #3 in the Coach's poll. The team's quarterback was Heisman winner Tim Tebow, playing in his Senior year.

With senior quarterback Tim Tebow and eleven defensive starters returning, the Gators had hoped to repeat as back-to-back national champions following their BCS National Championship at the end of the 2008 season. They finished with an undefeated 12–0 regular season, their first since 1995, but the Gators' 32–13 loss to the Alabama Crimson Tide in the SEC Championship Game derailed their national title hopes, and forced them to settle for a berth in the Sugar Bowl. At the conclusion of the 2009 season, the Gators were ranked No. 3 in both major polls.

On December 26, 2009, Gators athletic director Jeremy Foley announced that Urban Meyer would step down as the team's head coach for health and family reasons. The following day, Meyer stated that he would instead take an indefinite leave of absence, allowing him to resume his position as the head coach. Meyer returned to coach the Gators in spring practice in March 2010.

On January 11, 2009 during the national championship celebration at the University of Florida, quarterback Tim Tebow announced his intention to return for his senior season. This was followed on January 15 by linebacker Brandon Spikes who announced his intention to return as well. With Spikes' return, the entire two-deep of the Gators defense was set to return for the 2009 season. One major loss was All-America wide receiver Percy Harvin, who opted to leave the University of Florida to enter the 2009 NFL Draft.

The Gators also lost offensive coordinator and quarterback coach Dan Mullen, who became the head coach at Mississippi State following Sylvester Croom's resignation. Former offensive line coach Steve Addazio was named as Mullen's replacement, with Scot Loeffler hired to take on the role of quarterback coach.

Florida was voted #1 in both the preseason USA Today Coaches' Poll and the AP Poll. The Gators received the highest ever percentage of preseason #1 votes in the history of the AP Poll, which began in 1950.

Florida emerged after the last season game as undefeated for the entire regular season 12-0. What a great year. At 8-0, Florida had won the Eastern SEC. Now, it was time for the big SEC Championship game. Alabama was the foe. They had dominated the Western Division and were also undefeated going into the championship game. So, on Dec5, at the Georgia Dome in Atlanta, the two teams faced off. Only one would be SEC Champion; then move on to play for the National Championship.

On this particular day in December, #2 Alabama was the better team though playing #1 ranked Florida. Alabama got off to a great start and kept it up until they had beaten the Florida Gators by the score of L (13-32) before a nice crowd of 75,514. Alabama was crowned SEC Champions.
a
This defeat kept the Gators from the BCS Championship game but they did play in the January 1 Sugar Bowl against #4 Cincinnati, coached by Brian Kelly, who had just committed to replace Charley Weis at Notre Dame. The Gators were ranked #5. The game was played in the Louisiana Superdome in New Orleans, LA. The Gators had no problem with the Bearcats. W (51–24) before 65,207 fans.

2010 Florida Gators Football Coach Urban Meyer
<u>Outback Bowl Champs</u>

The 2010 Florida Gators football team was the One hundred-fourth season for Florida. It was the sixth and last for Coach Urban Meyer of six great seasons as the Football Gators head coach. This was another respectable year for the Gators, even with five losses.

The Gators competed in the Football Bowl Subdivision (FBS) of the National Collegiate Athletic Association (NCAA) and the Eastern Division of the Southeastern Conference (SEC). It was the Gators seventy-eighth with the powerful South-Eastern Conference (SEC). It was again an OK SEC showing with four SEC losses. Coach Meyer led the Gators to a Bowl berth and a regular season record of 8-5 and 4-4 in the SEC Eastern Division. Florida finished third among the six SEC Eastern Division teams. Coach Meyer ended his coaching career by leading the Gators to a 37–24 Outback Bowl victory over coach Joe Paterno's Penn State Nittany Lions,

Defending national champion Alabama, still ranked #1 would be a baptism of fire or a great win. On Oct 2, the battle occurred at Bryant-Denny Stadium in Tuscaloosa, AL. The #7 Gators could not keep up with Alabama and lost the game L (6–31) before a big crowd of 101,821. On November 13, Steve Spurrier's well-coached Gamecocks gained the victory at Ben Hill Griffin Stadium L (14-36).

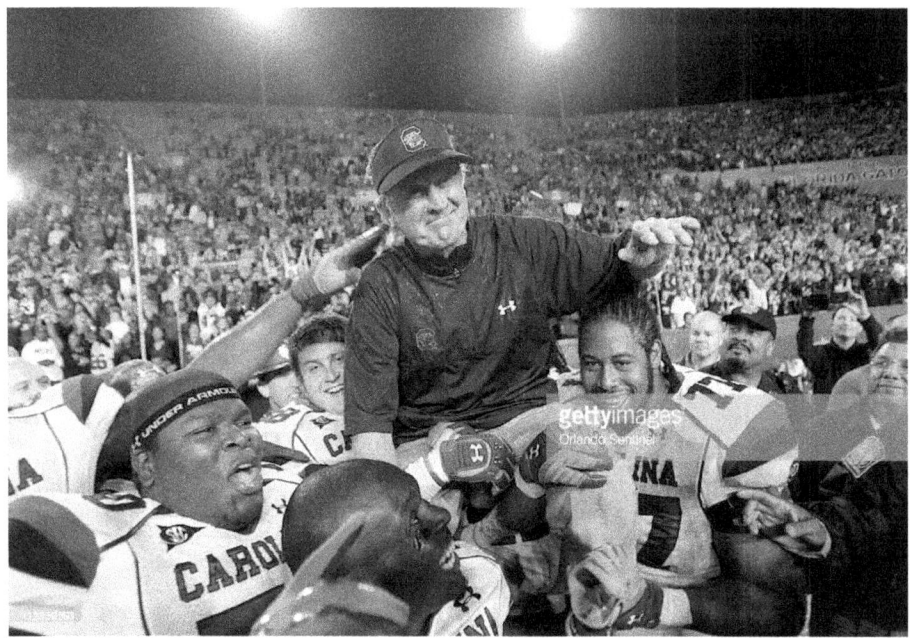

Outback Bowl

On January 1, somehow Florida, now an institution with a top name in football with a 7-5 record got to play in a major bowl – the Outback Bowl. At Raymond James Stadium. The Gators beat Joe Paterno's Penn State Nittany Lions that day W 37–24 before a crowd of 60,574 and a national TV audience. The Gators finished 8-5.

Urban Meyer, A Florida Coach who made an impact.

When Urban Meyer thought about leaving before this year began, he actually gave his notice but then took it back. He loves being a football coach but his style of coaching demands that he gives it his all. Like a maple tree whose sap can only produce so much syrup in a year, Meyer was tapped out. He needed to address his health and he did.

And, so in a combination of not being able to work as hard and not having his great 2009 team to drive the program, thus needing a rebuilding year like many programs, the Gators win # slipped lower than nine for the first time in his years with the Gators. Yet, it was still positive and quite respectable. Meyer needed real time off, however, to get his life and his future coaching act together and he could not do that with a university, any university pinning their next season on his ability to bring it all in.

I love using the words of others to describe what I feel. Here is a great article from ESPN.com that nets out the Urban Meyer departure from Florida. We all knew we would miss him as Urban Meyer's come along as infrequently as Steve Spurrier's do.

Urban Meyer stepping down at Florida

Dec 9, 2010
ESPN.com news services

GAINESVILLE, Fla. -- With his wife and two of his three children sitting a few feet away, Urban Meyer didn't have to look very far to be reminded why he's leaving one of the premier jobs in college football.

It's all about family.

Meyer resigned from Florida on Wednesday, stepping down for the second time in less than a year. His first attempt, which lasted just a day, was for health reasons. This time it's to be a better husband and father.

"At the end of the day, I'm very convinced that you're going to be judged on how you are as a husband and as a father and not on how many bowl games we won," Meyer said at a campus news conference.

"I've not seen my two girls play high school sports. They're both very talented Division I-A volleyball players, so I missed those four years. I missed two already with one away at college. I can't get that time back," he said.

Meyer will coach his last game for Florida in the Jan. 1 Outback Bowl against Penn State in Tampa.

The 46-year-old coach led the Gators to two national titles but briefly resigned last December, citing health concerns. He had been hospitalized with chest pains after the Gators lost to Alabama in last season's Southeastern Conference championship game.

"Last year was a knee-jerk reaction," Meyer said. "This year was just completely different."

Meyer called Florida athletic director Jeremy Foley on Saturday to tell him he was contemplating retirement. They met Tuesday to finalize his intentions.

Meyer signed a six-year, $24 million extension in 2009, meaning he's walking away from about $20 million in guaranteed salary. But Foley did agree to pay Meyer a $1 million retention bonus the coach would have received had he been employed on Jan. 31, 2011.

This time, Foley doesn't anticipate another change of heart. Urban Meyer is now coaching the Phio State Buckeyes.

Chapter 20 Will Muschamp Era 2011 to 2014

Coach # 23 William Larry Muschamp
Coach # 24 D J Durkin

Year	Coach	Record	Conference	Record
2011	Will Muschamp	7–6	SEC	3–5
2012	Will Muschamp	11–2	SEC	7–1
2013	Will Muschamp	4–8	SEC	3–5
2014	Will Muschamp	7–5	SEC	4–4
2014	D J Durkin, Interim			

Will Muschamp Getting Ready to lead the Gators onto the field

My objective in finding leading and closing articles for modern Florida coaches from outside the barriers of Wikipedia, a great source for everything. and others, is to provide insights for why a selection is made, and then for why it was either good or bad.

Excerpts from A Man and His Plan: Will Muschamp's Rise to Become a Head Coach Included a Personal Road Map to Guide Way

By Scott Carter

Posted: Wednesday, August 3, 2011
http://floridagators.com/news/2011/8/3/21078.aspx?print=true

GAINESVILLE, Fla. –The competitor we've seen in those highlights on the sideline was born in all those backyard battles with his older brothers, Mike and Pat.

...

On his 39th birthday a year ago, Muschamp envisioned a much different future as coach-in-waiting at Texas under Mack Brown. And then Urban Meyer resigned after the season. And then Jeremy Foley called. And then he told Brown about an offer to take over the Gators and how it all seemed to fit perfectly into his plan.

The next thing Muschamp knew he was standing in front of a packed room at the Swamp in December as Florida's new head coach. The plan was always to take over a high-profile program like the Gators someday.

...

When Muschamp talks about how he got here, he starts by going back to those sweaty battles with Mike and Pat. It didn't matter what sport they were playing; the Muschamp boys went at each other hard.

Will was the youngest and always out to prove himself. They played football in the fall, basketball in the winter and early spring, and baseball in the spring and summer.

...

Muschamp's interest in coaching grew into a real career option during his college career at Georgia. A walk-on safety, Muschamp's tenacity and team-first attitude earned the respect of Bulldogs Coach Ray Goff and his assistants.

Muschamp eventually earned a scholarship and often spent extra time watching film and learning all he could about the game, knowing that his future in the game was most likely on the sideline and not on the field.

"I wasn't good enough to play after college, and then you get in that crossroads, 'Well, what am I going to do with the rest of my life?' " Muschamp said. "I was always close to my coaches at Georgia. I was always very appreciative of the extra input they gave me about coaching."

...

Muschamp got his first break when he took a job as a graduate defensive assistant at Auburn under Terry Bowden. That's where he first met Fisher and Florida State offensive line coach Rick Trickett, future colleagues at LSU under Saban who later recommended Muschamp to for a job opening.

"It really soothed that yearning for competition, building a common purpose and being a part of something special," Muschamp said. "I'm very team-oriented. I love the team concept and football in my opinion is the ultimate team sport."

...

The story of how Muschamp and Saban first met has been well-documented. LSU was in Atlanta preparing to face Georgia Tech in the 2000 Peach Bowl.

Muschamp, shortly after his first season at Valdosta State, was in Atlanta visiting in-laws and called up Fisher to see if he could stop by the Georgia Dome and watch LSU practice.

So, on Christmas Day, Muschamp dropped by and was introduced by Fisher to Saban.

"I can remember plain as day," Fisher told the Birmingham News in 2010 prior to Saban's Alabama team defeating Muschamp's Longhorns in the BCS title game. "Nick pulled me aside and said, 'Who's that?' I said, 'Coach, he went to Georgia. Don't worry. He ain't gonna tell Georgia Tech anything.' "

A month later, LSU linebackers coach Sal Sunseri left for a job at Michigan State. Fisher urged Saban to consider Muschamp for the opening.

The big break Muschamp needed had arrived. It came via a phone call from Fisher.

"Would you be interested in coming to LSU?" Fisher asked.

"Of course," Muschamp replied.

"Well, we've recommended you for the job here coaching linebackers," Fisher told him.

Much like the way he landed at Florida, the wheels started spinning fast.

"Within that night, I talked to Nick and the next morning I was on a plane to Baton Rouge and was offered the linebackers job that night," Muschamp said. "In less than a 24-hour period my career certainly took a huge swing in a positive way."

Working for Saban is when Muschamp began to formalize his plan to eventually take over his own program. Saban was the perfect teacher at the perfect time.

"I learned total program management. He always talked to the staff about career advancement – be careful what you ask for, take the right job, be patient, it's a marathon not a race. All of those things really resonate with me today," Muschamp said. "I've had some head coaching opportunities, some that I didn't even pursue and some I had point-blank offered and turned down until the Florida job."

Muschamp's career has been stuck on fast-forward since he joined LSU. After a season coaching linebackers, Muschamp took over as defensive coordinator from 2002-04. When Saban left for the NFL, Muschamp served as Miami's assistant head coach for defense in

..

As he searched for a replacement for Meyer, [Florida AD] Foley also had a plan, one that included someone with a stellar reputation and familiarity with the SEC. Muschamp fit like a glove, and after a face-to-face meeting, Foley was sure he had found his man.

Meanwhile, Florida was a perfect fit for the vision that Muschamp had of his first job as a head coach.

He wanted a recruiting base that included a talent pool within a three- to five-hour radius from campus with which you could win the SEC. Check. He wanted great support of the football program from the administration, starting at the top with the school president. Check. He wanted resources and facilities in place to attract the kind of recruits you can win a national title with. Check.

The deal was done as soon as Foley offered the job in Muschamp's mind – and that's not even factoring into the equation his roots in Gainesville. The Muschamp family lived here for 10 years when Will was growing up.

Muschamp's hiring drew the attention of his SEC colleagues, including Saban and Dooley.

"Will is one of my favorites," Saban recently told reporters. "He's got great principles and values personally and philosophically as a football coach."

"I had mixed feelings," Tennessee coach Dooley said at SEC Football Media Days. "I was proud of him. He deserved it. He's earned it. But I'd rather him been at Texas because he's a friend of mine. I mean, that's just how it is. He's going to do a great job, there's no doubt in my mind.

"But we got to play each other every year and that's a big game for both programs."

Muschamp's reputation as a stickler for details followed him to Florida.

In his first staff meeting once his new coaching staff was complete, Muschamp handed out notebooks with the plan for his first 100 days as head coach. He has since devised a plan with George Wynn, his former Georgia teammate and Assistant Athletics Director of Football Operations for the Gators, which is mapped out all the way through next summer.

As he turns 40, Muschamp's master plan adds another milestone a month from today when he leads the Gators onto the field against Florida Atlantic on Sept. 3 – his first game as a head coach.

Copyright ©2017 Florida Gators

End of article excerpts.

2011 Florida Gators Football Coach Will Muschamp
<u>Gator Bowl Champs</u>

The 2011 Florida Gators football team was the One hundred-fifth season for Florida. It was the first year for Coach Will Muschamp of four seasons as the Football Gators head coach. This was a just under OK year for the Gators, with six losses.

The Gators competed in the Football Bowl Subdivision (FBS) of the National Collegiate Athletic Association (NCAA) and the Eastern Division of the Southeastern Conference (SEC). It was the Gators seventy-ninth with the powerful South-Eastern Conference (SEC). They played their home games at Ben Hill Griffin Stadium on the university's Gainesville, Florida campus. It was a less than OK SEC showing with five SEC losses. Coach Muschamp led the Gators to a Bowl berth and a regular season record of 7-6 and 3-5 in the SEC Eastern Division. Florida finished in third place among the six SEC Eastern Division teams.

Gator Bowl

On January 2, 2012 v Ohio State at EverBank Field in Jacksonville, Florida picked itself up by the bootstraps and decided to win and played to win the Gator Bowl W 24–17before 61,312.

2012 Florida Gators Football Coach Will Muschamp
Shared Eastern SEC Title Sugar Bowl Participation

The 2012 Florida Gators football team was the One hundred-sixth season for Florida. It was the second year for Coach Will Muschamp of four seasons as the Football Gators head coach. This two-loss year was great under anybody's standards and it was the best of Will Muschamp's four years at Florida. The team came alive.

The Gators competed in the Football Bowl Subdivision (FBS) of the National Collegiate Athletic Association (NCAA) and the Eastern Division of the Southeastern Conference (SEC). It was the Gators eightieth with the powerful South-Eastern Conference (SEC). They played their home games at Ben Hill Griffin Stadium on the university's Gainesville, Florida campus. It was a great year overall and in the SEC with just one-loss. Unfortunately, the loss came against Georgia and prevented the team from winning first place among the six SEC Eastern Division teams. Georgia came in #1.

Overall, Florida finished the season with 11–2, 7–1 SEC, sharing SEC Eastern Division title with Georgia. But, in head to head, Georgia had won and thus, they played for the SEC Championship. The team was invited to the 2013 Sugar Bowl, where they lost to the Louisville Cardinals, 33–23.

The Gators were a popular TV team in 2012. The October 20 game against South Carolina hosted ESPN's College Gameday. In addition, their road games against Texas A&M and Tennessee were also hosted by College GameDay.

With an 11-1 record, Florida had its pick of Bowls and chose the Sugar Bowl at the Superdome in New Orleans, LA. Their opponent was #21 ranked Louisville. The Gators were flat and lost the game L (23-33) before 54, 178 fans.

The following Sugar Bowl Game Recap is from
https://www.allstatesugarbowl.org/site559.php

79th Annual Allstate Sugar Bowl ~ January 2, 2013
#21 Louisville 33 (Final: 11-2, #13)
#3 Florida 23 (Final: 11-2, #9)

It was no fluke. This Sugar Bowl belonged to Louisville from start to finish. Terrell Floyd's 38-yard interception return on the game's first play set the tone; and the Gators never fully recovered.

"I cannot tell a lie," Floyd said of his snare of a deflected ball. "I was just in the right place at the right time."

How Louisville and Florida Met in the 2013 Allstate Sugar Bowl

It was 14-0 after Louisville's first offensive possession, when star quarterback Teddy Bridgewater, who constantly bought time with nimble foot work throughout the night, and completed 10 of his first 11 passes, drove his team 83 yards to the Florida 1, where Jeremy Wright scored on the ground. From then on, the Gators could get no closer than the 10-point margin in which the 79th Sugar Bowl ended.

The Cardinals soared to a 24-10 halftime lead, and so flummoxed were the Gators that they started the second half with an on-sides kick - unsuccessful, and made worse with two personal fouls on Florida. Bridgewater connected with Damon Copeland in the end zone and Louisville had a 30-10 lead 12 seconds into the second half.

Florida would miss a pair of field goals, making its task harder, but after John Wallace kicked a 30-yard field goal for the Cardinals in the fourth quarter, Gator speedster Andre Debose returned the kickoff 100 yards to keep Florida within range of a football miracle.

With time starting to run out, Florida quarterback Jeff Driskel - recruited over Bridgewater two years before - guided his team 97 yards. With 2:13 remaining Driskel hit Kent Taylor with a two-yard touchdown pass.

The Gators had scored 13 fourth-quarter points and now had an outside chance to make up a 10-point deficit and stave off an embarrassing defeat.

Improbably, they would need a two-point conversion at this point, then a successful on-sides kick, another touchdown and another two-point conversion to send the game into overtime - and avoid the stigma of becoming the biggest favorite ever to lose, not only in the Sugar but in any of the major postseason pairings in the 15-year BCS era.

Driskel took the snap and rolled out to look for another open receiver. But defensive back Marcus Smith shot in untouched and sacked Driskel - effectively ending the game, securing the 22rd-ranked Cardinals' greatest victory and dooming No. 3 Florida to a humiliating setback.

"That was our statement!" screamed Smith immediately afterward.

In the end, Louisville outhit, outsmarted, and out-executed its more heralded opponents for the entire night. After the 24-10 halftime lead, the Cardinals never allowed the Gators to muster one of their patented second-half surges.

The discombobulated Gators turned the ball over three times, and committed nine penalties for 98 yards, including one on their bench for unsportsmanlike conduct.

On this night, Bridgewater thoroughly outplayed the quarterback the Gators signed instead of him (Driskel was 16-of-29 for 179 yards with a pair of costly interceptions). Bridgewater was 20-of-32 for 206 yards and two touchdowns.

"He was the best player on the field," Strong said simply.

"I don't even feel like I'm here right now, " Cardinals senior center Mario Benavideo said with confetti raining down from the Superdome ceiling. "It's so unreal. . ... 90 percent of the people thought we didn't belong. My mom and dad were in the 10 percent."

Louisville cornerback Andrew Johnson, who had one of two interceptions of Driskel, exalted, "Winning this game is making history."

The game opened with a memorable coin toss as Florida was represented by the NFL's all-time leading rusher, Emmitt Smith, and 1997 Heisman Trophy winner Danny Wuerffel, while Louisville was represented by former football great Tom Jackson, as well as the man known as "The Greatest of All-Time," Louisville native Muhammad Ali.

Recap by Sugar Bowl historian Marty Mulé, an award-winning sportswriter who covered college football and the Sugar Bowl for the New Orleans Times-Picayune for 33 years.

2013 Florida Gators Football Coach Will Muschamp

The 2013 Florida Gators football team was the One hundred-seventh season for Florida. It was the third year for Coach Will Muschamp of four seasons as the Football Gators head coach. This eight-loss losing season was the worst record for the Gators since Charley Pell's first year when he went 0-10-1. This was the worst season of Will Muschamp's four years at Florida. The clock was ticking for Will

Muschamp after this season for sure. Many were surprised that he got another season.

The Gators competed in the Football Bowl Subdivision (FBS) of the National Collegiate Athletic Association (NCAA) and the Eastern Division of the Southeastern Conference (SEC). It was the Gators eighty-first with the powerful South-Eastern Conference (SEC). They played their home games at Ben Hill Griffin Stadium on the university's Gainesville, Florida campus. It was a dismal year overall and in the SEC with five losses.

Overall, Florida finished the season with 4-8, 3-5 SEC, in fifth place in the six-team SEC Eastern Division. There were no post-season honors for the Gators this year. They failed to become bowl eligible for the first time since 1990.

Nobody expected such a season from the Gators in 2013 or ever again. They had great success with the same coach in 2012, and so they were ranked No. 10 in both major polls coming into the 2013 season. They opened looking like a great team with a 24–6 home win over Toledo, then fell in a very close match 21–16 to in-state rival Miami in a game in which the Gators gained almost twice as many yards as the Hurricanes but committed 5 turnovers, including a crucial late interception in the red zone. OK, those things happen.

The Gators ended the season on a seven-game losing streak in which the offense struggled continually while major injuries ended the season for a dozen starting players, including Tyler Murphy and defensive leader Dominique Easley. Despite the hard luck, Gator fans were looking for a little more

For the first time since the winless 1979 team, the Gators finished the 2013 season with a losing record. Several other streaks were broken, including 22 consecutive seasons going to a bowl game and a 22-game win streak against Vanderbilt. The Gators could not even beat lower division teams such as a November loss to Georgia Southern. This was Florida's first ever defeat to a lower division team and its first loss to a current FCS team since the winless 1946 Gators lost to Villanova. These are not good firsts!

2014 Florida Gators Football Coach Will Muschamp

The 2014 Florida Gators football team was the One hundred-eighth season for Florida. It was the fourth and last year for Coach Will Muschamp of four seasons as the Football Gators head coach. This year was much improved from the 2013 eight-loss season but it was still one of the worst in over twenty years with 5 losses. The clock ran out of time after this season for Coach Muschamp after this season. He had bad breaks for sure in 2013, but he did not seem to have a Plan B.

The Gators competed in the Football Bowl Subdivision (FBS) of the National Collegiate Athletic Association (NCAA) and the Eastern Division of the Southeastern Conference (SEC). It was the Gators eighty-second with the powerful South-Eastern Conference (SEC). They played their home games at Ben Hill Griffin Stadium on the university's Gainesville, Florida campus. It was a respectable year overall but the SEC was not so good with four losses.

Overall, Florida finished the season with 7-5, 4-4 SEC, in third place in the six-team SEC Eastern Division. There were no post-season honors for the Gators this year. They failed to become bowl eligible for the first time since 1990.

This season's hopes came to an end on November 16, following an overtime loss at home against South Carolina. The OT loss to Coach Steve Spurrier's Gamecocks eliminated the Gators from the SEC East race. At this point, there were lots of rumors and multiple reports surfaced that Muschamp would not be the head coach in 2015.

He was permitted to coach the final two games of regular season play and the Gators did become bowl eligible after a win over Eastern Kentucky. The regular season ended with a loss to Florida State. Gators hate losing to Florida State. The Gators would go on to win the Birmingham Bowl against East Carolina and finish the season 7–5. After four seasons, Muschamp compiled a 28–21 overall winning record and a 17–15 SEC record

The 2013 season had lots of flaws. One of them was low point production from the offense. So, for the second year in a row, head coach Will Muschamp replaced the OC & the offensive line coach. He released offensive coordinator Brent Pease and offensive line coach Tim Davis. Muschamp replaced Pease with Kurt Roper, who led the Duke Blue Devils to their 1st 10-win season, the ACC title game, and the Chick-fil-A Bowl in 2013. Muschamp also replaced Davis with Mike Summers, and hired Coleman Hutzler as the new special team's coach. Muschamp was running out of time and he knew it. This season would do nothing to help preserve his position with the University.

In the final regular game of the 2014 season, Florida State beat Florida L (19-24) in a close game. Losing to Florida teams always hurts the most.

DJ Durkin Interim Gators Head Coach

As noted, Will Muschamp was fired Nov. 16, 2014, and after he coached the final two games of the regular season, he left the program. That left D J Durkin, Muschamp's defensive coordinator and in his fifth year as a Gators assistant, to take over as interim coach for the team's bowl game.

The Gators were invited to play East Carolina in the Birmingham Bowl on January 3 at legendary Legion Field in Birmingham Alabama. The Gators triumphed in a close game W (28-20). Durkin ran the team through their drills for about a month that culminated in a 28-20 win over East Carolina in the Birmingham Bowl on Jan. 3.

Chapter 21 Jim McElwain Era 2015-2017+

Coach # 25 Jim McElwain
Coach # 26 Randy Shannon

Year	Coach	Record	Conference	Record
2015	Jim McElwain	10–4	SEC	7–1
2016	Jim McElwain	9–4	SEC	6-2
2017	Jim McElwain	4-7	SEC	3-5
2017	Randy Shannon	4-7	SEC	3-5

Coach McElwain instructing the Gators

Florida hires Colorado State's Jim McElwain as Gators new coach
Can Jim McElwain turn around the Florida program?
By THAYER EVANS, Sports Illustrated
Tuesday December 2nd, 2014

Colorado State coach Jim McElwain has agreed to become the new head coach at Florida, the school announced on Thursday. The news was first reported by ESPN's Chris Low and confirmed by SI.com. McElwain called a team meeting with his Colorado State players.

McElwain, 52, had a 22-16 record in three seasons with the Rams and is well versed in the SEC. He served as the offensive coordinator at Alabama from 2008 to '11, a period during which the Crimson Tide won two national titles.

McElwain is a respected recruiter in the state of Florida, where he signed future first-round NFL draft pick Ha Ha Clinton-Dix in his final season with the Tide and also recruited former Alabama star quarterback AJ McCarron. He will need to hit the recruiting trail immediately in an attempt to salvage a 2015 class that is ranked last in the SEC, according to Rivals.com.

McElwain is the second consecutive Nick Saban disciple hired by the Gators. He replaces Will Muschamp, who was fired just over two weeks ago following a disappointing 28-21 record in four seasons, including a 6-5 mark this fall.

A Montana native, McElwain has a season of NFL coaching experience as the Oakland Raiders quarterbacks coach in 2006. He played quarterback at Washington from 1980-'83, and got his coaching start there as an assistant in '84.

He was also an assistant at Montana State, Louisville, Michigan State and Fresno State. McElwain had signed a five-year contract with Colorado State in August that paid him $1.5 million annually and included a $7.5 million buyout. His total compensation package at Florida will average $3.5 million annually over six years, per the school's official release.

"The University of Florida Athletic Association and Colorado State have agreed to a payment of $3 million over six years," the release reads. "Florida and Colorado State will also play a game in Gainesville between 2017-20 with a $2 million guarantee. Coach McElwain has agreed to a $2 million payment over time to Colorado State."

So far so good!

2015 Florida Gators Football Coach Jim McElwain
Eastern Division SEC Champs   Citrus Bowl Participant

The 2015 Florida Gators football team was the One hundred-ninth season for Florida. It was the first season Coach Jim McElwain, the current Football Gators head coach. This year was much improved from the 2014 five-loss season by his predecessor. Double digit season wins may be back in style. Things look good for the team and the new coach. We'll see.

The Gators competed in the Football Bowl Subdivision (FBS) of the National Collegiate Athletic Association (NCAA) and the Eastern Division of the Southeastern Conference (SEC). It was the Gators eighty-third with the powerful South-Eastern Conference (SEC). They played their home games at Ben Hill Griffin Stadium on the university's Gainesville, Florida campus. It was a great year overall. Florida finished the season with a 10-4 record; 7-1 SEC, in first place in the six-team SEC Eastern Division.

The Gators finish in the SEC was surprising at 7–1. The squad earned the team a berth in the 2015 SEC Championship Game, but ended the season on the short end of the big games with an overall record of 10–4 after losing both the SEC championship and the Citrus Bowl.

Before the season began—in fact back on November 16, 2014 with two regular season games remaining, Florida announced that head coach Will Muschamp would be replaced after the 2014 football season. When the time came to leave, Defensive coordinator D. J. Durkin served as interim head coach for the post-season. Between the regular season and the bowl game, the school selected Colorado State head coach and former Alabama offensive coordinator Jim McElwain to become the head coach for the 2015 season.

As we go through the season results, you will see that the 2015 schedule consisted of 7 home games, 4 away games and 1 neutral game in the regular season. The Gators hosted SEC foes Ole Miss, Tennessee, and Vanderbilt, and traveled to Kentucky, LSU, Missouri, and South Carolina. Florida had its their 93rd meeting with Georgia in their annual neutral site rivalry game in Jacksonville, Florida. This season was first since the 2008 national championship season in which Ole Miss returns to Ben Hill Griffin Stadium.

Gamecock games had become important

With the W (24-14_ over the Gamecocks this yearm, the Gators snapped a two-year losing streak to the Gamecocks, and finished with a perfect record against SEC Eastern Division opponents. It was also the first Florida–South Carolina game with both teams having first-year coaches since 2005, when Urban Meyer and Steve Spurrier were coaching the Gators and Gamecocks, respectively.

Well before this scheduled game Steve Spurrier, who the pundits referred to as the "visor-slinging, slick-talking "Head Ball Coach" who helped transform the way college football is played with his pass-happy "Fun 'n' Gun" offense," announced his resignation as coach of the South Carolina Gamecocks on Tuesday, Oct 13, 2015. Spurrier was direct and to the point:

"First of all, I'm resigning and not retiring," Spurrier said Tuesday. "I doubt if I'll ever be a head coach again ... but don't say I've retired completely. Who knows what will come in the future?" We all know that sooner than later this beloved coach is back in the Florida fold. Bravo! But for now, he's not at SC anymore.

Florida won the Eastern SEC Conference and played Alabama on Dec 5 for the SEC Championship. But, the 2015 National Champion Crimson Tide came in as #2 and they beat the Gators L (15-29) to capture the full SEC. The Gators managed to get a berth in the Citrus Bowl for a fine year of college level football.

For Gator fans, the words regretfully and regrettably best prefix how Alabama dominated the Gators in the 2015 SEC Championship game. The pundits claim that the Crimson Tide had unleashed all its weapons against the Gators, scoring off an interception and a blocked punt in the first half, snuffing out the Gators' last gasp with a goal-line stand, and wearing down Florida at the end with a dominant running game. That is really a good description though Gator fans would have hoped for more. Alabama is a tough team to beat no matter how well you play. Period.

The Crimson Tide had conjured up a 16-9 lead in the first quarter, despite being held to minus-7 yards and no first downs. Minkah Fitzpatrick returned an interception 44 yards for a touchdown, and

Josh Jacobs went 27 yards for a score with a blocked punt. A field goal was set up by another pick -- one of three thrown by Florida quarterback Austin Appleby in the first half. Florida could have won this game but they did not.

The Tide led 33-16 at halftime and iced the victory with scoring drives of 98 and 91 yards, sparked by a goal-line stand that finished off what the pundits would say was "the last gasp by the Gators."

Alabama finished with 174 yards rushing in the second half. The bulk of the carries went to bruising sophomore Bo Scarbrough, who had two short touchdown runs and finished with 91 yards on 11 carries.

So, let it be written, but Gator fans surely wish the writing were different.

Citrus Bowl

On January 1, 2016 at 1:00 p.m., #19 Florida played #17 Michigan at the Orlando Citrus Bowl in Orlando, FL and were soundly beaten L (7–41) before a crowd of 63,113.

The best quick explanation for what happened goes like this.

Jake Rudock threw for 278 yards and three touchdowns and Michigan's defense dominated throughout in a 41-7 victory over Florida on Friday in the Buffalo Wild Wings Citrus Bowl.

C'est la vie.

Florida's reenergized offense began to struggle toward the end of the season, as did the special teams. The Gators would need overtime to defeat Florida Atlantic, who finished 3–9 on the season. The Gators lost their final three games against rival Florida State, Alabama in the SEC Championship Game, and Michigan in the Citrus Bowl respectively, ending a Camelot season with a 10–4 record.

Florida's turnaround season earned McElwain the 2015 SEC Coach of the Year award. McElwain was also in contention for the 2015 AFCA Coach of the Year award by virtue of winning the regional

AFCA award. In 2016, McElwain's job was to do it all again or do it better. He almost did

2016 Florida Gators Football Coach Jim McElwain
SEC Eastern Division Champs Outback Bowl Champs

The 2016 Florida Gators football team was the One hundred-tenth season for Florida. It was the second season for Coach Jim McElwain as the current Football Gators head coach. This year, the team had one less win in the regular season and one more loss in the SEC.

The Gators competed in the Football Bowl Subdivision (FBS) of the National Collegiate Athletic Association (NCAA) and the Eastern Division of the Southeastern Conference (SEC). It was the Gators eighty-fourth with the powerful South-Eastern Conference (SEC). They played their home games at Ben Hill Griffin Stadium on the university's Gainesville, Florida campus. It was a great year overall. Florida finished the season with a 9-4 record; 6-2, in first place in the seven team SEC Eastern Division. Alabama, who lost the Championship game to Clemson in the playoffs, really put a whooping on Florida in the SEC Championship game (16-54). In post-season, the Gators then won the Outback bowl against Iowa.

Florida running back Mark Thompson (24) runs for yardage as he gets by Missouri safety Ronnell Perkins, center, and linebacker Michael Scherer (30) during the first half of an NCAA college football game, Saturday, Oct. 15, 2016, in Gainesville, Fla. John Raoux AP

2017 Florida Gators Football Coach Jim McElwain
2017 Florida Gators Football Coach Randy Shannon

The 2017 Florida Gators football team was the One hundred-eleventh season for Florida. It was the third season for Coach Jim McElwain as the current Football Gators head coach until his dismissal on October 28, after which defensive coordinator Randy Shannon served as the interim head coach until the end of the season. It was the program's second losing season since 1979.

The Gators competed in the Football Bowl Subdivision (FBS) of the National Collegiate Athletic Association (NCAA) and the Eastern Division of the Southeastern Conference (SEC). It was the Gators eighty-fourth with the powerful South-Eastern Conference (SEC). They played their home games at Ben Hill Griffin Stadium on the university's Gainesville, Florida campus. It was a poor year overall. Florida finished the season with a 4-7 record; 3-5, in fiftth place in the SEC Eastern Division.

The Gators played 7 home games, 3 away games, and 2 neutral site games in the regular season. The Gators hosted SEC opponents Tennessee, Vanderbilt, LSU, and Texas A&M. They will travel to Kentucky, Missouri, and South Carolina. They will face Georgia at a neutral site.

Florida's non-conference schedule consisted of three home games: Northern Colorado, UAB, and rivals Florida State. They faced Michigan at a neutral site in the Advocare Classic. Here are the 2017 seasons results in tabular form. (4-7)

Date	**Opponent**	**Site**	**Results**
September 2	Michigan*	AT&T Stadium, TX	L (17-33)
September 16	Tennessee	Home	W(26-20)
September 23	Kentucky	Commonwealth KY•	W (28-27)
September 30	Vanderbilt	Home	W (38-34_
October 7	LSU	Home	L (16-17)
October 14	Texas A&M	Home	L (17-19)
October 28	Georgia	EverBank in Jacksonville	L (7-42
November 4	Missouri	Faurot Fld, Columbia,MO	L(16-45)
November 11	South Carolina	Wms-Brice Stadium SC	L (20-28)
November 18	UAB*	Home FL	W (36-7)
November 25	Florida State*	Home	L (32-38)------

Chapter 22 Dan Mullen Era 2018- +

Coach # 27 Dan Mullen
Coach # 26 Randy Shannon

Year	Coach	Record	Conference	Record
2018	Dan Mullen	10–3	SEC	5-3

Coach Dan Mullen & QB Feleipe Franks getting signals straight

2018 Florida Gators Football Coach Dan Mullen
<u>Peach Bowl Champion</u>

The 2018 Florida Gators football team was the One hundred-twelfth season for Florida. It was the first season for Coach Dan Mullen as the current Football Gators head coach.IThe program overcame its losing season and they were back on track to winning football games.

The Gators competed in the Football Bowl Subdivision (FBS) of the National Collegiate Athletic Association (NCAA) and the Eastern Division of the Southeastern Conference (SEC). It was the Gators eighty-sixth season with the powerful South-Eastern Conference (SEC). They played their home games at Ben Hill Griffin Stadium on the university's Gainesville, Florida campus. It was a poor year overall. Coming off a 4-7 season, Florida finished this season with a 10-3 record; 5-3, in third place in the SEC Eastern Division. They were in the top ten nationally ranked teams this year #6 in the Coaches Poll and #7 in the AP.

Unranked at the beginning of the 2018 season, Florida had a lot of surprises with its new coach DanMullen. They were tough. In the second game of the season, things looked bad as the team lost to Kentucky for the first time since 1986. This snapped a 31-game winning streak in the series and this gave the pundits some doubt about the reality of the coming recovery year.

But, Florida went back on surprising the pundits with five wins in a row, including on the road against #23 Mississippi State and at home against #5 LSU. Before too long, they had risen to ninth in the AP Poll. They then lost two games to No. 7 Georgia and Missouri and ended the conference regular season tied for second in the SEC East Division at 5–3.

They closed out the regular season by defeating rival Florida State, always a welcome victory, and they were invited to the Peach Bowl, where they defeated #8 Michigan by a healthy core of 41–15. The team finished with an overall record of 10–3, and in the season's final AP Poll, the team was ranked in a tie for seventh, the highest finish for the school since 2009. In 2019, the pundits are expecting great things. So am I.

Florida's offensive field chief was redshirt sophomore quarterback Feleipe Franks. He had a fine year with 2,457 passing yards, 24 passing touchdowns, and 7 rushing touchdowns. His 31 total touchdowns was tied for third in the Southeastern Conference. Running backs Lamical Perine and Jordan Scarlett finished with 826 and 776 yards, respectively. Defensively, the team was led by defensive end Jachai Polite, who finished with 20 tackles for loss and was named first-team All-SEC. The Gators are back.

Best wishes to Coach Dan Mullen and the 2019 Gators

That's All Folks!

Thank you for choosing this book among the many that are in your options list. We sincerely appreciate it! As you may know, this is the fourth Gators football book we have produced in the last two years. The four titles are as follows:

Great Moments in Florida Gators Football
Great Coaches in Florida Gators Football
Great Players in Florida Gators Football
Florida Gators Championship Seasons

Amazon.com/author/brianwkelly

The best to you all – a great Gator Nation!

Other Books by Brian W. Kelly: (amazon.com, and Kindle)

Hope for Wilkes-Barre-John Q. Doe Next Mayor Wilkes-Barre PA: John Doe Plan, help create better city!
Democrat Secret for Power & Winning Elections: Open borders & amnesty & millions of new Dem Voters
The Cowardly Congress Whatever happened to Congress doing the work of the people?
Help for Mayor George and Next Mayor of Wilkes-Barre How to vote for the next Mayor &Council
Ghost of Wilkes-Barre Future: Spirit's advice for residents about how to pick the next Mayor and Council
Great Players in Air Force Football: Air Force's best players of all time
Great Coaches in Air Force Football: From Coach 1 to Coach Troy Calhoun
Great Moments in Air Force Football: From day 1 to today
Great Players in Navy Football: Navy's best including Bellino & Staubach
Great Coaches in Navy Football: From Coach 1 to Coach #39 Ken Niumatalolo
Great Moments in Navy Football: From day 1 to coach Ken Niumatalolo l
No Tree! No Toys! No Toot Toot! Heartwarming story. Christmas gone while 19 month old napped
How to End DACA, Sanctuary Cities, & Resident Illegal Aliens . best solution to wipe shadows in America.
Government Must Stop Ripping Off Seniors' Social Security!: Hey buddy, seniors can no longer spare a dime?
Special Report: Solving America's Student Debt Crisis!: The only real solution to the $1.52 Trillion debt
How to End DACA, Sanctuary Cities, & Resident Illegal Aliens . best solution to wipe shadows in America.
The Winning Political Platform for America Unique winning approach to solve big problems in America.
Lou Barletta v Bob Casey for US Senate   Barletta's unique approach to solving big problems in America.
John Chrin v Matt Cartwright for Congress Chrin has a unique approach to solve big problems in America.
The Cure for Hate !!! Can the cure be any worse than this disease that is crippling America?
Andrew Cuomo's Time to Go? "He Was Never that Great!": Cuomo says America never that great
White People Are Bad! Bad! Bad! Whoever thought a popular slogan in 2018 would be *It's OK to be White!*
The Fake News Media Is Also Corrupt !!!: Fake press / media today is not worthy to be 4th Estate.
God Gave US Donald Trump?   Trump was sent from God as the people's answer
Millennials Say America Was "Never That Great": Too many pleased days of political chumps not over!
White People Are Bad! Bad! Bad! In 2018, too many people find race as a non-equalizer.
It's Time for The John Doe Party… Don't you think? By By Elephants.
Great Players in Florida Gators Football… Tim Tebow and a ton of other great players
Great Coaches in Florida Gators Football… The best coaches in Gator history.
The Constitution by Hamilton, Jefferson, Madison, et al. The Real Constitution
The Constitution Companion. Will help you learn and understand the Constitution
Great Coaches in Clemson Football The best Clemson Coaches right to Dabo Swinney
Great Players in Clemson Football The best Clemson players in history
Winning Back America. America's been stolen and can be won back completely
The Founding of America… Great book to pick up a lot of great facts
Defeating America's Career Politicians. The scoundrels need to go.
Midnight Mass by Jack Lammers… You remember what it was like Great story
The Bike by Jack Lammers… Great heartwarming Story by Jack
Wipe Out All Student Loan Debt--Now! Watch the economy go boom!
No Free Lunch Pay Back Welfare! Why not pay it back?
Deport All Millennials Now!!! Why they deserve to be deported and/or saved
DELETE the EPA, Please! The worst decisions to hurt America
Taxation Without Representation 4th Edition Should we throw the TEA overboard again?
Four Great Political Essays by Thomas Dawson
Top Ten Political Books for 2018… Cliffnotes Version of 10 Political Books
Top Six Patriotic Books for 2018… Cliffnotes version of 6 Patriotic Boosk
Why Trump Got Elected!.. It's great to hear about a great milestone in America!
The Day the Free Press Died. Corrupt Press Lives on!
Solved (Immigration) The best solutions for 2018
Solved II (Obamacare, Social Security, Student Debt) Check it out; They're solved.
Great Moments in Pittsburgh Steelers Football... Six Super Bowls and more.
Great Players in Pittsburgh Steelers Football ,,,Chuck Noll, Bill Cowher, Mike Tomin, etc.
Great Coaches in New England Patriots Football,,, Bill Belichick the one and only plus others
Great Players in New England Patriots Football… Tom Brady, Drew Bledsoe et al.
Great Coaches in Philadelphia Eagles Football..Andy Reid, Doug Pederson & Lots more
Great Players in Philadelphia Eagles Football Great players such as Sonny Jurgenson
Great Coaches in Syracuse Football All the greats including Ben Schwartzwalder
Great Players in Syracuse Football. Highlights best players such as Jim Brown & Donovan McNabb
Millennials are People Too !!! Give US millennials help to live American Dream
Brian Kelly for the United States Senate from PA: Fresh Face for US Senate
The Candidate's Bible. Don't pray for your campaign without this bible
Rush Limbaugh's Platform for Americans… Rush will love it
Sean Hannity's Platform for Americans… Sean will love it
Donald Trump's New Platform for Americans. Make Trump unbeatable in 2020
Tariffs Are Good for America! One of the best tools a president can have

Great Coaches in Pittsburgh Steelers Football Sixteen of the best coaches ever to coach in pro football.
Great Moments in New England Patriots Football Great football moments from Boston to New England
Great Moments in Philadelphia Eagles Football. The best from the Eagles from the beginning of football.
Great Moments in Syracuse Football The great moments, coaches & players in Syracuse Football
Boost Social Security Now! Hey Buddy Can You Spare a Dime?
The Birth of American Football. From the first college game in 1869 to the last Super Bowl
Obamacare: A One-Line Repeal Congress must get this done.
A Wilkes-Barre Christmas Story A wonderful town makes Christmas all the better
A Boy, A Bike, A Train, and a Christmas Miracle A Christmas story that will melt your heart
Pay-to-Go America-First Immigration Fix
Legalizing Illegal Aliens Via Resident Visas Americans-first plan saves $Trillions. Learn how!
60 Million Illegal Aliens in America!!! A simple, America-first solution.
The Bill of Rights By Founder James Madison Refresh *your knowledge of the specific rights for all*
Great Players in Army Football Great Army Football played by great players..
Great Coaches in Army Football Army's coaches are all great.
Great Moments in Army Football Army Football at its best.
Great Moments in Florida Gators Football Gators Football from the start. This is the book.
Great Moments in Clemson Football CU Football at its best. This is the book.
Great Moments in Florida Gators Football Gators Football from the start. This is the book.
The Constitution Companion. A Guide to Reading and Comprehending the Constitution
The Constitution by Hamilton, Jefferson, & Madison – Big type and in English
PATERNO: The Dark Days After Win # 409. Sky began to fall within days of win # 409.
JoePa 409 Victories: Say No More! Winningest Division I-A football coach ever
American College Football: The Beginning From before day one football was played.
Great Coaches in Alabama Football Challenging the coaches of every other program!
Great Coaches in Penn State Football the Best Coaches in PSU's football program
Great Players in Penn State Football The best players in PSU's football program
Great Players in Notre Dame Football The best players in ND's football program
Great Coaches in Notre Dame Football The best coaches in any football program
Great Players in Alabama Football from Quarterbacks to offensive Linemen Greats!
Great Moments in Alabama Football AU Football from the start. This is the book.
Great Moments in Penn State Football PSU Football, start--games, coaches, players,
Great Moments in Notre Dame Football ND Football, start, games, coaches, players
Cross Country with the Parents A great trip from East Coast to West with the kids
Seniors, Social Security & the Minimum Wage. Things seniors need to know.
How to Write Your First Book and Publish It with CreateSpace. You too can be an author.
The US Immigration Fix--It's all in here. Finally, an answer.
I had a Dream IBM Could be #1 Again The title is self-explanatory
WineDiets.Com Presents The Wine Diet Learn how to lose weight while having fun.
Wilkes-Barre, PA; Return to Glory Wilkes-Barre City's return to glory
Geoffrey Parsons' Epoch... The Land of Fair Play Better than the original.
The Bill of Rights 4 Dummmies! This is the best book to learn about your rights.
Sol Bloom's Epoch ...Story of the Constitution The best book to learn the Constitution
America 4 Dummmies! All Americans should read to learn about this great country.
The Electoral College 4 Dummmies! How does it really work?
The All-Everything Machine Story about IBM's finest computer server.
ThankYou IBM! This book explains how IBM was beaten in the computer marketplace by neophytes

Amazon.com/author/brianwkelly
Brian W. Kelly has written 210 books. Thank you for buying this one.
Other Kelly books can be found at amazon.com/author/brianwkelly

www.ingramcontent.com/pod-product-compliance
Lightning Source LLC
Chambersburg PA
CBHW071650090426
42738CB00009B/1476